Serial Murder

Serial Murder
An Elusive Phenomenon

Steven A. Egger

WITH CONTRIBUTIONS FROM

Richard H. Doney,
David A. Ford,
Eric W. Hickey,
Kenna Kiger,
and Harold Vetter

New York
Westport, Connecticut
London

Library of Congress Cataloging-in-Publication Data

Egger, Steven A.
　　Serial murder : an elusive phenomenon / Steven A. Egger.
　　　p.　cm.
　　Includes bibliographical references.
　　ISBN 0-275-92986-8 (alk. paper)
　　1. Serial murders—United States.　I. Title.
　　HV6529.S47　1990
　　364.1′523′0973—dc20　　　　89-70949

Library of Congress Catalog Card Number: 89-70949
ISBN: 0-275-92986-8

First published in 1990

Praeger Publishers, One Madison Avenue, New York, NY 10010
An imprint of Greenwood Publishing Group, Inc.

Printed in the United States of America

The paper used in this book complies with the
Permanent Paper Standard issued by the National
Information Standards Organization (Z39.48-1984).

10 9 8 7 6 5 4 3 2 1

To Jo, Lynn, and Sara Egger
and to the memory of Beaner

Contents

Preface

The authors of this book represent an eclectic variety of disciplines coming together with a central focus—serial murder. The domain assumptions and current research efforts of criminology, victimology, sociology, psychology, computer science, oral history, police science, geography, and systems analysis are all found within these pages.

This work will present the reader with a careful development of state-of-the-art theory and research on the phenomenon of serial murder. The various chapters provide firm analytical bases for future study and research by social scientists into this elusive phenomenon. A synthesis of current literature and research is presented first, followed with special focus upon analysis of incidence and prevalence estimates, the etiology of victimization, and an overlooked psychopathology, dissociative states. Case studies of serial murderers provide the reader with micro-analyses resulting from both nomolithic and idiographic methodologies. The current law enforcement responses to serial murder are then presented in the form of a taxonomy followed by a discussion of the problem of linkage blindness. The work concludes by looking to the future of serial murder research and investigation. References are provided for each chapter and a comprehensive bibliography on serial murder concludes the work.

There is a caveat to the reader with no apology. The title of this work, *Serial Murder: An Elusive Phenomenon*, is not a "foregone conclusion" hidden from the reader until the last pages of the final chapter but rather a focal point that determines the theme of each chapter, a primary criterion for the editor's selection of contributing authors, and a given premise which each writer in his or her own way attempts to negate by adding body to the skeletal literature of serial murder.

Acknowledgments

This work would have been impossible without the contributing authors who shared a vision with the editor. These contributors were selected for their dedication to the search for facts, documentation, and data, to the exclusion of fancy and "educated guesses." The work would, however, never have been envisioned had it not been for two unique individuals from very diverse backgrounds and experiences. Without the assistance of Captain Bobby Prince of the Texas Rangers, I would not have been able to spend time with Henry Lee Lucas, a prolific serial killer. Bobby's faith in my efforts is immensely appreciated. I doubt I will ever meet a more dedicated and effective law enforcement officer. Without the many stimulating conversations with Simon Dinitz, Professor of Sociology, Ohio State University, when he was visiting Beto scholar at Sam Houston State University, many of the questions raised and to some extent answered on the pages that follow would never have reached print. Bobby and Si were the driving force for this work.

Other individuals have also been of great assistance. Sergeant Frank Salerno of the Los Angeles Sheriff's Office Homicide Division provided continuing assistance in my study of the "Hillside Strangler" case and provided solid and practical advice. Robert Keppel, Criminal Division, Washington State Attorney General's Office, provided many insights to the Ted Bundy case and the currently ongoing "Green River Killer" investigation. I am also indebted to Karen Pamplin, former analyst at the Regional Organized Crime Information Center in Nashville, Tennessee, who shared information on serial killings across the southwest and southeast.

Former Dean Carolyn Steel at Sangamon State University placed a great deal of faith in my ability to complete this work. Her support is gratefully appreciated. Barbara Herbek, the highly over-qualified secretary for the Social Justice Professions Program, spent many hours at her computer typing draft after draft as revisions were inserted. Her efforts and attention to detail are gratefully acknowledged. The support of my colleagues, the faculty of Sangamon State University, particularly the enthusiasm of Professor Barbara Hayler, Convenor of the Social Justice Professions Program, will always be appreciated and remembered. Last, but not least, my wife Jo deserves kudos for her meticulate and superb proofreading abilities with this work.

Serial Murder

A Critical Examination of the Phenomenon of Serial Murder

The first four chapters of this work encompass what we think we know and what we don't know about the phenomenon of serial murder. Chapter 1 is the result of an extensive search of the literature and research on this subject. It includes not only the works in academic journals but also the material from mainstream periodicals and monographs as well as journalistic accounts.

Chapter 1 first addresses the various definitions of serial murder followed by the more difficult question of attempting to determine accurate quantitative assessments of the extent of serial murder. Next, the behavior of those who kill serially is discussed. The victimology of serial murder follows. Finally, the varied and descriptive typologies and categories that have developed from serial murder research are presented.

In Chapter 2, Kenna Kiger cites the various estimates and calculations that attest to determining the actual numbers of serial killers and their victims. Kiger presents a cogent argument for a "dark figure" of the occurrences of serial killings in this country. Kiger raises many questions concerning the validity and reliability of various official data sources. Herein a critique is offered of estimates given by researchers, journalists, and others regarding serial murder victims, offenders, and missing persons who may be victims of serial murderers. Kiger correctly warns that without accurate assessments of the amount of serial murder in the United States, subsequent theories and policies will be undoubtedly circumspect.

Eric Hickey in Chapter 3 presents the analysis of his study of 203 serial murderers in the United State responsible for the killings of between 1,483 and 2,161 victims from the years 1795 to 1988. The types of victims, the relationship of offenders to their victims, and the age and gender of the victims is provided. Hickey notes that the number of victims per serial murderer is declining while local "stay-at-home" killers are increasing in number. Hickey concludes that victims of serial murder generally bear no culpability or have done little to precipitate their demise.

In Chapter 4, Harold Vetter pinpoints and then focuses upon the almost completely unexplored clinical area of dissociative states and processes and the antisocial personality disorder. Here the work of Rieber and Green (1988) and their identification of the four salient characteristics—thrill-seeking, pathological glibness, antisocial pursuit of power, and absence of guilt—of the true psychopath is presented. Vetter argues that the psychopath has a dissociative tendency which he or she cannot turn off. The author's search of the literature reveals a strong suggestion of the presence of dissociative processes in the serial murderer. Chapter 4 concludes with an argument for the use of the recently developed Bernstein-Putnam Dissociative Experiences Scale on serial murderers as a worthwhile beginning of more sophisticated psychological analysis of this aberrant and violent behavior.

1

Serial Murder: A Synthesis of Literature and Research

The chapter is presented in five sections. The first section addresses various attempts to define the phenomenon of serial murder. The second section discusses what is known regarding the extent and prevalence of the phenomenon in the United States. Much of the focus of this section becomes what is *not known* as well as some of the reasons for this lack of accurate information. The next section focuses exclusively upon those individuals who kill serially and whose behavior tends to match certain definitional expectations. The victims of serial murderers is the topic of the fourth section. The last section discusses the varied and descriptive typologies and categories that have developed from serial murder research, some of which, while generally lacking in empirical validity, are nonetheless becoming standard language for researchers or the mass media.

There is a large variety of homicides. The legal basis used by law enforcement agencies to count criminal activity is of very limited utility in differentiating and then defining types of homicides. As Farmer and Hooker (1987) have noted, this legal basis "artificially lumps together disparate activities under the single heading of "homicide" (p. 3). Such a general rubric suggests only the corpus delicti in a criminal statute and thus a type of criminal behavior. More specific explication and analysis of this behavior requires modifiers or adjectives. More to the point, the term "serial murder" denotes a very specific type of homicide.

DEFINITION OF A SERIAL MURDER

There have been some limited attempts to define or characterize serial murder or the serial murderer in the literature. As early as 1972 Cormier's definition of the term ''multicide'' appears closely synonymous with most of the general contemporary usage of the term ''serial murder.''

Multicide is a term used to define a number of homicides committed by one person, but spread over a longer period of time, say months or even years, and generally corresponds to an unfolding, deep-seated psychopathological process. The murderer usually selects a type of victim and repeats the murders periodically up to the time of arrest. (p. 71)

Egger's initial definition developed in 1983 was the first effort to comprehensively define the phenomenon:

Serial murder occurs when one or more individuals—in most known cases, male—commit a second murder and/or subsequent murder; is relationshipless (victim and attacker are strangers); occurs at a different time and has no connection to the initial (and subsequent) murder; and is frequently committed in a different geographic location. Further, the motive is generally not for material gain but is usually a compulsive act specifically for gratification of the murderer. A key element is that the series of murders do not share in the events surrounding one another. Victims share common characteristics, of what are perceived to be prestigeless, powerless and/or lower socio-economic groups (that is, vagrants, prostitutes, migrant workers, homosexuals, missing children and single and often elderly women). (Egger, 1984, pp. 8–9)

This definition has been modified by Egger (1985; 1986) and minor revisions were made in 1988:

A serial murder occurs when one or more individuals (males, in most known cases) commit a second murder and/or subsequent murder; is relationshipless (no prior relationship between victim and attacker); is at a different time and has no apparent connection to the initial murder; and is usually committed in a different geographical location. Further, the motive is not for material gain and is believed to be for the murderer's desire to have power over his victims. Victims may have symbolic value and are perceived to be prestigeless and in most instances are unable to defend themselves or alert others to their plight, or are perceived as powerless given their situation in time, place or status within their immediate surroundings (such as vagrants, prostitutes, migrant workers, homosexuals, missing children, and single and often elderly women).

Hickey (see Chapter 2) argues against the notion that serial murder must be considered a stranger-to-stranger crime or that gain be excluded from the murderer's motive. He further argues that females comprise a larger proportion of the serial murderer population than implied in Egger's definition above. Hickey (1986) found 14 percent of identified serial murderers from 1800 to 1986 to be female.

Ressler, Burgess, D'Agostino, and Douglas (1984) provide a very brief definition:

Serial homicide involves the murder of separate victims with time breaks between victims, as minimal as two days to weeks or months. These time breaks are referred to a "cooling off" period. (p. 7)

Levin and Fox (1985) in their book *Mass Murder* define the serial murderer as one type of mass murder. Their definition attempts to address the psychopathy of the murderer's behavior.

This individual travels around, sometimes from state to state, searching for victims whom he can rape and sodomize, torture and dismember, stab and strangle. Even these truly sadistic killers are, however, more evil than crazy. Few of them can be said to be driven by delusions or hallucinations; almost none of them talks to demons or hears strange voices in empty rooms. Though their crimes may be sickening, they are not sick in either a medical or a legal sense. Instead, the serial killer is typically a sociopathic personality who lacks internal control—guilt or conscience—to guide his own behavior, but has an excessive need to control and dominate others. He definitely knows right from wrong, definitely realizes he has committed a sinful act, but simply doesn't care about his human prey. (pp. 229–30)

In 1985 (the same year as the Levin and Fox book) the editors of *Forensic Science International* provided what could be considered a medicolegal definition of serial murder. This definition is an effort by the journal editors to alert the medicolegal or criminal investigator to suspect seriality of a murder when the following characteristics are present:

committed on young males or females in which there has been brutalisation and apparent suffering before death as evidenced by bondage, torture with elicitation of pain and suffering, sexual molestation, mutilation before or after death, a unique pattern to the injury, possibly ripping of the abdomen, castration or patterned cuts, bites or pulverisation of the body in a shallow grave, under branches, rocks or in garbage dumps or containers or in water. ("Serial Murders," 1985, p. 136)

Holmes and DeBurger (1988) in their book *Serial Murder* define serial murder by its central elements with emphasis on the murderer's traits:

• repetitive homicide, continuing if not prevented

• primarily one-on-one

• relationship (victim-perpetrator) usually one of stranger or slight acquaintance, strong affiliation seldom

• motivation is to kill; not conventional passion crime or victim-precipitated

• intrinsic motive (not apparent or clear-cut) and ordinarily not for passion, personal gain or profit (adapted from pp. 18–19).

Norris (1988) provides a definition that focuses almost exclusively upon the serial murderer but does provide the reader with implicit references within his definition to the serial murder event.

The serial murderer in an episodic frenzy can strike without warning. He often preys on the most vulnerable victims in his area and then moves on, leaving the police to find the missing persons and search for traces of the scant clues he has left behind. Because his killing is not a passion of the moment but a compelling urge that has been growing within him sometimes for years, he has completely amalgamated this practice into his lifestyle. It is as though he lives to kill, surviving from one murder to the next, stringing out his existence by connecting the deaths of his victims. Without this string of murders, he feels he will fall apart, that he will disintegrate psychologically. The remainder of his life is devoted to maintaining the mask of normalcy and sanity. (p. 19)

In the preface to the *Multi-Agency Investigative Team Manual*, which provides guidelines for managing a multi-agency serial murder investigation, serial murder is defined as:

a series of two or more murders, committed as separate events, usually, but not always, by one offender acting alone. The crimes may occur over a period of time ranging from hours to years. Quite often the motive is psychological, and the offender's behavior and the physical evidence observed at the scene will reflect sadistic, sexual overtones. (Brooks et al., 1988, vii)

Feminist scholarship has recently begun to examine serial murder as "sexual terrorism" (Cameron and Frazer, 1987, p. 165) or as a perpetuation of gynocide, the systematic crippling, raping and/or killing of women by men (Dworkin, 1976). Thus feminist scholars do not view serial murderers as a novel or emerging criminal in our society. Quite the contrary, they are viewed as little different from mass murderers of the past and the phenomenon is seen as merely a variant of sexual murder which continues in our society (see Cameron and Frazer, 1987; Caputi, 1987).

The news media have also made some attempts to define the phenomenon. Lindsey (1984) refers to serial murderers as "killers who strike again and again, sometimes traveling from city to city, choosing strangers as victims, then moving on to kill again" (p. 1). *Time* calls serial murderers "a new breed of killer . . . whose victims are numerous and whose crimes are geographically far-flung and committed over a period of many years" (Stanley, 1983, p. 47).

Most researchers draw a distinction between mass and serial murder, although the news media almost invariably fail to make such a distinction. Lunde (1976) distinguishes the mass murder from the serial murder, with the latter referring to a crime in which a number of victims are killed, usually by one person in a single episode, and the former as referring to a number of murders by a single person over a period of months or, occasionally, years. Each killing is usually a discrete episode, but there is usually a common motive, method, and/or type of victim (p. 47).

Bartol (1980) argues that Lunde fails to suggest anything other than a temporal distinction between mass and serial murder and refers to both as mass murder. U.S. Justice Department officials, however, draw a distinction between mass murderers, whose multiple killings usually occur in one location at one time, and serial murderers, who kill repeatedly over a period of time, often over a wide geographical area (Lindsey, 1984).

In addition to drawing the distinction between serial and mass murder it is also necessary to identify the serial murderer as a unique actor who can be differentiated from other murderers. Norris (1988) describes the unique characteristics of the serial murderer:

—the lack of rational behavior with regard to appreciating the consequences of personal violence, and the compulsive premeditation with regard to each successive victim—is what sets the serial murderer apart from other killers.(p. 39)

Holmes and DeBurger (1988) identify six variables that differentiate the serial murder event from other murder events. Based upon a relatively small number of cases ($N = 44$) the following distinctions are made:

1. killers are between 25 and 35 years of age
2. victims almost always female and killers male
3. intraracial
4. no geographic variation
5. primarily involve two persons of similar status and
6. a stranger-to-stranger relationship (adapted from pp. 21, 24).

While Levin and Fox (1985) use mass murder as a generic term to encompass both serial and what they refer to as "simultaneous" (p. 13) murderers, they do attempt to draw a distinction. For them, serial killers slay their victims on different occasions and simultaneous killers act in one specific episode. Levin and Fox (1985) state that the murderer, the setting, the situation, the motivation, and public reaction are all important characteristics of mass murder. They further state that the degree of difficulty in solving the crime is the most obvious distinction of the serial murder.

Newsweek magazine differentiates between serial and mass murder by describing only the former as an act in which the killer explodes in one homicidal rampage (Starr et al., 1984). Darrach and Norris (1984) state in *Life* that "unlike traditional mass murderers, who suddenly crack under pressure and kill everybody in sight, serial murderers kill and kill and kill, often for years on end"

(p. 58). *Time* magazine (1983) contrasts its own definition of the serial murderer to the mass murderer, '' [who] confines his spree to one general area and strikes over a relatively short period of time'' (Stanley, 1983, p. 47). *Time's* prime example of a mass murderer is Angelo Buono, Jr., the so-called Hillside Strangler.

Two of the most recent works examining serial murder surprisingly fail to specifically define the phenomenon for the reader. While Holmes and DeBurger (1988) do not offer a specific definition, they do enumerate five central elements or components which they argue to be present in serial murder: repetitiveness, one-on-one, a stranger-to-stranger relationship, a motivation to kill, and an intrinsic motivation system. Keppel (1989), in a very brief book presenting summaries from appellate court transcripts on serial murder cases, makes no attempt to define serial murder.

There appears to be an assumption in most of the literature that serial murder or the serial murderer are well-defined terms. The limited number of definitions and distinctions made between mass and serial murders that differ from one another would certainly indicate otherwise. The working definition of serial murder (Egger, 1988) provided earlier and the definition offered by Levin and Fox (1985) are somewhat different but substantively similar. Cormier's (1975) term ''multicide'' appears consistent with these two definitions of serial murder. The Ressler et al. (1984) definition seems to be consistent with all of these definitions. Definitions offered in the news media appear to be very general and simplistic.

Lunde (1976) and Levin and Fox (1985) provide distinctions between mass and serial murder regarding the temporal aspects, the commonality of motive, method, and type of victim (serial), the setting, the situation, and the solvability. Levin and Fox (1985) also clarify the aspect of setting by indicating that while serial murderers kill at different times, they may kill in one place as well as moving from place to place. They cite John Wayne Gacy as an example of this type of serial murderer. The limited distinctions found in the news media are contradictory and confusing, at best. *Time's* example of Angelo Buono, Jr. as a mass murderer is indeed in conflict with its own media counterparts' distinctions as well as definitions of serial murder and the serial murderer found in the literature.

Even the more sophisticated definitions (see Egger, and Levin and Fox above) are limited as to what arrested serial murderers articulate and what can be ascertained from an unsolved and hypothetically connected series of homicides. All attempts at a comprehensive definition are limited empirically and ethnographically by the very nature of the phenomenon under study. Future research into serial murder should provide more comprehensive definitions from which to analyze homicides so long as the information derived is aggregated and not simply of a repetitive nature.

EXTENT AND PREVALENCE OF SERIAL MURDER

How many serial murderers are there? How many people do they kill? Is serial murder on the increase? The literature provides no decisive answers to any of these questions. Is serial murder a contemporary phenomenon or a recently discovered problem with a history? The literature provides a clearer answer to this question.

Serial murder, as indicated earlier, is a stranger-to-stranger crime. Thus, one must look to this category of homicide to attempt to determine the number of serial murders, since no evidence is found of extensive monitoring or tabulating of this phenomenon in the literature. Homicides have typically been separated into three categories: about one-third are between intimates—family members or lovers; one-third are between acquaintances; and one-third are between strangers. In recent years, the rate in the last category has risen dramatically while the other two have remained relatively stable (Meredith, 1984). Franklin E. Zimring, director of the University of Chicago's Center for Studies in Criminal Justice, says this classification needs to be examined much more carefully. He states, ''That's as specific as police agencies get with that category [between strangers], and it's not enough. We need to know who these strangers are and why the rate is going up'' (Meredith, 1984, p. 44).

Morris and Bloom-Cooper (1964) find in analyzing victim-killer relationships of homicides in England between 1957 and 1962 that it was ''abundantly clear that homicide 'out of the blue', in which the victim is struck down without reacting in any way, is exceptionally rare'' (p. 325). This is apparently changing, at least in the United States. Block (1977) found that the proportion of violent incidents involving intimates and acquaintances had dropped between 1956 and 1976, while the proportion involving strangers had risen. Godwin (1978) finds a dramatic increase in stranger-to-stranger killings, and he argues that these types of slayings are becoming more and more prevalent, quadrupling in the last decade (p. 7). Gilbert's (1983) analysis of homicides in San Diego found that between 1970 and 1980, nearly 50 percent of all homicide victims did not know their killers. During this period, there was a 60 percent increase in all reported violent crimes, and the criminal homicide rate increased from 7.8 to 10.2 per 100,000 population (U.S. Department of Justice, 1981).

In examining the supplementary homicide reports from 1976 to 1985, Maxfield (1988) found that 16.5 percent of the homicide victims were killed by strangers (no prior relationship) and in an additional 28.6 percent the relationship was recorded as unknown. Thus, it would appear that serial murder accounts for a portion of each of these groups.

In 1987, 20,096 criminal homicides were reported nationally to the FBI for a rate of 8.3 per 100,000 population. Of this total, in approximately 5,948 cases the relationship of victim to offender was unknown, and in 2,649 of these cases the victim and offender were reported to be strangers (U.S. Department of Justice, 1988). Thus, the number of stranger-to-stranger homicides was in excess of 2,649 and not more than 5,948 for 1987. The number within this group committed by the serial murderer is unknown.

It is interesting to note that Holmes and DeBurger (1985) claim that ''an estimated 5,000 people each year are victims of serial killers'' (p. 14). This statement grossly misinterprets the available data on homicide and seems to reflect, at the very least, an invalid analysis. The authors qualify this claim in their later book in which they state, ''Between 3,500 and 5,000 persons are slain by serial murderers each year in this country'' (Holmes and DeBurger, 1988, p. 19). Further, the authors contend this claim is a ''reliable approximation [sic]'' based upon data available and various experts.

Norris (1988) agrees with earlier estimate of Holmes and DeBurger (1985):

In 1983 alone, according to the FBI, approximately five thousand Americans of both sexes and all ages—fifteen people a day and fully twenty-five percent of all murder victims—were struck down by murderers who did not know them and killed them for the sheer ''high'' of the experience. The FBI calls this class of homicide serial murders and their perpetrators recreational or lust killers. (p. 15)

This attribution to the FBI in 1983 is apparently a reference to the author's analysis of the *Uniform Crime Report* (U.S. Department of Justice, 1983) and not statements by FBI officials. Norris provides no reference citation within his text, list of references, or bibliography to his work.

The Centers for Disease Control (1982) analyzed all homicides reported to the Federal Bureau of Investigation between 1976 and 1979. Results of this analysis revealed that during this period 13 percent of the homicides were committed by strangers and in 29 percent of the offenses the offenders were unidentified. In analyzing the same data for circumstances of the homicides, 20 percent were found to be indeterminable. In most instances, serial murders would be found within these categories since they are stranger-to-stranger and frequently not determined.

The *Uniform Crime Report 1987* notes that now almost 25 percent of the reported criminal homicides were committed with unknown motives. Almost all the serial murders are encompassed within this 25 percent, or about 5,024 murders. The *Vital Statistics of the National Center for Health Statistics* concentrates on cause and nature of death, but its statistics are not collected to reveal motive or relationship between victim and offender; neither do police agencies collect or maintain data and information of this type. Darrach and Norris (1984) found at least 120 serial killers had been captured or singled out by the police in the last 20 years; however the authors did not indicate how this number was determined or derived.

The number of serial killers operating at any one time in this country is an often debated subject; however only very rough estimates have been made. Thirty-five is frequently the estimate attributed to the U.S. Government (see Kiger, Chapter 3). Robert Ressler of the FBI's Violent Criminal Apprehension Program sees this estimate as being very low. Ressler argues that approximately 70 different serial homicide patterns have been identified at one point in time. When unidentified patterns are added to this number, active serial killers may number in the hundreds (Brandl, 1987).

It would appear that the mass media are currently the only source from which to quantify serial murders in this country. Serial murders come to the attention of the print media when a serial murderer is apprehended and his killings are revealed or when a series of murders occurs within a relatively small geographical area and their multiplicity becomes evident over time. Press attention and column space thus provide a source for identifying and accumulating a more aggregate picture of this phenomenon. Fox and Levin (1983) utilized this data source in examining multiple murders. They state, "Because of the newspaper publicity associated with extreme acts of aggression, we believe that our selection procedure uncovered most of the acts of multiple murder committed during the time period under investigation" (p. 3). The information collected from this data source (42 mass murderers between 1974 and 1979) was also apparently used by Levin and Fox (1985) in their book on mass murder. Dominick (1984) found that newspapers devote a great deal of column space to a few sensational crimes, especially the more spectacular homicides. Without extensive survey research to provide an inventory of serial murders from each law enforcement jurisdiction, newspaper research is the only currently available means to collect this datum. The problem with this approach is that many unsolved and less spectacular murders are potentially serial in nature. Without the serial murderer and his confession, numerous unsolved murders will remain separate distinct homicide events and, thus, will receive little, if any, attention in major newspapers.

A great deal of cross-checking and backtracking is necessary in this type of newspaper content analysis. Two strategies can be utilized in the initial search: a search for an identified serial murderer or a search for identified serial murders. The former, used by Egger (1984) in a preliminary search of the *New York Times Index* from January 1978 to June 1983, revealed a total of 54 serial murderers who had reportedly killed four or more persons and been identified by the paper during this time period.

Simonetti (1984) examined a much larger timespan than Egger utilizing his search criteria. In her search of the *New York Times Index* from January 1970 through November 1983, she found only 38 cases of serial homicide between 1978 and 1983. Simonetti went one step beyond Egger's preliminary search and examined the actual news article on microfilm. She claims to have eliminated a number of cases because they were mass murders or the victims were not strangers to the offender (p. 11).

Simonetti (1984) overlooks the fact that Egger was searching for murderers and she was searching for murder cases. Notwithstanding this, a sixteen-case discrepancy does appear to be large since in many known cases the serial murderer appears to be acting alone. Simonetti's data from 1970 to 1983 contradict this assumption, finding approximately 25 percent of the cases identified involved two or more perpetrators (1984, p. 11). However, Simonetti provides no case documentation in order to verify these results.

This apparent discrepancy of findings from two researchers using the same secondary material, the *New York Times*, highlights the problematic nature of newspaper research. (Further, this discrepancy underscores not only the validity problems of data collection interpretation but also the fragile nature of serial murder research using newspaper accounts as a primary source of data.)

(Any attempt to determine the number of serial murder victims is fraught with the same problems of determining the number of serial murderers.) In addition, known victims of homicide will probably not be identified as serial murder victims unless their demise has occurred in a relatively small geographical area such as in the "Green River Murders" in the Pacific Northwest area, or unless their assailant has been apprehended and confesses to the murders as in the cases of Lucas, Gacy, Bianchi, and other serial murderers. In addition, the victims of serial murder are sometimes not found, or if found, it may be next to impossible to determine their identity. Alfred Regnery, former administrator of the Office of Juvenile Justice and Delinquency Prevention, U.S. Department of Justice, contends that many missing children are the victims of serial murderers. He stated, "Because the bodies of the victims are not always found, we have no idea what the real number is" (*Houston Post*, Nov. 11, 1983, p. 1). Robert O. Heck, a U.S. Justice Department official, has stated that each year more than 4,000 bodies are found abandoned on lonely hillsides, in city dumpsters, or beside rural roads and are never identified (Lindsey, 1984). However, Heck's statistics are only an estimate and have absolutely no empirical basis as there is no mechanism for collecting such information. In discussing the number of serial killers, Levin and Fox (1985) state, "Indeed, one can only speculate that many of the more than five thousand unsolved homicides in the nation each year are the work of a few very effective killers" (p. 186).

Whether or not the incidence of serial murder is increasing is a question frequently addressed in the contemporary literature with a great deal of focus on the increase of stranger-to-stranger or motiveless homicides. Those who contend that there is such an increase apparently base their argument largely on the increase in the number of apparently motiveless killings over the last 15 years (Nelson, 1984). Law enforcement officials assert that history offers nothing to compare with the spate of such murders that has occurred in the U.S. since the beginning of the 1970s. These officials will concede that more murders than are generally recognized could have occurred in the past. They may have gone unnoticed because detectives in widely scattered jurisdictions did not connect the crimes. However, officials still maintain that the increase of murders with no apparent motive is definitely increasing (Lindsey, 1984). Lindsey states:

In 1966, according to the department [of Justice], almost 11,000 murders were committed in the United States. No apparent motive could be deduced for 644 of the total, about 5.9 percent. The other killings involved disputes with friends or family members, robberies or other murders where the motive was readily apparent. (By 1982, the last year for which statistics are available, more than 23,000 murders were committed and the number for which there was no apparent motive had climbed to 4,118 or 17.8 percent of the total. (Lindsey, 1984, p. 7))

Riedel and Zahn (1985) found homicide cases in the United States between 1976 and 1978, in which the victim-offender relationship was unknown, had increased from 24 to 30 percent over the three-year period (p. 10). Riedel and Zahn suggest this trend may indicate an increase in stranger homicides.

An analysis of all recorded homicides in Manhattan, New York during 1981 found homicides involving strangers were twice as prevalent as homicides involving family members. This seems to suggest that homicidal encounters between strangers are becoming much more common in large metropolitan areas (Messner and Tardiff, 1985). This research appears to be consistent with the research and analysis of Zahn and Riedel (1983, 1985) who found stranger murders to be underreported. Riedel (1987) suggests that the increase of homicides with unknown relationships may be due to a larger proportion of stranger homicides. He concludes by stating, "Limited evidence suggests stranger homicides are increasing" (Riedel, 1987, p. 257).

Jenkins (1988c) also seems to argue for an increase in serial murders in this country. He found only two cases between 1950 and 1970 in which the victims numbered ten or more. However, since 1970 he identified 39 such cases.

Sonnenschein (1985) refers to murders with no apparent motive as random and senseless and his comparison of these murders based on the FBI's *Uniform Crime Report* between 1965 (5.4%) and 1981 (17%) reveals a 14 percent increase in this category over the seventeen-year period.

Ressler et al. (1984), in a paper presenting the results of a two-year study on serial or series murder, state:

The beginning of such stranger, motiveless murders was first noticed by the media in the mid-sixties when the "Son of Sam" killer, David Berkowitz stalked victims in New York and gunned them down with a .44 pistol without apparent motive. Since that time there has been a considerable upswing in these types of murders and in the past decade the rate has climbed to an almost epidemic proportion (p. 1).

To illustrate the scope of this problem, Ressler et al. (1984) cite a newspaper indexing report on the occurrence of mass murders and serial murders in the years 1982, 1983, and through July 1984. They conclude that the figures from this report "dramatically illustrate the increase in mass murders as well as the category of serial murders" (p. 3). While the information presented from this newspaper indexing report by Ressler et al. does tend to show an increase in serial murders, with 10 in 1982, 27 in 1983, and 12 in the first seven months of 1984, there are severe limitations to this data. First of all, the total murders in the first seven months of 1984 may reflect a decrease if seasonal variation of serial murders is discounted. This total of 12 murders in seven months reflects an average of only 1.7 per month, compared to 2.25 per month for the previous twelve months and 0.83 for 1982. If the incidence of murders is linear then the total serial murders for 1984 would be fewer than 22. While linearity of serial murder occurrences is, of course, not assumed, the limited time frame of 31 *[handwritten margin notes:]* does not deny that serial murder does question a limited prediction   ✗✗

months is not sufficient, given the data presented, to conclude that serial murder is increasing, implying a definite trend in this phenomenon. True, the data reflect an increase within the thirty-one-month period, based upon twelve-month increments or a portion thereof. This does not, however, represent a trend. Even more problematic is the fact that the data presented by Ressler et al. represent only that data reported as occurrences of serial murder and subsequently reported in the newspapers indexed in the report.

Ressler, Burgess, and Douglas (1988) cite an increase in the number of murders committed for unknown motives reported in the FBI's *Uniform Crime Reports* from 8.5 percent of all murders in 1976 to 22.5 percent in 1986 (p. 2). They argue that many sexual homicides may be reported in this unknown motive category. These authors further state that "it is the belief of both investigators and clinicians that the majority of serial murders are sexual in nature" (Ressler, Burgess, and Douglas, 1988, p. 3). From this somewhat limited analysis, serial murder appears to be increasing.

For some, the increase of serial murder is combined with an increase in mass murder and referred to as multiple murder. Elliott Leyton argues that there has been a dramatic increase in multiple murders in the United States since the late 1960s (Leyton, 1986).

Whereas there was one multiple murderer in the 1950s, by 1984 the United States was producing one multiple murderer a month. One Department of Justice official recently estimated that there are as many as 100 serial killers currently operating in the country ("Why Mass Murderers Kill," 1986, p. 7).

Leyton (1986) states in his book *Compulsive Killers: The Story of Modern Multiple Murder* that in the early 1980s the multiple-murder rate in the United States was on a "meteoric rise" (p. 22), when the homicide rate was beginning to abate. In a footnote to this argument, Leyton readily admits the unreliability and unavailability of statistics for multiple murder and the further weakness of these numbers is due to those not captured and the reliability of reporting police jurisdictions. This footnote certainly tends to weaken Leyton's own argument for a "meteoric rise" or a dramatic increase in multiple murders. (Others mentioned herein who provide the same basic argument for an increase could also be held accountable to Leyton's footnote, to a lesser or greater extent.)

The U.S. Justice Department has hesitated to refer to serial murder as an epidemic, but the volume of cases of serial murder has brought more attention to the phenomenon (Starr et al., 1984). However, Roger Depue, FBI director of the newly formed National Center for the Analysis of Violent Crime, states, "It isn't just a matter of being more aware of [serial murders]. The actual number seems to be increasing" (Starr et al., 1984, p. 100).

Others who argue that serial murder is increasing attribute the increase to the violence on television or the growth of sadistic pornography. Pierce Brooks, a recognized homicide expert, thinks the increased mobility of Americans is partly to blame for the rise in serial homicides. Brooks states, "We are becoming more of a society of strangers" (Berger, 1984, p. 1).

Zahn (1980) also notes that there is a definite increase in stranger murders and in cases where the offenders remain unknown (p. 124). Zahn further states that "with careful monitoring of these types of homicides that are occurring differing allocations to solve the problems associated with these types might occur" (p. 128). The problem, however, is that there is no such monitoring on a national scale. The *Uniform Crime Report* and preliminary content analysis of newspaper accounts reveals that the occurrence of serial murder is a persistent, and possibly increasing phenomenon in our society. It is possible, however, that serial murder is stable in rate and any "increase" is the result of rising awareness and reporting procedures of the media. Yet no resources are being allocated to examine the extent or prevalence of this phenomenon. The number of serial murders or the extent to which they can be attributed to this increase has not been documented.

Dietz (1986) states, "Claims to the contrary notwithstanding, there is no empirical evidence that the frequency of serial killers is increasing or is higher in the United States than in other countries" (p. 486). He argues that although detection of serial killers may be increasing, rates are not known, and the study of trends or comparisons is not yet possible.

Norris (1988) argues that the number of serial killers has increased since 1960. Masters (1985) also finds a "rash of cases" (p. 251), beginning in the early 1960s. He concludes that these murderers "are becoming less rare and may well come to represent a type of 'motiveless' criminal who belongs predominantly to the twentieth century" (Masters, 1985, p. 251). Wilson and Seaman (1983) concur, finding such crimes rare prior to 1960. However, a few serious researchers would appear to support Linedecker's (1988) claim of less than 12 serial killers in the United States between 1900 and 1950.

There is a general impression that serial murder has emerged only in the last few years. However, this perception cannot be supported (Gest, 1984; Starr et al., 1984). Hickey's (1985) historical literature review refutes the notion that serial murderers are a product of contemporary society. Hickey (1985) found 117 serial murderers as far back in U.S. history as the early 1800s and he concluded:

First, the data unequivocally contradicts the assumption that serial murderers are a recent phenomenon. Regardless of their typologies, serial murderers can be traced back 200 years. Secondly, the emergence of serial murderers to the public view is made possible by our advancing technology, but they probably have always existed and operated in the United States (p. 11).

While Leyton (1986) argues rather unconvincingly that the United States produces proportionately more serial murderers than any other industrial nation, the phenomenon is certainly not unique to this country. Hickey (1985) found 47 serial murderer cases in foreign countries (p. 3). The Ratcliffe Highway murders in London in 1811 (see James and Critchley, 1971) is one early example in England. Franklin (1965) provides numerous examples of European and U.K.

murderers, which today would be referred to as serial, such as Bela Kiss (early 1900s, Hungary); Henri Desire Landru (1919, France); Peter Kurten (1929, Germany); Dr. Marcel Petiot (1941, France); Gordon Cummins (1942, England); and John Reginald Christie (1950, England). Of course, the most famous serial murderer was "Jack the Ripper," who operated in the late 1800s in London, England and who recently was compared to the "Yorkshire Ripper" (see Chapter 5).

Smith (1987) describes a number of serial killers from southern and southeast Asia, Europe, and England. Smith concludes by stating, "One thing appears certain, serial killing represents a world-wide problem which isn't going away" (Smith, 1987, p. 4).

PEOPLE WHO KILL SERIALLY

The killing of a stranger is not seen as principally motivated by previous interpersonal frictions in the killer-victim relationship, but rather as the outcome of some other interpersonal motive. More than dyadic relationship killings, these cases create a principal cultural concern with motivational and materialistic factors rather than with the consequences to society of numerous homicides (Lundsgaarde, 1977). Lundsgaarde (1977) found patterns indicating that those who kill intimates were better off than those who kill strangers. Many received much more lenient sentences and some were not even prosecuted. Similarly, Black (1988) notes that in the United States during the late 1970s "those convicted of killing a stranger were considerably more likely to receive a sentence of capital punishment than those convicted of killing a relative, friend or acquaintance" (p. 12). Daly and Wilson (1988) explain this sentencing disparity by pointing to the public's preference for more severe penalties for predatory attacks upon strangers "because they [the public] perceive themselves as potential victims, and perhaps also because such killings are perceived as volitional and deterrable" (pp. 273, 274). Black concurs and argues that relational distance is a very powerful predictor of legal behavior. There is every reason to believe that individually and collectively, members of our society respond in like fashion to the relational distance of the killer and his victim. Thus, tolerance for the act of homicide is greatly reduced as the relational distance between the killer and victim is increased.

As Egger (1984) observed, if one loses a family member, loved one, or friend as a result of a killing in which victim and attacker had a prior relationship, such a relationship tends to mitigate the loss for the survivors in that it provides some sense of rationality for the act. Where relational distance is great, no sense of rationality can be found for the act and tolerance levels approach zero.

To kill a stranger not only defies an understanding of the rationality for such an act but tends to accentuate a general level of fear due to the apparent randomness of victim selection. Lundsgaarde (1977) states the problem succinctly: "The killer who chooses a stranger as his victim overtly threatens the preservation of social order" (p. 140).

Not a great deal is known about serial killers who choose strangers as victims. Zahn (1981) states, "The sum of homicide literature is repetitive, but it is not cumulative" (p. 111). Such is apparently the state of our knowledge of people who kill serially.

Intrinsic to the identity of the serial murderer is the etiology of such behavior; however, identity of the murderer is of primary importance to law enforcement. This is generally attempted through the development of modus operandi information but is frequently due to a "fluke" or luck (Levin and Fox, 1985). Nevertheless, the identification is imperative to stop the killer. Etiological considerations may be important but are a more long-range objective. As these murderers are identified, apprehended, and studied, some description of them has developed. Older references in the literature tend to reflect a Freudian orientation to this phenomenon.

J. Paul de River categorizes this group of killers as "lust killers" who suffer from a deviation or perversion of the sexual impulse (1949, p. 99). They are "cold, calculating and egotistically sadistic" (p. 120). Guttmacher (1960) states that many of these sadistic killers vent their hostile impulses through cruelty to animals; however, their real hatred is not against animals, but against their fellow man.

In discussing these compulsive homicides, Revitch and Schlesinger (1981) posit that the majority of these crimes have an underlying basis of sexual conflicts and that most of the sex murders belong to this group. Serial murderers, according to Lunde (1976), are sadist murderers who are apt to repeat their crimes. He describes the sadist murderer as one who kills, mutilates, or abuses his victims to achieve sexual pleasure and may choose victims with specific occupations or characteristics. Lunde (1976) states, "They usually have few normal social and sexual relationships. In fact, they often have had no experience of normal sexual intercourse" (p. 53). The sadist murderer is one of the most common types of killers of strangers and, of all types of murderers, is the most likely to repeat his crime, according to Lunde. Brittain (1970) describes the sadistic murderer as one "excited by cruelty, whether in books or in films, in fact or fantasy" (p. 202). Levin and Fox (1985) state, "The serial killer, motivated by sex and sadism, is hardly deterrable. His sociopathic disposition favors immediate gratification, regardless of the consequences" (p. 225).

Dr. Helen Morrison, who has reportedly interviewed a number of serial murderers, argues against the sexual theme of serial murder. She states, "The incidence of sadomasochistic sex is very high. The incidence of mass murders is not, at least in the sheer number of perpetrators" (McCarthy, 1984, p. 1). Storr (1972) also discounts the sexual nature of sadomasochism or cruelty. He argues that "sado-masochism is less 'sexual' than is generally supposed, and is really a 'pseudo-sexual' activity or preoccupation, much more concerned with power relations than with pleasure'' (Storr, 1972, pp. 74–75). The emphasis on power relations or control was, for Levin and Fox (1985), an important characteristic of serial murderers. They state:

Domination unmitigated by guilt is a crucial element in serial crimes with a sexual theme. Not only does sadistic sex—consensual or forcible—express the power of one person over another, but in serial homicides, murder enhances the killer's sense of control over his victims. (p. 72)

Levin and Fox (1985) contend that the murderer is trying to achieve a feeling of superiority over the victim and to triumph or conquer by destruction. Further, that ''as the serial killer becomes more and more secure with his crime, however, he may also become increasingly more sadistic and inhumane'' (p. 67). They argue that ''the pleasure and exhilaration that the serial killer derives from repeated murder stem from absolute control over other human beings'' (p. 68). The psychological need to control and the wish to command the fate of those around them is, for Fox and Levin (1985), often evident in serial murderers.

As Egger (1985) has noted, the motivational dynamics of serial murder seem to be consistent with research on the nature of rape. This similarity becomes even more evident when one realizes that ''it may take only a small increase in the desperation of the assailant or resisting victim to convert a violent rape into a murder'' (West, 1987, p. 19).

There is still no consensus among behavioral scientists, even when they look at the same data, for the reasons why so many Americans kill each other (Rose, 1979, p. 81). Banay (1956) notes that the reasons given for the act of homicide by the individual are misleading since the true cause is masked by other ''logically'' understandable explanations. Banay concludes simply that there is no logic in murder (p. 193).

Elliott Leyton (1986) expands upon a frequently cited explanation for homicide. Leyton, an anthropologist, identifies relative deprivation, which he also extends to absolute deprivation, as the provocation for the multiple murderer's frustration. From a cultural perspective, the multiple murderer (Leyton includes both mass and serial murderers) is then

a profoundly conservative figure who comes to feel excluded from the class he so devoutly wishes to join. In an extended campaign of vengeance, he murders people unknown to him, but who represent to him in their behavior, their appearance, or their location the class that has rejected him. (p. 23)

Leyton (1986) argues that multiple murders are a ''kind of sub-political and conservative protest which nets the killer a substantial social profit of revenge, celebrity, identity and sexual relief'' (p. 26), ''and is viewed by them as a mission or crusade.'' For Leyton, these killings are, ''a kind of rebellion against the social order'' (p. 26); ''a protest against their [the killers] perceived exclusion from society'' (p. 27).

Leyton (1986) concludes by rejecting arguments of sexual excitement or of conquest over the victim. The motivation is rather a solution to those problems resulting from denied ambition. Multiple murderers act "to relieve a burning grudge engendered by their failed ambition" (p. 298).

Colin Wilson (1972) would appear to agree with Leyton: "If man is deprived of meanings beyond his everyday routine, he becomes disgusted and bitter, and eventually violent. A society that provides no outlet for man's idealist passions is asking to be torn apart by violence" (p. 233).

Wilson and Seaman (1983) carry this line of thinking one step further by attempting to examine the thoughts of those who commit murder. While the argument for unmotivated resentment as a prerequisite for such violence is extended and further developed, the authors also attach an explanation for what they label as "motiveless viciousness" (p. ix). Such violence, as frequently committed by the serial killer, is the result of Sartre's magical thinking, that is, thinking that cannot possibly accomplish its objective (Wilson and Seaman, 1983, p. xii). However, such an etiological argument seems specious given the fact that such thinking is apparently nothing more than a lack of self-control and an unwillingness to delay gratification. Explications of this nature are indeed almost trite and frequently found in much of the more mainstream true-crime literature.

Abrahamsen (1985) describes David Berkowitz (Son of Sam) as "a human being inexorably driven to destroy himself and others" (p. xii). Abrahamsen found Berkowitz to have total indifference to the fate of his victims and to have an urge to kill (and confess when the time was ripe). Berkowitz as his own detective became, in a sense, the victim as well as the victimizer through his own confessions (p. 215). Such a description could easily have been given of other well-known serial killers like Henry Lee Lucas and John Wayne Gacy.

Norris (1988) in *Serial Killers* presents a list of behavior patterns which he offers as the epistemology of the "serial killer syndrome" (p. 212). These 22 patterns are symptoms of episodic aggressive behavior which for Norris provide a profile of predisposition. Norris contends that these patterns or profiles are the "combined symptomatology of hundreds [sic] of serial killers" (p. 242). It would seem that the reader must accept such statement as fact based upon Norris's assertion of having interviewed more than a dozen serial killers (p. 210) and that the remaining data for such a synthesized symptomatology stems from interviews of secondary data sources. Such acceptance from a critical layperson, notwithstanding the expectations of a scholarly analysis, is indeed difficult, given the total lack of empirical documentation, footnotes, or references in Mr. Norris's work.

The word "psychopath" is frequently used by psychologists and psychiatrists to described the behavior of the motiveless serial murderer. They also use the term "sociopath." Both terms have now been replaced. *The Diagnostic and Statistical Manual of Mental Disorders*, first published in 1952 by the American Psychiatric Association, referred to a "sociopathic personality" (code 52). The third and revised edition of this manual (1987) refers to such behavior as "antisocial personality disorder" (code number 301.70, p. 317).

Levin and Fox (1985) found the terms "sociopath" and "psychopath" used interchangeably to describe serial murderers repeating acts of brutality and sadism due to a lack of conscience or guilt. Sociopaths or psychopaths are not mentally ill or grossly out of touch with reality. They are not able to experience love or empathy due to family rejection and needs frustration. They lack a sense of moral guilt and are unable to postpone drives for immediate gratification. These people cheat and lie as well as rape and murder (Levin and Fox, 1985).

Dr. Joel Fort, a psychiatrist who testified at the trial of serial murderer Edmund Kemper in Santa Cruz, California, defined the sociopath as having

a morality that is not operating by any recognized or accepted moral code, but operating entirely according to expediency to what one feels like doing at the moment or that which will give the individual the most gratification or pleasure. It includes an absence of conscience. (Godwin, 1978, p. 300)

For example, Luke Karamazov, convicted serial killer, is described by Hilberry (1987) as "on the whole . . . well satisfied with his own composure, his lack of feeling [for his victims]" (p. 88). Hilberry quotes Karamazov as stating, "I had a certain detachment, if you can visualize. There has to be some part of me left out" (p. 88).

Dr. Emanuel Tanay, a forensic psychiatrist, notes that the serial killer does not give any visible signs of derangement, even under the most expert examination. Tanay interviewed Theodore Bundy and found no overt psychopathology in examining him (Berger, 1984). Dr. Helen Morrison, who reportedly spent 800 hours with John Wayne Gacy, believes the serial killer is a new personality type (Berger, 1984).

Cleckley (1976) identifies a number of marks or attributes of psychopaths, whose behavior is not readily understood in terms of mental deficiency, neurosis, or psychosis. These primary attributes include unreliability, insincerity, pathological lying, and egocentricity; poor judgment and impulsivity; lack of remorse, guilt, or shame; an inability to experience empathy or concern for others, or to maintain affectionate attachments; impersonal and poorly integrated sex life; and an unstable life style with no long-term plans. Beyond such general attributes, the psychiatric and psychological literature, due to its individualistic case approach to the study of such people and their classification, does not readily facilitate aggregate analysis of the serial murderer's characteristics. Dr. John Liebert, a psychiatrist at the University of Washington, has stated, "We have some basic clinical knowledge of serial murderers that allows us to rule people out. What we don't have is how to rule them in" (Berger, 1984, p. 1).

Theories regarding inadequate socialization or childhood trauma are frequently cited in the homicide literature and often referred to regarding the serial murderer. Storr (1972) states that human cruelty (which describes the acts committed by serial murderers, i.e., torture, mutilation, dismemberment, etc.) is "a phenomenon which can only be understood if we take into account the fact that many people suffer from persistent feelings of powerlessness and helplessness which date from a very early period in childhood'' (p. 76). Reinhardt's (1962) case studies of multicides (mass and serial murders) found a prevalence of neglect and early years spent in wretched states of social and psychological deprivation.

They gave preponderant evidence of never having experienced normal communication with a dependable, understanding part of the social world about them. They had no workable system of social or personal frames of reference. (p. viii)

Willie (1975), who concurs with Reinhardt, found the most common feature of the family backgrounds of the murderer to be the violent punishing practices inflicted upon the child, and that there ''appears to be no other factor which is as specific in the family backgrounds of homicidal offenders'' (p. 168).

Hazelwood and Douglas (1980) state that:

Seldom does the lust murderer come from an environment of love and understanding. It is more likely that he was an abused and neglected child who experienced a great deal of conflict in his early life and was unable to develop and use adequate coping devices (i.e., defense mechanisms). (p. 4)

Ellis and Gullo (1971) found in their extensive reading of the case histories of murderers:

Whenever sufficient material is given on the murderer's background, it is consistently found that (1) his upbringing particularly in relation to being treated kindly by his parents and his being emotionally close to them and to his other family members, left much to be desired; and (2) from an early age, he acted peculiarly, especially in his interpersonal relations with others, and began to get into some kind of school, social or vocational difficulties. (p. 158)

Burch and Cavanaugh (1986) conducted an analysis of 11 clinical studies of multiple murders involving a number of serial murderers. They found no specific relationship between multiple murder and any particular psychiatric diagnosis or theory of criminology (p. 17).

Serial murderers are frequently found to have unusual or unnatural relationships with their mothers. Lunde (1976) notes, ''Normally there is an intense relationship with the mother. Her death is often one of those fantasized during adolescence. Later on, she may become one of the victims'' (p. 53). ''Many serial murderers have had intense, smothering relationships with their mothers—relationships filled with both abuse and sexual attraction'' (''The Random Killers,'' Nov. 26, 1984, p. 105).

Bjerre (1981), in his classic study of murder, states:

Time after time during my studies among murderers I was struck by the fact that just the most brutal criminals—men who, however different their psychological natures may have been in the beginning, and who had a stereotyped incapacity to conceive their fellow creatures as anything but dead matter or as the means to the satisfaction of their animal lusts; in other words men who for a long time had been cut off from any sort of association with humanity—were nevertheless frequently attached to their mothers by bonds which seemed even stronger than those which one ordinarily finds between mother and son. (p. 81)

(One characteristic of the serial murderer not addressed in the literature is that there are very few instances in which a serial murderer is a female. Instances of female mass murderers can be found but relatively few serial murderers have been identified (see Hickey, 1986). This sexual differentiation may lead researchers to study maleness and its socialization as an etiological consideration. However, the lack of this obvious distinction has apparently precluded such study.)

Neither is the sexual preference or orientation a consistent correlate when known serial murderers are examined. As West (1987) notes, "there is no reason to suppose that the likelihood of becoming homicidal is associated with a particular sexual orientation" (p. 194). For example deSalvo, Bundy, or Kemper preferred females as sexual partners and as prey while Gacy, Nilsen, or Corll preferred males in these roles.

Serial murderers are considered to be very mobile, moving from city to city and state to state.)Robert Keppel, chief criminal investigator for the Washington State Attorney General's Office who investigated the Theodore Bundy case and is currently involved in investigating the "Green River Killings" in the Pacific Northwest area, characterizes serial murderers as tending to be highly mobile, ready to move quickly to another town after committing several killings that might lead to their detection (Lindsey, 1984). Theodore Bundy is reported to have left victims across the country from Seattle, Washington to Pensacola, Florida. Henry Lee Lucas remains a very strong suspect in killings that have occurred in 27 different states (see Chapter 7). Levin and Fox (1985) found serial murderers to have become more geographically mobile, like society in general.

(Most known serial murderers traveled continually) Where the average person might put 10,000 to 20,000 miles a year on his car, some serial murderers have traveled 100,000 to 200,000 miles a year by automobile (Sonnenschein, 1985). However, it should be noted that not all serial murderers are as mobile and may commit their killings within a relatively small geographic area. For instance, John Wayne Gacy committed his killings in and around the suburbs of Chicago. Robert Hansen committed his killings within the Anchorage, Alaska area, even though he buried his victims in rural areas outside Anchorage.

(Ressler et al. (1984) found that a number of serial murderers have been fascinated with law enforcement.)They found several who had posed as law enforcement officers, held positions as security guards, or worked as auxiliary police. Some serial murderers are so fascinated by detective work that they school themselves in police procedures (Gest, 1984). Examples of this fascination found in the literature were: Theodore Bundy, who worked for the King County Crime Commission in Washington; Wayne Williams, who often photographed crime scenes; John Wayne Gacy had a police radio in his home; and Edmund Kemper, who frequented a bar near police headquarters and questioned off-duty officers about the murders he had committed. Robert Keppel states that "a lot of them [serial murderers] seem to know something about police routine and are kind of police buffs" (Lindsey, 1984, p. 7).

SERIAL MURDER VICTIMS

(Little is known regarding the victims of serial murderers other than they are almost always strangers to the murderer) (For a somewhat different perspective and a more extensive discussion of serial murder victimization, see Chapter 2.) As Wolfgang and Ferracuti (1967) found in comparing solved and unsolved homicides, a higher proportion of the latter involved victims who were strangers to their assailants. Frequently, the pattern of a serial murderer is revealed through his choice of victims. In a preponderance of known cases, the victims seem to be young females presumably chosen to satisfy the lust of the serial murderer. The victims are sometimes young males as in the cases of John Wayne Gacy and Elmer Wayne Henley. It has been estimated that 50 percent of unidentified bodies in county morgues or medical examiners' offices across the country are young children or adolescents (C. Wingo, personal communication, July 1983). We do not know how many of these bodies represent victims of serial murderers.

In most cases, the victims are selected solely on the fact that they crossed the path of the serial murderer and became a vehicle for his hypo-arousal and pleasure (Egger, 1984). Victims may be self-selecting only from their existence at a place and point in time. This is apparently the only known precipitating factor. Definitions of serial murder discussed earlier in this chapter suggest some commonalities among victims. Egger's (1984) original working definition identifies prestigelessness, powerlessness or membership in lower socio-economic groups as common characteristics of serial murder victims. Levin and Fox (1985) seem to agree with Egger and state, "Serial killers almost without exception choose vulnerable victims—those who are easy to dominate" (p. 75). "The serial killer typically picks on innocent strangers who may possess a certain physical feature or may just be accessible" (p. 231). The examples provided by Egger (1984), "vagrants, prostitutes, migrant workers, homosexuals, missing children, and single and often elderly women" (p. 9), would seem to portray this vulnerability or innocence.

Sherman, Gartin, and Burger (1989) found predatory stranger offenses to be partially dependent upon the availability of vulnerable victims at a particular geographic location. The extent to which a person is responsible for his or her own vulnerability seems to be one of the determining factors in precipitating the homicide. Luckenbill (1977) found that in about two-thirds of the homicide encounters he studied, the interaction that led to the homicide was initiated by the victim. Allen (1980) refers to their victim role as "subintentional" death. This concept of victim precipitation was originated by von Hentig in 1948. Today victim precipitation is considered a major cause or certainly a contributing factor of homicide by most criminologists. However, the extent to which victim precipitation occurs in serial murder can only be speculated upon since very little information is usually available regarding the pre-homicide interaction between offender and victim.

Sagarin and Maghan (1983), in discussing the susceptibility and vulnerability of victims, state:

The vulnerability of an individual or group to criminal depredations depends upon an opportunity factor as well as an attractiveness factor. Extreme risks are run by people who appear at the "right time" and the "right place," from the offender's point of view. Hence certain lifestyles expose individuals and their possessions to greater threat and dangers than other. (p. 241)

Karmen (1983) provides examples of these high-risk life styles: homosexuals cruising downtown areas and bathrooms; cult members soliciting funds on sidewalks and in bus stations; and released mental patients and skid row alcoholics wandering the streets at odd hours (pp. 241–42). The same could possibly be said for hitchhikers, lost or runaway children, migrant workers, and single and often elderly women.

Jenkins and Donovan (1987) found four primary "hunting grounds" favored by serial killers. These areas also reflect four different types of victims sought out by serial killers: female prostitutes from "red-light" areas; men involved in casual homosexual contacts; men frequenting skid-row areas of big cities; and women living on college campuses.

Sagarin and Maghan (1983), in discussing homosexuals as victimizers and victims note that

the offender's rage against society is deflected and targeted on those who are victimized as the offender is. . . . Victimization appears to produce a rage that feeds an offender mentality, and offenders then choose victims who are the most vulnerable, closest (spatially and socially), and offer the greatest opportunities. (p. 160)

If these concepts of susceptibility or vulnerability and victim-victimizer are combined, an extrapolation is possible in examining the victims of the serial murderer. If many serial murderers were victimized in childhood, as indicated above, and vulnerable due to their childhood situation, they may in fact have chosen victims like their earlier selves or from the same general life style, from which to victimize. Sagarin and Maghan (1983) states, "One common thread that emerges from most victim/offender studies is that both parties are usually drawn from the same group or background" (p. 242). However, it must be noted that there were no serial murder, victim/offender studies found in the literature other than anecdotal material or conclusions based upon very few serial murder cases. Therefore, no valid conclusions can be drawn from the literature regarding victim/offender relationships in this context.

The victim/offender relationships have been found to be highly correlated with homicide location in urban areas. Most stranger homicides tend to occur on the street or in a commercial establishment (Riedel and Zahn, 1985). As noted earlier, serial murders are found within this category in the group of homicides where offender/victim relationship is unknown.

Some blame the mobility of U.S. society for making victims more available to serial murderers. "It's not unusual for people—especially if they're drug users—to just up and leave home," says Commander Alfred Calhoun of the Quachita Parish Sheriff's Office in Monroe, Louisiana. "Many become victims because they're hitchhiking or wandering in deserted places" (Gest, 1984, p. 53). Robert Keppel contends that since many serial murderers are charismatic, they can convince their victims to go with them for some reason: "They pick people they can have power and control over, small-framed women, children and old people" (Lindsey, 1984, p. 7).

Psychiatrist Helen Morrison contends that the "look" of the victims is significant. She states, "If you take photos, or physical descriptions of the victims, what will strike you is the similarity in look." Morrison also theorizes that some nonverbal communication exists between victim and killer: "There's something unique in that interaction" (McCarthy, 1984, p. 10). Morrison believes that the victims of serial murderers were symbolic of something or someone deeply significant in the murderers' lives. Some psychologists have said that the victims specifically represent cruel parents against whom some murderers feel they cannot directly take revenge (Berger, 1984).

Dr. Morrison says the serial murderer does not distinguish between human beings and inanimate objects (Berger, 1984). This characteristic may be similar to the contract killers, whom Dietz (1986) describes as depersonalizing their victims (p. 115). Lunde (1976) found dehumanization of the victims, or perception of them as objects by the sexual sadist murderers. He argues that this "prevents the killer from identifying with the victims as mothers, fathers, children, people who love and are loved, people whose lives have meaning" (Lunde, 1976, p. 61).

Few serious researchers of homicide would disagree with Carolyn Block (1987), who succinctly states, "Homicide is a function of the vulnerability of the potential victim and the strength of the potential offender" (p. 163). This is certainly true for serial homicide as well.

CATEGORIES AND TYPOLOGIES

An examination of the spatial dimensions of serial murder reveals a multitude of geographic and chronological patterns that provide us with little similarity among victims or offenders. The frequency of these events may occur within hours or in some cases months or years apart. The only source, in most cases, is the memory of the murderer himself through his confessions. Nevertheless, some limited typologies and/or categories of serial murder have been proposed.

Burgess et al. (1986) contend that this development of a typology of murderers is essential to enhance law enforcement investigative efforts, to focus more clearly on professional intervention efforts, and to facilitate a dialogue between appropriate disciplines to encourage suspect profiling research.

Zahn and Sagi (1987) provide a very convincing argument for subdividing the stranger homicide category due to its heterogeneous nature. They suggest additional variables in order to form more homogeneous categories to include drug and alcohol use, history of violence or mental illness, nature of disputes, and presence of psychotic disturbance.

When one refers to the serial murderer it is frequently understood that such an individual has some degree of mobility. Cecil Wingo, chief investigator for the Harris County, Texas Medical Examiner, describes serial murderers in geographic terms. He has coined the terms "megastat" and "megamobile." The "megastat" commits killings over time in a single static urban environment. The "megamobile" is mobile, moving over great stretches of geography as he commits his killings (Egger, 1984). Holmes and DeBurger (1985) use the terms "geographically stable" and "geographically transient." They define the former as one who typically lives in a particular area and kills his victims within the general region of his residence and the latter as one who travels continually throughout his killing career. Holmes and DeBurger further differentiate between these two types, stating that for the "geographically stable" serial murderer, "very frequently, the motive is sexual in nature and the predator may slaughter a selected group of victims" (p. 6). This assertion is, however, based upon only three cases (John Wayne Gacy, Albert Fish, and Wayne Williams) and appears to be of very questionable validity.

Hickey's (1985) geographic typology of serial murder is a more fully developed attempt. He identifies three different types: the "traveling or mobile," the "local," and the "place-specific." Hickey states,

Mobile murderers are those individuals, almost exclusively male, who move from city to city and across state lines, killing victims at random, or seeking out a specific type of victim. . . . These killers tend to appear friendly and helpful to their victims and usually take considerable precaution against being caught, i.e. Edmund Kemper. (p. 9)

[T]he local serial murderer stays in close proximity to his city or community. Again, almost exclusively male, these killers usually have a specific type of victim, i.e. prostitutes in the Green River Killings or the young males in the Atlanta Child Murders. (p. 10)

[T]he place-specific murderer, or the killer who repeatedly murders in the same place. This type of killer usually operates in nursing homes, hospitals or in private homes. Either male or female these murderers kill for reasons of financial security, "mercy" killing, hatred of a particular group of people such as infants, handicapped or the elderly as well as motives of violence and sex...i.e. Ed Gein; John Gacy...i.e. Herman Webster Mudgett. (p. 10)

Hickey's (1985) typology is based upon an historical literature review in which he reports to have identified "117 men and women in the United States who can be identified as serial murderers. An additional 47 serial murderer cases were collected from foreign countries" (p. 3).

Holmes and DeBurger (1988) in a later work also present four major homicidal behavior patterns of serial murderers. The visionary motive type is a psychotic whose acts are commanded by an unseen force. The mission-oriented type is attempting to do something about a situation needing correction. The third pattern, killers with hedonistic motives, encompasses three subcategories: the lust-oriented, whose central focus is sexual gratification; the thrill-oriented, who desires thrills or excitement; and the comfort-oriented, whose main objective is to enjoy life. The fourth behavior pattern is the power/control-oriented type whose primary drive is to exert power and control over others.

Gee (1988) has developed three classifications of multiple murder based upon the problem such murders present for the forensic pathologist.

In one a number of people are killed secretly and their bodies concealed; in the second the deaths are contrived so as to appear to be natural or accidental; in the third no attempt is made to conceal the obvious serial homicides. (p. 53)

Legal classifications of murder (first degree, second degree, etc.) and classification based upon assailant-victim relationships tend to ignore many of the dynamic aspects of the event in the study of serial murder. The classification of murder regarding its motive appears to have provided a somewhat more productive method of examining serial murder. Jesse (1924, p. 13) in her classic study of motive provides six "natural" groups of motives:

1. gain
2. revenge
3. elimination
4. jealousy
5. lust of killing
6. conviction

Jesse (1924) describes her fifth group by dividing it into: lust-murders in which the satisfaction of lust is the actual killing, without any sexual connection with the victim; and lust-murders committed at the same time or directly after the sexual act as part of the sexual gratification.

Megargee (1982) classifies aggressive acts into those of instrumental or extrinsic motivation, in which the aggressive or violent behavior serves as a means to some end, and angry or intrinsic motivation, in which the injury to the victim is an end in itself. It is his first classification that concerns us here, as the motive of sexual gratification is frequently identified in cases of serial murder.

Dietz (1986) has developed a typology for serial killers who have killed five or more victims in five or more killing incidents. This criterion is used by Dietz, who argues that killers with a smaller number of victims are more heterogenous. Dietz's typology is:

1. psychopathic sexual sadists—males suffering from antisocial personality disorders and sexual sadism
2. crime spree killers—those who kill repeatedly during a series of crimes motivated by the search for excitement, money, and valuables
3. functionaries of organized crime operations—including traditional organized crime, various types of gangs, contract killers, illegal mercenaries and terrorists
4. custodial poisoners and asphyxiators—most are caretakers of the debilitated or children in hospitals, houses of babysitters, foster parents and baby power of nineteenth-century England
5. supposed psychotics—who claim to be acting at the direction of command hallucinations or under the influence of compelling delusions (adapted from pp. 487–88).

Guttmacher (1960) refers to purely sadistic homicides as lust-murders. Karpman (1954) describes the perpetrators of lust-murders as nearly always psychotic and sexually impotent. J. Paul de River (1958) defines lust-murder as homicide in which death has occurred through torture brought about to relieve sexual tension. The lust-murderer only gains sexual gratification through physical injury or torture of the victim (p. 99). Lust-murder is further described by de River as being accompanied by acts of perversion such as vampirism, cannibalism, and necrophilia (p. 40). Nettler (1982) refers to this as intentional lust-murder or sadistic murder.

Hazelwood and Douglas (1980) describe two types of lust murderers. The organized nonsocial is seen as a totally egocentric amoral individual who can be superficially charming and manipulative of others. His crimes are committed with method and "expertise." The disorganized asocial type is described as a "loner" with feelings of rejection who has great difficulty in interpersonal relationships. His killings are less cunning and done on impulse. He generally selects female victims, although male victims are not unknown.

Nettler (1982) provides a further description of the lust-murderer:

[F]or such men, the act of killing of a woman is itself sexually stimulating. . . . Many have intercourse, in varied fashion, with the corpse before and after mutilating it. . . . The distinctive significance of sadistic killers is that they commit "butcher murders" without being psychotic. By legal standards, they are in touch with reality. They do not kill under the direction of a delusion. (p. 131)

Revitch and Schlesinger (1978) refer to lust-murders as compulsive homicides that are stimulated through a combination of social pressures, resulting in the weakening of authority and controls. However, a lust-murder does not necessarily mean serial murder, which often appears to be random and motiveless.

SUMMARY

Few definitions of serial murder have been developed. Numerous assumptions have been made regarding the term "serial," but few have specifically defined this adjective when used to modify the terms "murder" or "murderer." Frequent references to serial murder are made using the term "mass," to describe a number of victims. This is particularly true for the press and electronic media. The lack of differentiation between the terms "mass" and "serial" murder results in general confusion as to what is meant by a serial murder. The working definition (Egger, 1988) provided herein and the definition offered by Levin and Fox (1985) appear to be the most extensive definitions of the phenomenon of serial murder. The accuracy of these definitions is, however, yet to be determined due to the lack of empirical data and information.

The extent and prevalence of serial murder in this country is as yet unknown. There have been numerous estimates made regarding the annual incidence of this phenomenon and the number of serial murderers at large at any one time. However, the estimates are based upon extrapolations from total homicides in a given year, from very questionable analysis of *Uniform Crime Reports* data or from those specifically and formally identified by the criminal justice system as serial murderers. The number of serial murder victims is based only upon the confessions of serial murderers or the identification of a pattern of serial murders. Whether or not the phenomenon of serial murder is on the increase has not been empirically determined. Many references are made to an increase, but research is limited by the fact that serial murder per se is not reported in official crime or mortality statistics. Media reports are the only information base from which to determine an increase as well as the extent and prevalence of serial murder. Such an information base is indeed questionable. Historical research (Gest, 1984; Hickey, 1985, Franklin, 1965) reveals numerous reports of serial murder and refutes the notion that serial murder is a contemporary phenomenon.

Serial murder is predominantly a stranger-to-stranger crime. Thus, the research on the serial murderer focuses on the individual who attacks victims not known to him. Practically all of the psychological research conducted on serial murderers is done from a case-study specific approach and there has been little or no effort to combine or collate this research material in order to make general observations or correlates on a large population of serial murderers. The terms most generally used to describe the serial murderer are "psychopath" or "sociopath." However, these terms themselves are subject to a great deal of disagreement among psychologists and psychiatrists. The theories of inadequate socialization are the most frequently cited as explanations of the serial murderer's behavior.

There is a paucity of research on the serial murder victim. In almost all known cases they have been strangers to the serial murderer. Their selection by the serial murderer appears to be random in nature. There is some suggestion and limited research to indicate that victim selection is based upon vulnerability or symbolic representation as perceived by the murderer.

Legal classifications of homicide are not useful in describing or categorizing serial murder. The range of geographical or chronological patterns found in serial murder provides only a few typologies or categories which are limited in nature and scope. Many identified serial murderers have been found to be extremely mobile; however, some may commit their killings within a relatively small geographical area (e.g., John Wayne Gacy). Research into the mobility of the serial murderer results in only a very general differentiation. General typologies relating to the "motive" of the serial murderer result in such terms as "lust" or "sadistic" and are not specifically unique to the phenomenon of serial murder. The way in which the serial murderer is organized (Hazelwood and Douglas, 1980) provides a simple dichotomy and may be more useful to law enforcement investigative efforts.

REFERENCES

Abrahamsen, D. (1985). *Confessions of Son of Sam*. New York: Columbia University Press.

Allen, N. H. (1980). *Homicide: Perspectives on prevention*. New York: Human Sciences Press.

American Psychiatric Association. (1987). *Diagnostic and statistical manual of mental disorders* (3rd edn., revised). Washington, DC: American Psychiatric Association.

Banay, R. S. (1956). "Psychology of a mass murder." *Journal of Forensic Science 1*, 1.

Bartol, C. R. (1980). *Criminal behavior*. Englewood Cliffs, NJ: Prentice-Hall, Inc.

Berger, J. (1984, September 8). "Mass killers baffle authorities." *New York Times*.

Bjerre, A. (1981). *The psychology of murder: a study in criminal psychology* (reprint of 1927 edn.). New York: De Capo Press.

Black, D. (1988). *Sociological justice*. New York: Oxford University Press.

Block, C. R. (1987). *Homicide in Chicago*. Chicago: Loyola University of Chicago.

Block, R. L. (1977). *Violent crime: Environment, interaction and death*. Lexington, MA: Lexington-Heath.

Brandl S. G. (1987, October). "The management of serial homicide investigations: Considerations for police managers." Paper presented at the meeting of the Midwestern Criminal Justice Association, Chicago, IL.

Brittain, R. P. (1970). "The sadistic murderer." *Mental Science and the Law, 10*, 198–207.

Brooks, P. R., Devine, M. J., Green, T. J., Hart, B. L., and Moore, M. D. (1988). *Multi-agency investigative team manual*. Washington, DC: U.S. Department of Justice.

Burch, K. A. and Cavanaugh, J. L., Jr. (1986). "The study of multiple murder: preliminary examination of the interface between epistemology and methodology." *Journal of Interpersonal Violence, 1* (1), 5–23.

Burgess, A. W., Hartman, C. R., Ressler, R. K., Douglas, J. E., and McCormack, A. (1986). "Sexual homicide: A motivational model." *Journal of Interpersonal Violence, 1* (3), 251–72.

Cameron, C. and Frazer, E. (1987). *The lust to kill: A feminist investigation of sexual murder*. New York: New York University Press.

Caputi, J. (1987). *The age of sex crime*. Bowling Green, OH: Bowling Green State University Popular Press.

Cleckley, H. (1976). *The mask of sanity*. St. Louis: C. V. Mosby Co.

Cormier, B. M., Angliker, C. C. J., Boyer, R., Mersereau, G. (1972). "The psycho-dynamics of homicide committed in a semispecific relationship." *Canadian Journal of Criminology and Corrections, 14*, 335–44.

Daly, M. and Wilson, M. (1988). *Homicide*. New York: Aldine De Gruyter.

Darrach, B., and Norris, J. (1984, July). "An American tragedy." *Life Magazine*, pp. 58–74.

de River, J. P. (1949). *Crime and the sexual psychopath*. Springfield, IL: Charles C. Thomas.

Dietz, P. E. (1986). "Mass, serial and sensational homicides." *Bulletin of the New York Academy of Medicine, 62* (5), 477–91.

Dominick, J. R. (1984). *Mass Communication*. Beverly Hills, Ca.: Sage.

Dworkin, A. (1976). *Our blood: Prophecies and discourses on sexual politics*. New York: Harper and Row.

Egger, S. A. (1984). "A working definition of serial murder and the reduction of linkage blindness." *Journal of Police Science and Administration, 12*(3), 348–57.

———. (1985). *Serial murder and the law enforcement response*. Unpublished dissertation, College of Criminal Justice, Sam Houston State University, Huntsville, Texas.

———. (1986, November). *Utility of the case study approach to serial murder research*. Paper presented at the American Society of Criminology Annual Meeting, Atlanta.

———. (1988). Definition of serial murder revised. (work in progress).

———. (1989). "Serial murder." In W. C. Bailey (ed.), *The encyclopedia of police science*. New York: Garland Publishing Company, pp. 578–81.

Ellis, A. and Gullo, J. (1971). *Murder and assassinations*. New York: Lyle Stuart Inc.

Farmer, D. J. and Hooker, J. E. (1987). *Homicide policy and program analysis: Understanding and coping in local government* (Commonwealth Papers). Richmond, VA: Virginia Commonwealth University, Center for Public Affairs.

Fox, J. and Levin, J. (1983). *Killing in numbers: An exploratory study of multiple-victim murder*. Unpublished manuscript.

Franklin, C. (1965). *The world's worst murderers*. New York: Taplinger Publishing Co.

Gee, D. J. (1988). "A pathologist's view of multiple murder." *Forensic Science International, 38*, 53–65.

Gest, T. (1984, April 30). "On the trail of America's 'serial killers.' " *U.S. News & World Report*, p. 53.

Gilbert, J. (1983). "A study of the increased rate of unsolved criminal homicide in San Diego, California and its relationship to police investigative effectiveness." *American Journal of Police, 2*, 149–66.

Godwin, J. (1978). *Murder USA: The ways we kill each other*. New York: Ballantine Books.

Guttmacher, M. (1960). *The mind of the murderer*. New York: Grove Press, Inc.

Hare, R. D. and McPherson, L. (1984). "Violent and aggressive behavior by criminal psychopaths." *International Journal of Law and Psychiatry, 7*, 35–50.

Hazelwood, R. and Douglas, J. (1980, April) "The lust murderer." *FBI Law Enforcement Bulletin*, pp. 1–5.

Hazelwood, R. R., Ressler, R. K., Depue, R. L., and Douglas, J. E. (1987). "Criminal personality profiling: an overview." In R. R. Hazelwood and A. W. Burgess (eds.), *Practical aspects of rape investigation: A multidisciplinary approach*. New York: Elsevier, pp. 137–49.

Hickey, E. W. (1985). "Serial murderers: Profiles in psychopathology." Paper presented at annual meeting of Academy of Criminal Justice Sciences, Las Vegas, Nevada.

———. (1986). "The female serial murderer." *Journal of Police and Criminal Psychology, 2*(2).

Hilberry, C. (1987). *Luke Karamazov*. Detroit: Wayne State University Press.

Holmes, R. M. and DeBurger, J. (1985). "Profiles in terror: The serial murderer." *Federal Probation, 49*, 29–34.

———. (1988). *Serial murder*. Newbury Park, CA: Sage.

James, P. D. and Critchley; T. A. (1971). *The maul and the pear tree: The Ratcliffe Highway Murders 1811*. London: Constable & Co.

Jenkins, P. (1988a). Review of *Compulsive killers: The story of modern multiple murder*. *Journal of Criminal Justice, 16*, 151–54.

———. (1988b). "Myth and murder: The serial killer panic of 1983–5." *Criminal Justice Research Bulletin, 3*(11).

———. (1988c). "Serial murder in England 1940–1985." *Journal of Criminal Justice, 16*, 1–15.

———. (1989). "Serial murder in the United States 1900–1940: A historical perspective." *Journal of Criminal Justice 17*, pp. 377–92.

Jenkins, P. and Donovan, E. (1987, July–August). "Serial murder on campus." *Campus Law Enforcement Journal*, pp. 42–44.

Jesse, F. (1924). *Murder and its motive*. New York: Alfred A. Knopf.

Karpman, B. (1954). *The sexual offender and his offenses*. New York: Julian Press.

Keppel, R. D. (1989). *Serial murder: Future implications for police investigations*. Cincinnati: Anderson Publishing.

Kozenczak, J. R. and Henrikson, Karen M. (1987, August). "In pursuit of a serial murder." *Law and Order*, pp. 81–83.

Levin, J. and Fox, J. A. (1985). *Mass murder*. New York: Plenum.

Leyton, E. (1986). *Compulsive killers: The story of modern multiple murders*. New York: New York University Press.

Lindsey, R. (1984, January 21). "Officials cite a rise in killers who roam U.S. for victims." *New York Times*, pp. 1, 7.

Linedecker, C. L. (1988). *Thrill killers: True portrayals of America's most vicious murderers*. New York: Paper Jacks.

Lunde, D. T. (1976). *Murder and madness*. Stanford, CA: Stanford Alumni Association.

Lundsgaarde, P. (1977). *Murder in space city*. New York: Oxford University Press.

Masters, B. (1985). *Killing for company: The case of Dennis Nilsen*. London: Jonathan Cape.

Maxfield, M. G. (1988, November). "Homicide circumstances 1976–1985: A taxonomy based on supplementary homicide reports." Paper presented at the annual meeting of the American Society of Criminology, Chicago.

McCarthy, K. (1984, July 7). "Serial killers: Their deadly bent may be set in cradle." *Los Angeles Times*, p. 1.

McIntyre, T. (1988). *Wolf in sheep's clothing: The search for a child killer.* Detroit: Wayne State University Press.

Megargee, E. I. (1982). "Psychological determinants and correlates of criminal violence." In M. E. Wolfgang and N. A. Weiner (eds.), *Criminal violence.* Beverly Hills, CA: Sage.

Meredith, N. (1984, December). "The murder epidemic." *Science, 84,* pp. 43–48.

Messner, S. F. and Tardiff, K. (1985). "The social ecology of urban homicide: An application of the 'routine activities' approach." *Criminology, 23*(2), 241–67.

Morris, T. and Bloom-Cooper, L. (1964). *A calendar of murder.* London: Michael Joseph.

Nelson, T. (1984). "Serial killings on increase, study shows." *Houston Post,* pp. 1, 11.

Nettler, G. (1982). *Killing one another.* Cincinnati, OH: Anderson.

Newton, M. (1988). *Mass Murder: An annotated bibliography.* New York: Garland.

Norris, J. (1988). *Serial killers: The growing menace.* New York: Doubleday.

Reinhardt, J. M. (1962). *The psychology of strange killers.* Springfield, IL: Charles C. Thomas.

Ressler, R. K. et al. (1984). "Serial murder: A new phenomenon of homicide." Paper presented at the annual meeting of the International Association of Forensic Sciences, Oxford, England.

Ressler, R. K., Burgess, A. W., Hartman, C. R., Douglas, J. E., and McCormack, A. (1986). "Murderers who rape and mutilate." *Journal of Interpersonal Violence, 1*(3), 273–87.

———. (1986). "Sexual homicide: A motivational model." *Journal of Interpersonal Violence, 1*(3), 251–72.

Ressler, R. K., Burgess, A. W., and Douglas, J. E. (1988). *Sexual homicide: Patterns and motives.* Lexington, MA: Lexington Books.

Revitch, E. and Schlesinger, L. B. (1978). "Murder: Evaluation, classification, and prediction." In I. L. Kutash et al. (eds.), *Violence: Perspectives on murder and aggression.* San Francisco, CA: Jossey-Bass, pp. 138–64.

———. (1981). *Psychopathology of homicide.* Springfield, IL: Charles C. Thomas.

Riedel, M. (1987). "Stranger violence: Perspectives, issues, and problems." *The Journal of Criminal Law & Criminology, 78*(2), 223–58.

Riedel, M. and Zahn, M. A. (1985). *The nature and patterns of American homicides.* Washington, DC: National Institute of Justice.

Rose, H. M. (1979). *Lethal aspects of urban violence.* Lexington, MA: Heath and Co.

Sagarin, E. and Maghan, J. (1983). "Homosexuals as victimizers and victims." In D. E. MacNamara and A. Karmen (eds.), *Deviants: Victims or victimizers.* Beverly Hills, CA: Sage, pp. 147–62.

"Serial Murders: Another forensic challenge." (1985). *Forensic Science International, 27,* 135–42.

Sherman, L. W., Gartin, P. R., and Burger, M. E. (1989). "Hot spots of predatory crime: Routine activities and the criminology of place." *Criminology, 27* (1), 27–55.

Simonetti, C. (1984). *Serial murders: 1970–1983*. Unpublished M. A. thesis, State University of New York at Albany, Albany, New York.

Smith, Harold E. (1987). "Serial killers." *Criminal Justice International, 3* (1), 1, 4.

Sonnenschein, A. (1985, February). "Serial killers." *Penthouse*, pp. 32, 34–35, 44, 128, 132–34.

Stanley, A. (1983, November 14). "Catching a new breed of killer." *Time*, p. 47.

Starr, M., et al. (1984, November 26). "The random killers." *Newsweek*, pp. 100–106.

Storr, A. (1972). *Human destructiveness*. New York: Basic Books, Inc.

United States Department of Justice. (1981). *Uniform crime report*. Washington, DC: U.S. Government Printing Office.

United States Department of Justice. (1983). *Uniform crime report*. Washington, DC: U.S. Government Printing Office.

United States Department of Justice, Federal Bureau of Investigation. (1988). *Uniform crime reporting handbook*. Washington, DC: U.S. Government Printing Office.

Usher, A. (1975). "Sexual violence." *Forensic Science, 5*, 243–55.

von Hentig, H. (1948). *The criminal and his victim*. New Haven, CT: Yale University Press.

West, D. J. (1987). *Sexual crimes and confrontations: A study of victims and offenders*. Brookfield, VT: Gower.

"Why mass murderers kill." (1986, April 21). *Maclean's*, pp. 6–7.

Willie, W. S. (1975). *Citizens who commit murder: A psychiatric study*. St. Louis: Warren H. Green.

Wilson, C. (1969). *A casebook of murder*. New York: Cowles Book Co.

––––––. (1972). *Order of assassins: The psychology of murder*. London: Rupel and Hart-Davis.

Wilson, C. and Seaman, D. (1983). *The encyclopedia of modern murder: 1962–1982*. New York: Putnam.

Wilson, P. R. (1987). " 'Stranger' child-murder: Issues relating to causes and controls." *International Journal of Offender Therapy & Comparative Criminology, 31*, 49–59.

Wolfgang, M. E. (1958). *Patterns in criminal homicide*. Philadelphia: University of Pennsylvania Press.

Wolfgang, M. E. and Ferracuti, F. (1967). *The subculture of violence*. London: Tavistock.

Zahn, M. A. (1980). "Homicide in the twentieth century." In J. A. Inciardi and C. Faupel (eds.), *History of crime: Implications for criminal justice policy*. Beverly Hills, CA: Sage.

––––––. (1981). "Homicide in America: A research review." In I. L. Barak-Glantz and R. Huff (eds.), *The mad, the bad and the different: Essays in honor of Simon Dinitz*. Lexington, MA: Lexington Books.

Zahn, M. A. and Sagi, P. C. (1987). "Stranger homicide in Nine American cities." *The Journal of Criminal Law & Criminology, 78*(2), 377–97.

2

The Darker Figure of Crime: The Serial Murder Enigma

KENNA KIGER

The focus of homicide research in criminology as well as the popular press has been on felony-murder (e.g., killings that occur during a robbery or burglary) and the ''crime of passion'' homicide that occurs usually between acquaintances or family members as a result of a personal dispute. Much of this research has utilized the FBI's Uniform Crime Report (UCR) homicide data as well as the Supplemental Homicide Report (SHR). Another source of homicide data that has been used (usually to validate UCR findings) is the annual mortality data collected by the National Center for Health Statistics.

Although innovative procedures have been designed to make the UCR and SHR data useful for such homicide studies, these data sources are not adequate for the study of an important and largely neglected social problem—serial murder.

This chapter presents some of the limitations of existing data sources in the study of serial homicides (see Egger in this volume for a comprehensive definition) and critiques the estimates cited by researchers, journalists, and others concerning serial murder victims, offenders, and missing persons.

Much of the focus of the recent research on serial murder has been on qualitative or descriptive case studies (Rule, 1980; Cahill, 1986; Linedecker, 1980; D. O'Brien, 1985). In addition, a number of researchers have constructed typologies of the motives and crime scenes (Holmes and DeBurger, 1988; Ressler et al., 1984; Snider and Clausen, 1987) in an attempt to subclassify the phenomenon. Although idiographic research provides useful insights into the lives and possible individual-level etiology of serial murderers, it is also important to accurately quantify the problem. Without accurate quantitative assessments of the extent of serial murder, we will be unable to develop informed typologies, theories, and policy decisions. Indeed, we run the risk of creating a social problem, the magnitude of which may be greatly exaggerated.

ESTIMATES OF SERIAL MURDER

Levin and Fox (1985) see mass and serial murder as "America's growing menace" and a recent *Newsweek* article (November 26, 1984) claims that there is an epidemic of serial murder in the United States. Roger Depue, director of the National Center for the Analysis of Violent Crime, suggests that serial murder is increasing and that the volume of recent cases is not simply due to media attention (Starr et al., 1984). Another official estimate cited by a team of researchers from the FBI's Violent Criminal Apprehension Program (Ressler et al., 1984) also confirms that the phenomenon of serial murder is on the increase, based on a search of newspaper indices of multiple murder. In addition to claiming that there is an epidemic of serial murder, there are several numerical estimates cited as having come from "official" sources.

The authors of a *Maclean's* magazine article claimed that the FBI estimates that *unknown* serial murderers claim as many as 6,000 victims in the United States each year, leaving one to believe that this number should be added to the total number of victims resulting from known serial offenders (July 8, 1985). Robert O. Heck, a Justice Department official, said that there are as many as 4,000 serial murder victims each year, over half of whom are under the age of 18. Heck went on in a news interview to say that this phenomenon has escalated to epidemic proportions and concluded with an ominous message that "there's something going on out there" (Lindsey, 1984).

One of the most recent estimates of the extent of serial murder victimization suggests that the number of victims ranges from 3,500 to 5,000 victims annually (Holmes and DeBurger, 1988). This estimate, according to the researchers, is calculated by summing the following: the "known" number of serial murder victims, an estimate of between one-quarter and two-thirds of the 5,000 murder victims whose killer is unknown, and a "probable proportion" of missing children who have become serial murder victims (Holmes and DeBurger, 1988: 19). These authors emphasize that their range is only an estimate but at the same time claim it to be a reliable one. One can only assume that by a reliable estimate, these authors mean an accurate estimate. It should be noted that one could conceivably have a reliable and yet invalid/inaccurate estimate of a particular phenomenon. These same authors also offer an estimate of the number of active serial murder offenders in the United States based on their consultation with "experts" (*sic*) and a computation of an average number of victims per offender. They suggest that there are currently 360 active serial murderers in this country. Most recently, Norris (1988) claims that the FBI estimate of active serial killers is 500. According to Norris, this number represents those offenders that are "at large and unidentified'' (p. 19). With reference to this and other frequently cited FBI estimates, to this author's knowledge, the basis for these estimates has never been made available for the use of independent researchers. It is possible to imagine that the FBI has collected sufficient information on the victims of un-solved murders for comparison with the correlates of known serial murder victims and that estimates might then be extrapolated from this information. However, the research community as a whole has not been able to validate these findings. Other more conservative estimates of the number of active offenders currently operating in the United States have ranged from 30 (Starr et al., 1984) and 35 (Levin and Fox, 1985) to 100 (Leyton, 1986). Thus, the current estimated range of existing active offenders, depending upon the chosen source, ranges from 30 to 500!

Obviously, a consensus does not exist, not even among official estimates, concerning the annual number of serial murder victims or offenders. Lest the reader think this synopsis of the dissensus too harsh, there is no doubt that the nature of this phenomenon makes estimation difficult and any absolute numbers representing a reliable reflection of the scope of the problem, impossible.

The sources of data that have been used to arrive at these various estimates vary at the least with reference to sample bias and size, data collection procedures, and the definition of serial murder. Many samples involve only known or ap-prehended serial offenders, an obvious selection bias. In addition, their claims of a victim count may be suspect and unreliable. Other studies have relied on a secondary analysis of newspaper indices and other periodicals, searching for stories involving serial homicides. Newspaper stories are problematic sources of data because they are obviously dependent upon editorial decisions and because they may sensationalize (not to mention glorify) this phenomenon in order to increase circulation.

Only when lone homicides have been linked as the work of one offender will these incidents appear as serial homicides in a newspaper. The term "linkage blindness" has been used by Egger (1984) to refer to "the lack of sharing or coordination of investigative information relating to unsolved murders and to the lack of adequate networking among law enforcement agencies" (Egger, 1984: 348). The well-documented difficulties of law enforcement personnel to link these series homicides (Egger, 1984) must certainly be reflected in the mainstream coverage of crime. Thus, those who rely only on newspaper indices to collect their data are using a sample that most certainly suffers from an unknown and possibly unacceptable amount of selection bias.

In addition to the problem of sample bias, there is the problem of very small sample sizes in the current research on serial murder. The sample sizes have ranged from Elliott Leyton's (1986) sample of six, which was the basis of his theory on the cause of modern multiple murder, to 36, as used by the FBI in its study of incarcerated offenders who had committed serial killings (Ressler et al., 1984). The method employed in the FBI study was to interview convicted offenders using a 57-page protocol instrument. Levin and Fox researched 42 cases of serial and simultaneous homicide, and Hickey had a sample size of 143 (from 1800–96) in his study of serial murder victimization (Hickey, 1987). Norris (1988) researched 260 serial killers for his recent book, but used only 12 cases to develop his biosocial profile of a serial killer. Holmes and DeBurger (1985) studied seven serial murderers to develop their typology and used a sample of 110 offenders as the basis of their recent book (Holmes and DeBurger, 1988).

Part of this sample size variation is due to the specific time periods and lengths that are used as well as the data source, that is, newspaper coverage of murders, biographies, apprehended serial offenders, interviews, and so on. However, some of the discrepancy is due to the definition of serial murder that the researchers use. In addition to the conceptual muddle that exists due to the lack of distinction between serial and mass murder, there is the definitional problem of the number of homicides that must occur before the killings are recognized as part of a series. The arbitrariness of the designation of the number of killings that must occur before the incidents are counted as serial murder makes generalizations of and comparisons between available studies difficult at best. For example, Levin and Fox (1985) searched various newspaper indices for serial killings involving at least 4 victims. Egger (1984), whose definition of serial murder has reportedly been used by the FBI, proposes that a serial murder has occurred when a second and subsequent murder occurs; thus, a sample based on this definition would conceivably include serial homicides involving as few as 2–3 victims. Holmes and DeBurger (1988) do not specifically define the number of murders that must occur before they would categorize an offender as a serial murderer. Their definition is based on what they refer to as the "elements" of serial murder, such as the fact that it is repetitive and occurs usually between strangers or slight acquaintances. These authors claim that the serial murderer "kills again and again and will continue to kill if not prevented" (p. 18). The extent to which this statement is unfounded is unknown as is the number of serial murder offenders who desist and are never discovered by the authorities. Cases such as the Zodiac (Graysmith, 1976) illustrate that serial murder offenders may be known to exist and may not be apprehended by the police possibly because they discontinue their criminal careers.

The above mentioned data gathering processes (many of which are innovative) have been developed because the sources of data used to study "normal" homicides do not serve the needs of researchers, law enforcers, and policymakers attempting to respond to serial murder. The next section will attempt to discuss the limitations of these data sources and to outline some of the problems with other data that have been used that may add insight into the extent of serial murder victimization such as missing persons, unsolved homicides, and the unidentified deceased.

UNIFORM CRIME REPORTS AND SUPPLEMENTAL HOMICIDE REPORTS

The FBI's Uniform Crime Reports (UCR) consist of data collected annually from law enforcement agencies across the United States. Ideally, these reports reflect all criminal offenses that come to the attention of the police. Although local reporting by police agencies is considered to be voluntary, the current reporting rate reflects 97 percent of the total United States population (FBI, 1984b). These reports give annual information on both Part I offenses (murder and non-negligent manslaughter, forcible rape, robbery, aggravated assault, burglary, larceny-theft, motor vehicle theft, and arson), as well as the "less serious" offenses—Part II crimes such as embezzlement, forgery, vandalism, and so on. The Uniform Crime Reporting Handbook (FBI, 1980) details the definitions of these various crimes to aid law enforcement personnel in classifying and recording the various offenses. The information gathered by local agencies is then sent on to the FBI either directly or through a state-level data compilation program.

Much has been written concerning the inadequacies of the UCR system (see R. O'Brien, 1985). Many of these inadequacies, such as the hierarchical "counting rule" (i.e., counting only the most serious offense per incident), the lack of detail on victim and offender characteristics (with the exception of homicide), and the omission of many federal and white-collar crimes, would probably not affect a study of serially committed homicides. However, the UCR data collection procedures make it virtually impossible to assess serial murder incidence and prevalence.

The FBI collects its UCR data in such a way that tracking an individual offender is not possible. Specifically, because these data are based on crime incidents as opposed to offenders, multiple crimes committed by one offender are not possible to track. The lowest level of aggregation available is that of the individual law enforcement agency and not the individual offender. Thus, it would be impossible to link serial homicides that had been committed by one offender.

As mentioned earlier, UCR crimes represent only those crimes that are known to police. With reference to serial murder victims, the UCR cannot count undiscovered or hidden bodies. Moreover, the police decision as to whether or not a homicide has occurred (much less a homicide series) based upon the discovery of an unidentified body may be affected by the condition of the body, as well as a variety of other factors. In cases in which the body is badly decomposed, the manner and cause of death is often not ascertainable. A decomposed body then is unlikely to be included in a UCR count of homicide, regardless of the cause of death. When a body is discovered that has been dead for a number of years, the time of death is to be approximated by the coroner or medical examiner (National Center for Health Statistics, 1987). If a body is determined to have been a homicide victim who was murdered three years previously, it is unlikely that the homicide count for that year is updated to reflect this discovery, based on the way the various agency records are collected.

Much has been written about other factors that affect police decisionmaking (Black, 1970; Smith and Visher, 1981; Visher, 1983; Wilson, 1978). While factors such as organizational pressures, police/offender interactions, the seriousness of the offense, and the level of police professionalization may affect the decisions made by law enforcement personnel, it is unlikely that these factors would affect homicide classification procedures. The notable exception may at times be certain organizational pressures not to alarm the public when a serial murderer is thought to be active in an area.

Unlike other crimes that are part of the UCR's reporting, additional homicide information is made available in a supplemental data report. The Supplemental Homicide Report (SHR) data, collected as part of the UCR, provide some details about the victim, offender, and circumstances of the homicide. The SHR unit of analysis is the homicide incident, thus allowing for the possibility of more than one victim. Recent innovations, such as those by Williams and Flewelling (1987), attempt to deal with one of the most troublesome aspects of the SHR, that of missing data. Information that may be missing for a single homicide incident may include such characteristics as the motive of the homicide and the victim/offender relationship. Williams and Flewelling note that across U.S. cities the average amount of missing data on homicides is 25 percent. The nature of serial homicide may make it especially susceptible to the missing data problem and thus be seriously underrepresented in these data. Homicide situations in which the victim and the offender do not know one another are more likely to have missing information. Thus, the missing data problems are not randomly distributed and are more likely to occur in incidents of stranger homicide. Additionally, in incidents in which the motive for the homicide is unknown (as opposed to being committed in the course of another felony), there is also more likely to be information missing on the victim/offender relationship (Williams and Flewelling, 1987).

The SHR unit of analysis is the homicide incident and thus allows for the count of more than one victim. While this makes the SHR useful concerning the study of mass or simultaneous killings, it still does not allow the linking of multiple victims over time to one offender. Mass-murder situations could be assessed by analyzing the single offender/multiple victims and multiple offenders/ multiple victims categories (see SHR codebook). Although the SHR's reporting system allows for the study of simultaneous homicides, it may also be the case that because of reporting procedures, simultaneous homicides are not recorded as such.

Much has been said about the UCR/SHR inability to tap the "dark figure of crime," or those crimes not reported to the police. However, this limitation has been directed almost entirely at crimes other than motor vehicle theft and homicide (Hindelang, 1974; Skogan, 1975; R. O'Brien, 1985). Both the homicide and motor vehicle thefts as reported by the UCR are widely accepted as reliable reflections of the actual number of these crimes (R. O'Brien, 1985; Messner, 1983; Gove et al., 1985). Because studies that compare the number of homicides as recorded by police with the number of homicides according to coroners' assessments of the cause of death (i.e., vital statistics) find a reasonable correlation (Bowers and Pierce, 1975; Cantor and Cohen, 1980), the validity of these measures is accepted based on this convergence. But, as noted by Williams and

Flewelling (1987), (the SHR suffer from an extensive missing data problem as well as a lack of reporting. Thus, the reliability and validity of these data sources must be evaluated.)

The inability of the UCR figures to reflect anything except the number of deaths labeled as homicides by the police is presented by Blackman and Gardiner (1986). In a number of ways the UCR may inaccurately reflect the actual number of deaths, the most important of which is that the UCR is only a body count (Blackman, and Gardiner 1986). (Due to the nature of victim disposal in serial murders, an unknown proportion of serial murder victims' bodies are hidden and may never come to the attention of the police or coroner, thus representing a "dark figure" of serial murder.)As with any data, homicide data are only as reliable as the source from which they are taken. As illustrated by the continuing discovery of victims of the Green River Killer in the Seattle area, many of these victims had never been reported missing, and others had been buried for years prior to their discovery (Garcia, 1987). Also unknown is the number of dead bodies found each year whose identity remains anonymous. Serial murder data within these national statistics becomes not only a dark but a murky figure.

As discussed earlier, the SHR does give information concerning the victim/ offender relationship and the circumstances or motive of the homicide. A time-series analysis of these relationships indicates that the nature of homicide is changing. There has been a dramatic increase in the number of homicides in which the victim and offender are strangers or their relationship is unknown (Godwin, 1978). Contrary to Starr et al. (1984) who suggest that as many as two-thirds of the 5,000 unsolved homicides per year may be committed by serial killers, the actual proportion of these homicides that may be attributable to serial murder is unknown.

In addition to the changes in the relationship between victims and offenders, the motives underlying homicide have also changed. Egger's (1984) analysis of UCR data shows a 270 percent increase in homicides with unknown motives. Contrary to Norris (1988), a homicide in which the motive is unknown cannot be assumed to have been committed for the "sheer high" of the experience. It should be noted that although the motive codes used by the FBI are limited, we should not think that any homicide is without motive. The motives of a serial murderer may not be revenge or greed and may not fit into an FBI category, but these individuals do have motives in their madness. Based on the level of complexity of other possible motives, the FBI categories may need to be expanded to include the various motivations of the serial murderer.

Recent annual UCR figures indicate that approximately 5,000 people each year are murdered by someone whom the police initially code as a stranger. With reference to the coding decisions made by police, an unknown number of homicides that are originally coded as unknown offender and motives, are un-doubtedly cleared at a later date and found to have been for profit and committed by family, acquaintances, and so on. The process by which police go back and recode these homicides is of questionable reliability. Rather than assuming that a large proportion of the unsolved murders with unknown motives are the work of serial murderers, many of the stranger homicides with unknown motives may very well be an increase in felony-murders. This inference is supported by the fact that in other UCR homicides, felony-murders are most likely to occur between strangers (Williams and Flewelling, 1987). It is more likely that the serial murders fall into the category of homicides in which the relationship between the victim and offender as well as the motive is unknown (uncodable) that may be attributable to serial murder. Certainly, attributing all or even most of the stranger and unknown homicides to serial murderers is at this time not warranted, notwithstanding the previously mentioned estimates. A more con-servative estimate of the UCR recorded homicides, a proportion of which may be serial homicides, would be the stranger and unknown homicides with unknown motives. Based on calculations of the number of reported homicides in 1985 (FBI, 1986), this would amount to 3,636 cases of homicide, a proportion of which may match known serial murder victim profiles. Certainly the UCR is not the only sample from which estimates of serial murder victims may come. The unidentified dead, hidden dead bodies, and an undetermined number of missing persons may also add to our total.

Accompanying the change in the nature of homicide has been a reduction in the "clearance rate" for homicide. A case is considered cleared when an indi-vidual is arrested for a reported offense or when certain other clearance-related events occur. These include the charging of an individual, a suicide by a suspected individual, a deathbed confession, the killing of a suspected individual by police or a citizen, a confession while in custody, and so on (FBI, 1988). Thus, actual clearance rates may be somewhat lower than those published by the FBI due to false confessions and inaccurate accusations by prosecutors of an individual's connection to a crime or crimes. In addition, police jurisdictions use different criteria for calculating clearance rates and thus cross-jurisdictional comparisons are questionable (Spelman, 1988). Currently about 75 percent of all homicides are cleared by arrest (or other). This rate represents an all-time low, with a high of 93 percent occurring in 1962 (FBI, 1961; 1986).

Undoubtedly, much of the correlation between increases in stranger and un-known homicides and the clearance rate is due to the linkage blindness that exists in law enforcement (Egger, 1984). Successful homicide investigations are undoubtedly enhanced by situations in which the victim and offender are linked by personal networks of family or acquaintances, employment, leisure activities, and so on. A lack of these networks, as is usually the case with unknown motive, stranger/unknown offender serial murders, exacerbates the problems in solving a homicide and thus decreases the overall clearance rate.

Vital Statistics

As previously mentioned, mortality data gathered by the National Center for Health Statistics (NCHS), Division of Vital Statistics, has been utilized by homicide researchers to assess the reliability and validity of UCR homicide data (Cantor and Cohen, 1980). Homicides recorded by the NCHS are acquired from death certificates as completed by coroners, physicians, or medical examiners. Although the absolute numbers of homicides as recorded by the UCR and NCHS differ, this difference is for the most part due to the definition of homicide that is being used. Deaths coded as homicides by coroners are not based on any assessment of criminality, but rather whether the death occurred due to the intentional infliction of injury by another person (National Center for Health Statistics, 1987). In addition, the NCHS has complete coverage of the national population and thus sampling procedures used by the NCHS may be more representative than those of the UCR. Cantor and Cohen (1980) concluded that the question of absolute convergence of these two sources is less important than the trends of each and that it makes little difference which source is used when testing the effects of variables hypothesized to be related to homicide rates. Data gathered by the NCHS offer little if any additional insight into the estimates of annual victims of serial murder. Unlike the homicide data gathered by the Supplemental Homicide Reports, mortality data from the NCHS does not reveal the motive or the relationship between the victim and offender. However, the information that coroners across the country may have—the number of unidentified bodies found each year—would increase the accuracy of recent estimates of the prevalence of serial murder

Unidentified Bodies

As with the estimates of the annual number of serial murder victims in the United States, the number of unidentified dead found each year varies depending on the source. Robert O. Heck claimed that each year as many as 4,000 abandoned dead bodies are found and never identified. He believes serial murderers are responsible for a considerable number of these 4,000 (Lindsey, 1984). The American Bar Association's (ABA) president, in a presentation to the U.S. House of Representatives, stated that an even larger number of unidentified dead bodies were found each year (5,000) and that this number represents only dead children (U.S. House, 1985).

Although it is not mandatory that coroners report the discovery of an unidentified body to any sort of national clearinghouse, at least one state, California, has a fairly accurate assessment of the number of "unidentified deceased" through their Missing/Unidentified Deceased Program. Based on information received from county coroners, only 56 unidentified juvenile remains were found in the period 1980–84. As Best (1987a) noted, California has more than its share of homicides, runaways, and unidentified dead and one could extrapolate, based on these 56 individuals in a 5-year period, that approximately 11 juveniles per year are found in California and probably not more than 100 in the United States as a whole. This is hardly the 5,000 claimed by Child Find and the ABA president!

The National Crime Information Center (NCIC) of the FBI maintains a record of all unidentified deceased reports that they receive. In 1987 there were 396 entries of unidentified deceased into this file, with 271 identifications or cancellations, leaving only 125 unidentified individuals at year end. This file has been "on line" since June 30, 1983, and as of June 1, 1988 had accumulated 1,632 active or uncleared cases. As noted by an NCIC official, not all police departments and/or coroners use this NCIC service and thus these figures must be an underestimate of the number of unidentified deceased found each year (Miller, R., personal communication, 1988).

The NCIC also has a missing person file that can be cross-matched with descriptive data given on the unidentified. These descriptive data for both missing and unidentified persons include blood type, dental characteristics, broken bones, birth marks, and so on (NCIC, 1985). However, for this program to serve its designated purpose, law enforcement and other officials must be willing to complete time-consuming forms and enter this information with the NCIC. According to a recent survey, approximately 50 percent of the coroners in Illinois are funeral directors, police officers, janitors, and so on, many of whom have had no formal training for the position (Bauer, 1988). Thus, the information received from coroners and reported to agencies such as the NCIC may be deficient with reference to the reliability of information concerning the cause of death, time of death, and so on.

As has been illustrated, there is a lack of sharing of information concerning unidentified deceased in the United States and this, in part, has led to citations of unfounded figures. There may be no better issue to illustrate how unfounded figures can become gospel than that of the missing children movement.

Missing Persons

In their attempt to estimate the annual number of serial murder victims in the United States, Holmes and DeBurger (1988: 19) suggested that a "probable proportion" of missing children should be factored into the total. Aside from their neglect of missing adults in this formula, one can ask, "How many missing children are there, and what is a probable proportion of these that may be serial murder victims?"

Many estimates of the number of missing children paint a missing children problem of enormous proportions. There are over 100 state and national child search agencies, with at least as many estimates of missing children. Recently, several dramatic missing-children cases, including the disappearance of Etan Patz (who has never been found) and the murder of Adam Walsh, have served to direct public attention to the issue of missing and exploited children. This issue was also used by the Republican Party as part of their 1984 party platform, as a social problem in need of national attention and funding (U.S. Department of Justice, 1984). Currently, the missing-children problem has fallen under the scrutiny of a variety of researchers, as a social problem that has been constructed by the media and a few for-profit agencies and whose magnitude has been greatly exaggerated (Best, 1987a, 1987b; Altheide and Fritz, 1987).

The U.S. Department of Health and Human Services has estimated the number of missing children at 1.5 million per year (Karlen, 1985). Other child-search agencies as well as the Office of Juvenile Justice and Delinquency Prevention (OJJDP) of the U.S. Justice Department also estimate the number of missing children to be 700,000 to 2 million per year (OJJDP, 1988). However, studies indicate that 90–95 percent of this figure represents runaways, many of whom return home in 24 hours (Department of Health and Human Services, 1983; FBI, 1984a; U.S. Department of Justice, 1986). Also, some juveniles may run away more than once a year and thereby be counted repeatedly.

With reference to serial murder, the significant cases of missing children would be those children who had been abducted by strangers. The most notorious (and unfounded) estimate of stranger abducted children was that of Child Find, a New York private child-search agency. In a *New York Times* interview (Staff, 1982), this organization claimed that 50,000 children are abducted by strangers each year. They also estimated that 10 percent (5,000) of these children are found dead each year, 10,000 are found alive, and the remaining 35,000 are never to be seen or heard from again (p. 77). U.S. Senator Paul Simon reiterated this figure, also claiming that 50,000 stranger abductions of children was a conservative estimate (U.S. House, 1981). John Walsh, whose son was abducted and murdered, estimated the number to be 20,000–50,000 stranger abductions each year, with 80 percent of these children murdered within two days. Were this actually the case, we would have 16,000–40,000 children murdered by strangers each year (Thornton, 1983). This number is in sharp contrast to the one extrapolated from the California Supplemental Homicide Report. Based on the California figures, probably fewer than 300 children nationwide are killed by strangers in a given year. As noted by Best (1987a), since the publication of these newer studies, agencies such as Child Find and others have reduced their numbers to ranges of 600–1,000.

Recent figures obtained from the National Center for Missing and Exploited Children (January 1988) show that from June 13, 1984 through June 1, 1988 (a 42-month period), the center recorded 17,511 cases of missing children. Of these 17,511, 455 were thought to be stranger abductions and 75 of these children were found dead (NCMEC, 1988). For a 42-month period, this would be approximately 20 children per year killed by strangers. Assuming this estimate to be a low one and the California SHR figure a high one, the range of plausible estimates is 20–300 children killed by strangers annually. The outrageously excessive estimates in the missing-children area lead us to be suspicious of all of these estimates and to wonder what would be Holmes and DeBurger's (1988) probable proportion of these ridiculous missing-children figures.

The National Crime Information Center collects and disseminates data for missing persons as well as the previously mentioned unidentified deceased file. The 1982 Missing Children Act established this missing-children mandate and even though the FBI does not have jurisdiction over many of the reported cases, parents still have the right to have their child listed with the NCIC file. Recently the NCIC numbers have been rapidly changing, in part due to the increased use by law enforcement agencies through the mandate. From 1982 to 1983, following the mandate, there was a 21.8 percent increase in reporting, followed by a 45.0 percent increase in 1984. This increase has since levelled off and the most recent increase (1987) was a 10.6 percent change in reporting (Miller, 1988). Missing-person records are entered based on four different categories, with stranger abductions of children and adults being included in the "involuntary missing." An activity report generated by the NCIC for May 1988 indicated that during this month, 6,192 cases of involuntarily missing persons were reported to the agency, with 2,218 of these cases being cancelled. Thus, 3,974 cases were still active (NCIC, 1988). The total thus far for 1988 of all missing persons (which would include runaways, voluntarily missing adults, etc. is 63,340 (NCIC, 1988). These active records include an undetermined number of people who are no longer missing, but the NCIC or local law enforcement agency has not been and possibly will never be notified. People are not as interested in informing the police that their 16-year-old son returned home as they are to have him recorded as missing.

ESTIMATION AND EXTRAPOLATION

If we are to use the numbers of missing persons, unidentified deceased, and homicides between strangers with unknown motives in our attempt to assess the incidence of serial murder then it is important to have reliable estimates of what these figures are. Based on available data, we should be circumspect in our conclusions concerning serial murder victimization. We forego the temptation to provide "true" estimates of the annual number of serial murders in the United States. We must agree, however, with the conclusion drawn by Joel Best (1987b) that there currently is no evidence to support the claims of thousands of children abducted and murdered each year by strangers. Once a figure has been cited by an "expert," "official," or "authority," these figures are printed again and again, without the necessary qualifications with which they were originally intended. Although the nature of serial murder makes estimation difficult, flamboyant and unverified figures only sensationalize the problem and thus obstruct realistic policy formulation. Figures that are extrapolated from very small samples need to be qualified as such (e.g., Holmes and DeBurger, 1988) and thus definitive statements based on these extrapolations should be avoided.

Sudnow (1965) in his analysis of a public defender system illustrated the importance of viewing the daily activities and decisionmaking of "rate-producing agencies" as social activities. An ethnography of recordkeeping would illustrate the processes by which events are translated by decisions prior to becoming official records. Decisions as to whether a death is a suicide, a lone homicide, or part of a series are made by individuals who may be operating under different definitional standards. Official statistics are created by human beings. Thus one should employ a sociological analysis in their development and recognize the limitations and implications of these record-producing processes and what they mean for theory and policy formulation.

SUMMARY

The social constructionist perspective of how the mass media help to create social problems—especially in the missing children issue and the extent of serial murder victimization—can be applied here to illustrate the ways in which the claims made by individuals and organizations can enlarge the magnitude of a problem (Spector and Kituse, 1987). To the natural horror and outrage which themselves lead to magnification are added the various organizational vested interests. As noted by Best, "Big numbers mean big problems" (1987b: 1). To avoid exaggeration of an existing situation, there should be some accountability of researchers and the media and some verification process of the numbers that they cite as official, particularly if our policies depend on the magnitude of the problem. Once a story has been circulated and a figure cited, many times an update is not presented that would negate the former claims (Altheide and Fritz, 1987).

The incidence of serial murder in the United States is currently unknown, as is the prevalence of active offenders. During the development of this chapter, the Police Executive Research Forum published a pamphlet dealing with the upcoming revisions of the Uniform Crime Reporting system, some of which may improve the UCR data with reference to the study of serial murder. Part of these revisions will include detailed data on the nonfamily/stranger abduction of children, including the offender's motive, the victim's age, and so on. Another improvement in the system will be that additional information on victim characteristics and the victimization incident will be available. In addition, horizontal tracking systems that will better enable law enforcement personnel to track offenders within large metropolitan areas are currently being implemented. All contacts within large metropolitan areas will be part of a file that is accessible to all jurisdictions in the area, thus reducing "linkage blindness." In addition to these revisions, there are a number of other UCR improvements that will add to the overall quality of these records as well as make them more accessible and useful to law enforcement and other users (Spelman, 1988).

With reference to the missing-person issue, a final report by the OJJDP, due in 1989, will present the results of a national incidence assessment of missing children. This report will include the results of a telephone survey of 40,000 households across the country, concerning their experiences with missing children. Also reported will be the results of a study of nonfamily abductions as recorded by police in a sample of 20 U.S. counties and an assessment of the number of "throwaway" (abused and neglected) children. This study should provide the most reliable estimates available of the extent of the missing-children

problem, including stranger abductions and thus adding insight into the level of serial murder victimization of missing children. The National Crime Information Center also provides a file for the discoveries of unidentified deceased as well as missing persons. Better use of this service by all law enforcement agencies and coroners across the country would increase the reliability and usefulness of this tracking system.

A crucial activity if any of these data sources is to accurately reflect the unidentified deceased and missing is the unfounding process. There should be periodic follow-ups on all reports of missing persons to insure that the individual is still missing. In addition, better use of the cross-matching service made available by the NCIC for comparing the missing persons file and unidentified deceased may help to solve active cases.

There are various levels to the problems created by serial murder. This phenomenon may be increasing either absolutely or relatively to other violent crimes. If it is increasing, which has yet to be reliably shown, this will lead to decreases in law enforcement efficiency due to the involvement of strangers in this crime. Many of the victims of serial murder are lower-status individuals (vagrants, prostitutes, children) and thus a lack of attention (and funding) for this phenomenon may be viewed as a form of discrimination. Offenders convicted of serial murders will very likely spend most of their lives in prison as well as exhausting appeals processes in states with the death penalty, presenting an added burden to our already strained criminal justice system. Recent negotiations and plea bargainings that have occurred with serial killers in an attempt to discover their victims may well present questions of ethics (Comiskey, 1983). If it is the absolute number of serial murder victims or missing children that represents the scope and seriousness of the problem, then we are in desperate need of an objective assessment of the actual conditions that exist. There is no question of the repugnancy of this phenomenon, no matter what its numbers, and the intent here is certainly not to trivialize the consequences of this aberrant behavior. Although the focal point of this chapter has been to illustrate the ways in which the numbers may be exaggerated and to "debunk" some existing and potential myths, Jenkins (1988) notes that recent Justice Department figures may even underestimate the number of active offenders, while overestimating the number of victims. Jenkins also suggests that the creation of a serial murder panic may not only serve to support recent federal funding decisions (National Center for the Analysis of Violent Crime) but may also be an indicator of a shift in public attitudes concerning the causes of crime. Rather than blaming the social environment of certain groups and individuals, society now sees (as Jenkins calls them) "semi-human monsters" as responsible for many homicides. If these ideological shifts about the causes of crime are inaccurate, we may well be funding programs to track "semi-human monsters" who are responsible for only 2–3 percent of the annual homicides (Jenkins 1988). Jenkins thus illustrates the potential for ineffectual policies, the focus of which may be misdirected. Rather than a focus on the possible low estimate of 2–3 percent (350–526 homicides, based on 1985 figures) of annual homicides that are committed by serial murderers, at least as much consideration might be given to the study of the structural, cultural, and social conditions that facilitate this behavior.

Each year an undetermined number of the homicides, as reported by the UCR and the NCIC, represent the victims of serial murderers. Innovations of existing data sources and the creation of new sources will better enable us to assess the nature and extent of this phenomenon and to make substantive as well as methodological gains. In addition to researching the correlates of serial murder victimization, an accurate assessment of the amount of serial murder victimization that occurs each year in this country is necessary prior to the development of informed theories and policy decisions.

REFERENCES

Altheide, D. L. and Fritz, N. J. (1987). "The mass media and the social construction of the missing children problem." *The Sociological Quarterly, 28*(4), 473–92.

Bauer, S. (1988, September 12). "All new coroners to be tested." (Champaign, IL) *News-Gazette*, p. 3.

Best, J. (1987a). "Calculating the numbers of children abducted by strangers: Dark figures and child victims." Paper presented at the Pacific Sociological Association Meeting, Seattle.

————. (1987b). "Dark figures and missing children: Defining stranger abduction." Paper presented at the American Society of Criminology Meeting, Montreal, 1987.

————. (1988). "Missing children, misleading statistics." *The Public Interest, 92*, 84–92.

Black, D. J. (1970). "The production of crime rates." *The American Sociological Review, 44*, 18–27.

Blackman, P. and Gardiner, R. (1986). "Flaws in the current and proposed uniform crime reporting program regarding homicide and weapons use in violent crime." Paper presented at the annual meeting of the American Society of Criminology, Atlanta.

Bowers, W. J. and Pierce. G. L. (1975). "The illusion of deterrence in Issac Ehrlich's research on capital punishment." *Yale Law Journal, 85*, 187–208.

Cahill, T. (1986). *Buried dreams*. New York: Bantam Books.

Cantor. D. and Cohen, L. E. (1980). "Comparing measures of homicide trends: Methodological and substantive differences in the Vital Statistics and Uniform Crime Report Time Series 1933–1975." *Social Science Research, 9*, 121–45.

Comiskey, R. J. (1983) "Paying a murderer for evidence, commentaries on the issue." *Criminal Justice Ethics*, Summer/Fall, 47–56.

Department of Health and Human Services, Office of Inspector General. (1983). *Runaway and homeless youth, national program inspection*. Hyattsville, MD: Public Health Service.

Egger, S. A. (1984). "A working definition of serial murder and the reduction of linkage blindness." *Journal of Police Science and Administration, 12*(3), 348–57.

Federal Bureau of Investigation, United States Department of Justice. (1961). *Crime in the United States. Uniform Crime Reports 1960*. Washington, DC: U.S. Government Printing Office.

————. (1980). *Crime in the United States. Uniform Crime Reports 1979*. Washington, DC: U.S. Government Printing Office.

————. (1984a, January). *The missing children*. Washington, DC: U.S. Government Printing Office.

————. (1984b). *Crime in the United States. Uniform Crime Reports 1983*. Washington, DC: U.S. Government Printing Office.

————. National Crime Information Center. (1985). *Missing person file data collection entry guide*. Washington, DC: U.S. Government Printing Office.

————. (1986). *Crime in the United States. Uniform Crime Reports 1985*. Washington, DC: U.S. Government Printing Office.

————. (1987). *Uniform Crime Reports. 1978–1984: Supplementary homicide report*. Washington, DC: U.S. Government Printing Office.

————. (1988). *Uniform crime reporting handbook*. Washington, DC: U.S. Government Printing Office.

Garcia, C. (1987, July 27). "Casting a net at Green River: A serial murder manhunt remains a study in frustration." *Time*, p. 61.

Godwin, J. (1978). *Murder USA: The ways we kill each other*. New York: Oxford University Press.

Gove, W. R., Hughes, M., and Geerken, M. (1985). "Are uniform crime reports a valid indicator of index crimes?: An affirmative answer with minor qualifications." *Criminology, 23*, 451–501.

Graysmith, R. (1976). *Zodiac*. New York: Berkley Books, St. Martin's Press.

Hickey, E. W. (1987). *The etiology of victimization in serial murder: An historical and demographic analysis*. Submitted for publication.

Hindelang, M. J. (1974). "The uniform crime reports revisited." *Journal of Criminal Justice, 2*, 1–17.

Holmes, R. and DeBurger, J. (1985, September). "Profiles in terror: The serial murderer." *Federal Probation, 49*, 29–34.

Holmes, R. M. and DeBurger, J. (1988). *Serial murder*. Newbury Park, CA: Sage.

Jenkins, P. (1988). "Myth and murder: The serial killer panic of 1983–85." *Criminal Justice Research Bulletin, 3*(11), 1–7.

Karlen, N. (1985, October 7). "How many kids missing?" *Newsweek*, pp. 30–31.

Levin, J. and Fox, J. A. (1985). *Mass murder: America's growing menace*. New York: Plenum.

Leyton, E. (1986). *Compulsive killers: The story of modern multiple murders*. New York: New York University Press.

Lindsey, R. (1984, January 21). "Officials cite a rise in killers who roam U.S. for victims." *New York Times*, pp. 1, 7.

Linedecker, C. L. (1980). *The man who killed boys*. New York: St. Martin's Press.

McKay, S. (1985, July 8). "Coming to grips with random killers." *Maclean's*, pp. 44–45.

Messner, S. F. (1983). "Regional differences in the economic correlates of the urban homicide rate: Some evidence on the importance of cultural context." *Criminology, 21*, 477–88.

National Center for Missing and Exploited Children. (1988). Memorandum.

National Center for Health Statistics. (1986). *Annual summary of births, marriages, divorces and deaths: United States. Monthly Vital Statistics Report* (report no. 13DHHS). Hyattsville, MD: Public Health Service.

————. (1987). *Medical examiner's and coroner's handbook on death registration and fetal death reporting* (DHHS Publication no. PHS87–1110). Hyattsville, MD: Public Health Service.

National Crime Information Center. (1985). *Missing person file, data collection entry guide*. Washington, DC: U.S. Government Printing Office.

————. (1988, May). *Unidentified persons report: Missing persons report*. Washington, DC: U.S. Government Printing Office.

Norris, J. (1988). *Serial killers: The growing menace*. New York: Doubleday.

O'Brien, D. (1985). *Two of a kind: The hillside stranglers*. New York: Signet.

O'Brien, R. (1985). *Crime and victimization data*. Beverly Hills: Sage Publications.

Office of Juvenile Justice and Delinquency Prevention. (1988). *OJJDP update on research*. Washington, DC: U.S. Government Printing Office.

Ressler, R. K. et al. (1984). "Serial murder: A new phenomenon of homicide." Paper presented at the annual meeting of International Association of Forensic Sciences, Oxford, England.

Rule, A. (1980). *The stranger beside me*. New York: Signet.

Skogan, W. G. (1975). "Measurement problems in official and survey crime rates." *Journal of Criminal Justice, 2*, 1–17.

Smith, D.A. and Visher, C. A. (1982). "Street-level justice: Situational determinants of police arrest decisions." *Social Problems, 29*, 167–77.

Snider, D. and Clausen, T. (1987). *A typology of serial murder*. Unpublished manuscript.

Spector, M. and Kituse, J. (1987). *Constructing social problems*. New York: Aldine de Gruyter.

Spelman, W. (1988). *Beyond bean counting*. Washington, DC: Police Executive Research Forum.

Staff. (1982, December 5). "Child abductions a rising concern." *The New York Times*, p. 77.

Staff. (1985, September 9). "Are serial killers on the rise?" *U.S. News and World Report*, p. 14.

Staff. (1988, January 3). "Experts say mass murders are rare but on the rise." *The New York Times*, pp. 10, 15.

Starr, M. et al. (1984, November 26). "The random killers." *Newsweek*, pp. 100–106.

Sudnow, D. (1965). "Normal crimes: Sociological features of the penal code in a Public Defender office." *Social Problems*, 255–77.

Thornton, J. (1983, October 24). "The tragedy of America's missing children." *U.S. News and World Report*, pp. 63–64.

U.S. Department of Justice, Office of Juvenile Justice and Delinquency Prevention. (1984). *Missing/abducted children, serial murder tracking and prevention program*, Sam Houston State University.

————. (1986, March). *America's missing and exploited children: Their safety and their future*.

U.S. House of Representatives. (1981). *The Missing Children Act. Hearings held by the Subcommittee on Civil and Constitutional Rights*. Committee on the Judiciary, November 18, 30.

————. (1985). *Oversight hearing on the Missing Children's Assistance Act*. Hearings held by the Subcommittee on Human Resources, Committee in Education and Labor, May 21.

Visher, C. A. (1983). "Gender, police arrest decisions, and notions of chivalry." *Criminology, 21*, 5–28.

Williams, Kirk R. and Flewelling, Robert L. (1987). "Family, acquaintance, and stranger homicide: Alternative procedures for rate calculations." *Criminology, 25*(3), 543–60.

Wilson, J. Q. (1978). *Varieties of police behavior: The management of law and order in eight communities*. Cambridge, MA: Harvard University Press.

3

The Etiology of Victimization in Serial Murder: An Historical and Demographic Analysis

ERIC W. HICKEY

The apparent rise in the modern serial or multiple murderer has incited interest in various social sciences, and researchers have begun to explore the social, psychological, and biological makeup of these offenders in order to establish accurate profiles. To date, the body of knowledge remains small when compared with the number of unanswered questions pertaining to serial murder, especially the extent of the phenomenon. Jenkins (1988) argues that to a great degree the panic surrounding the phenomenon of serial murder during the early 1980s stemmed more from misinterpretation of *Uniform Crime Report* data than an actual surge of new cases. Besides methodological issues, Jenkins also notes that armed with this 'new wave' of mass murderers the Justice Department was able to justify the creation of a National Center for the Analysis of Violent Crime, including VICAP, or Violent Criminal Apprehension Program. While the controversy continues over the extent of serial murder, the need for more research has gathered momentum. In addition, comparable data on victims of crime, especially those of homicide, are limited. Researchers have recognized for some time the need to understand the victim and his/her involvement with the offender. Hewitt (1988) reviewed the body of literature of victim-offender relationships in homicides based upon data from a large heterogeneous population. He then examined demographic characteristics of victims and offenders in the often publicized community of Middletown (Muncie, Indiana) and found the victim-offender relationships to be similar to those in larger cities. Studies in victimization assist in clarifying the victim side of the offender-victim relationship, measure in part the degree of vulnerability and culpability of certain victims, and often reveal the social dynamics of criminal acts. Case study analysis in serial murder has begun to provide researchers with insightful information, however tenuous. Elliot Leyton (1986) for example, in his book *Hunting Humans*, provides an in-depth investigation into the lives and minds of a few contemporary serial killers and their relationships with their victims. The purpose of this research is to contribute to this body of knowledge by focusing on the victims of serial murders and demographic factors associated with victimization. These data will allow us to determine the variations, if any, between victims of homicides in general and victims of multiple murderers. Second, from a historical perspective, we are able to challenge current notions pertaining to serial murderers and their victims by drawing on this data base of homicide victims.

EMERGENCE OF SERIAL MURDER

According to statistics collected by the Federal Bureau of Investigation, there were 18,690 murders and non-negligent manslaughter cases in 1984. Over the past 20 years we have seen the murder and non-negligent manslaughter rates increase 300 percent while police clearance rates for this crime have declined from 93 percent in 1962 to 74 percent in 1982 (FBI, 1984). The homicide rate, 8.3 per 100,000 in 1987, appears to be one of the highest of any country in the world. While Eitzen and Timmer report that the majority of those slain die in domestic and community conflicts, they also suggest that perhaps one-third of all murders are perpetrated by strangers (1985, pp. 130–31). Due to a marked increase in stranger-to-stranger homicides, perhaps as many as 25 percent of all murders go unsolved each year. The increasing numbers of serial murders are believed by some experts to constitute many of these unsolved cases (Holmes, 1988, pp. 19–20).

While the recent "emergence" of serial murders has attracted considerable attention by researchers, relatively little attention has been accorded their victims. This may be due to a lack of consensus regarding the defining of serial murder. Egger (1985) defines serial homicide as "relationshipless (victim and attacker are strangers)." However, by providing an operational definition of serial murder that encompasses victims who did have relationships with their attackers, we may well enhance our limited data and understanding of this genre of victimization. For instance, Hickey (1986), simply by including all offenders who through premeditation killed three or more victims over a period of days, weeks, months, or years, was able to identify several women as serial killers. The thrust of current research appears to narrow operational definitions of serial murder without any documented assurances that the focus does not exclude pertinent data. To suggest that all victims of serial murder are strangers, that the killers operate primarily in pairs, or do not kill for financial gain is derived more from speculation than verifiable evidence, given the current state of serial murder research.

In essence, serial murders should include any offenders, male or female, who kill over time. This includes murderers who, on a repeated basis, may kill within the confines of their own home; for example, a woman may poison several husbands, children, or elderly people in order to collect insurance. In addition, serial murderers are also those men and women who may be mobile and operate within the confines of a city or state or even travel through several states as they seek out victims. Consequently, some victims will have a personal relationship with their killers and others will not, while some victims are killed for pleasure and some merely for gain. Of greatest importance from a research perspective is the establishment of commonality among the victims, if possible. As Egger (1985), in his own definition of victims, insightfully observes, "victims . . . are perceived as powerless given their situation in time, place, or status within their immediate surrounding (such as vagrants, prostitutes, migrant workers, homosexuals, missing children, and single and often elderly women)" (p. 3). Commonality among those murdered may include several factors, any of which may prove heuristic in determining the reasons for their victimization.

METHOD

The data for this chapter were gathered from historical materials through a biographical case study analysis of serial murderers by examining biographical texts, almanacs, and newspapers dealing with serial murderers and their victims. Given the nature of the data, we were prevented in our research methodology from conducting random sampling. But as Glaser and Strauss (1967) have convincingly argued, there are systematic methods in conducting qualitative research that may point toward theoretical explanations for social behavior. Their notion of "grounded" theory as a methodology included what Glaser and Strauss refer to as "constant comparisons." By examining different groups or individuals experiencing the same process we learn to identify structural uniformities. Grounded theory stresses a systematic, qualitative field method for research. First, we were interested in constant feedback; more specifically in this research, cases of serial murder were sought out within a specified time frame. These cases were identified through as many avenues as possible, including newspapers, journals, bibliographies, biographies, and computer searches of social science abstracts until the process became repetitive or redundant and new information ceased to be found.

Unfortunately, one can never be sure of the precise moment when the feedback process should be halted. We were confident that systematic searches of several different sources of information would generally yield most of the existing data. In a broader definition of serial murder the researcher might envision a variety of serial-related killings which technically could be included in this type of research. These categories could include individuals who work as enforcers within the realm of organized crime, political and/or religious terrorists who kill repeatedly, and members of street gangs. We might also include those who repeatedly tampered with food and medicinal products to bring death to persons who ingest the tainted goods. Other categories broadly defined could also include those who practice euthanasia or carry out abortions in clinics. From an historical perspective we might also include the gunslingers of the old West who frequently killed in order to promote themselves and their lifestyles. Finally, there are the growing lists of 'mass murderers' who methodically annihilate entire families, people in restaurants or bars, or randomly shoot people on streets, campuses, or parks. They too have committed multiple homicides and could be added through definitional imperatives to this assorted homicide offender list. Other definitional considerations for cases to be included or excluded may be generated from a variety of taxonomies including motives, methods, or specific numbers of victims.

While each of these typologies and perspectives may be meritorious, this study excludes them as part of its overall operational definition. Instead, each time a case appeared in a text or news report in which an offender had been charged with killing three or more individuals over a period of days, weeks, months, or years, they were included in our study.

A few exceptional cases were also included in which the offenders were reported to have killed only two victims but were suspect in other slayings or in which evidence indicated their intent to kill others. In order to justify inclusion the homicides had to be deliberate, premeditated acts in which the offender selected his or her own victims and acted under his/her own volition. Often a distinct pattern emerged in the method of killing or in the apparent motives for the murders. Usually the murders were to some degree motivated by sex, money, vengeance, hatred, or an urge to kill. Each case was analyzed for specific data including the time frame and geographic distribution of the criminal behavior, number of victims, relationship of victim to offender, age and sex categories of particular victims, and the degree of victim facilitation.

Spanning the time frame between 1795 and 1988, the findings from these data represent the victims of 34 women and 169 men in the United States. They are responsible for a minimum of 1,483 homicides and a maximum of 2,161 homicides. This specified victim range is a result of a few serial murderers who have killed so many that only close approximations to the actual number can be ascertained. Difficulty occurs in accurately determining the number of victims of serial murderers, especially when we are dealing with a few offenders who have allegedly killed over 100 people. The problem is compounded when the majority of these particular cases appeared in the nineteenth century, when record keeping was not as accurate or efficient. Often data sources are not consistent in reporting figures for these "super" serial killers. In addition, some of these victim data may have been exaggerated due to the sensational nature of the crimes. Consequently these few killers were excluded from our study, as were unsolved cases of homicide where serial murder was suspect. While we recognize these data do not represent an exhaustive study of serial murderers, we do believe them to represent, excluding the Federal Bureau of Investigation records, one

Figure 3.1
Distribution of Offenders in United States by Decade, 1795–1988
$N = 203$

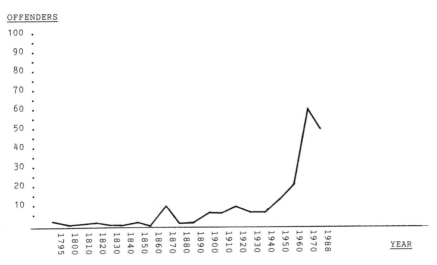

of the largest and most varied assortment of multiple killers ever assembled. Hampered by the ever present "dark figure" of crime, the total number of serial murders will in all probability never be known.

PREVALENCE OF SERIAL MURDERS AND VICTIMS

To date very little empirical research has appeared addressing the extent of the serial murder phenomenon. In part this stems from the difficult task of accumulating information on specific cases. In recent years we have begun to see researchers analyzing collections of case studies, drawing their samples primarily from the past 20 years (Leyton, 1986; Levin and Fox, 1985). These data have been particularly helpful in illustrating the diversity amongst serial killers, but the need to measure the extent of the problem still exists.

One of the most perplexing questions researchers find themselves asking is how many serial murderers have killed or are presently killing in the United States. Agents from the FBI indicate that a conservative figure places the number of offenders currently active in the United States at 35 but may be as high as 100 or more. This does not mean there are 35–100 new offenders each year but rather that that number may be active in a given year. From the 203 offenders in our study 67 percent committed their murders over at least one or more years. For this group the median number of years for an offender's homicide spree was 4.3 years. Controlling for gender, 75 percent of female offenders continued their killing through one or more years, with a median of 8.4 years. Male data indicated 65 percent of their group spanning one or more years, with 4.2 years as the median. One possible explanation for females doubling their male counterparts in the amount of time they were free to kill may be due in part to their methods of killing and the types of victims selected.

Between 1795 and 1988 the 'rise' of the serial killer found its surge during the past 25 years. Our projected number of offenders between 1980 and 1989 will be slightly lower than those in the previous decade. In all likelihood we should expect to see a continued increase in the numbers of cases of serial murder past the year 2000 but not with the surge illustrated during the 1970s. Certainly media attention has been instrumental in creating public awareness of this particular type of offender. It is unlikely, however, that media attention alone is responsible for this recent 'emergence' of serial killing.

By comparing time frames in this study, we find that over half of the 159 cases appeared since 1970. While we recognize there will always exist the ''dark figure'' or unknown cases, these data may be viewed as indicating trends in serial murder. One of the trends indicates a nearly ten-fold increase in the number of cases during the past 20 years in comparison with the previous 174 years. While the debate continues over causal explanations for this dramatic rise in serial murder, we must also be cognizant of the victims. The dynamics of victimization will in all likelihood enable researchers to better understand the etiology of serial murder.

DEMOGRAPHICS OF VICTIMIZATION IN SERIAL MURDER

As indicated in Table 3.2 the number of known victims of serial murder has risen markedly since 1950. For those who fall prey to these offenders their plight is a deplorable one indeed, but the odds of becoming a victim are minuscule when compared with the population as a whole. Of all types of crimes, homicide has one of the lowest victimization rates. If we were to take all of the victims in this study between the years 1975–1988 and assume for a moment that these deaths occurred in one year instead of the actual fourteen-year span, the homicide rate for serial murder would still only be approximately 0.2 per 100,000 population. Inversely proportional to the nominal risk of falling prey to serial murderers is the amount of fear and public awareness of this phenomenon. We stand a greater risk of domestic homicide and a much greater risk of other violent crimes than we do of dying at the hands of a serial killer.

Having minimized the risk the general population experiences we must recognize that rates will vary considerably when we control for specific segments of the population. In short, some of us are at much greater risk than others. As noted in Table 3.2, the number of victims per case has steadily declined over the years. This may in part be explained by greater accuracy in police investigations and efficiency in apprehension of offenders.

Table 3.1
Number of Serial Murder Cases and Offenders in the United States 1795–1988

Years	No. of Cases	No. of Cases Per Year	No. of Offenders	Percent	No. of Offenders Per Year
Total	159	.82	203	100	1.0 (194 yrs.)
1795-1969	76	.45	95	47	.55(174 yrs.)
1970-1988	83	4.2	108	53	5.4 (20 yrs.)

Table 3.2
Victim-Serial Murderer Comparisons in the United States, 1795–1988

Years	No. of Cases	No. of Cases Per Year	No. of Victims	No. of Victims Per Case	No. of Victims Per Year
Total	159	.82	1,483-2,161	9-14	8-11 (194 yrs.
1795-1824	5	.16	44-47	9	1-2 (30 yrs.)
1825-1849	2	.08	58	29	2 (25 yrs.)
1850-1874	8	.32	64-150	8-19	3-6 (25 yrs.)
1875-1899	7	.28	97-214	14-31	4-9 (25 yrs.)
1900-1924	14	.56	184-251	13-18	7-10 (25 yrs.)
1925-1949	13	.52	133-174	10-13	5-7 (25 yrs.)
1950-1974	51	2.04	492-675	10-13	20-27 (25 yrs.)
1975-1988	59	4.21	411-592	7-10	29-42 (14 yrs.)

Table 3.3

Distribution of Serial Murderers by State 1795–1988 (N = 203 offenders)

STATE		# OF CASES WHERE ONE OR MORE VICTIMS WERE KILLED
California		50+
Texas Florida New York Illinois		16-25
Georgia Ohio		11-15
Washington Oregon Utah Colorado Kansas Oklahoma Louisiana Alabama Tennessee	Kentucky Indiana Michigan Pennsylvania Massachusetts Connecticut New Jersey Virginia	6-10
Idaho Montana North Dakota Nevada Arizona New Mexico Alaska Wyoming Nebraska Minnesota Wisconsin	Missouri Arkansas Maryland Mississippi North Carolina South Carolina West Virginia Delaware Vermont Rhode Island New Hampshire	1-5
Iowa South Dakota Hawaii Maine		none recorded in this study

The four states in our study reporting zero cases of serial murder all have small populations. Generally, states with larger populations and large metropolitan areas are more likely to report cases of serial murder. Except for California, the most populous state, there does not appear to be regionality in serial killing. Instead, serial murder appears to be correlated with population density more than regional variations. Inevitably, we expect to find cases in every state. California reported more than double the cases found in any other state between 1795–1988 and that trend appears to have continued in recent years.

Following California, four states, two northern and two southern, reported having between 16 and 25 serial homicide cases. In group three we again see representation from both the north and south. In each succeeding group of states we see an equitable distribution from each region of the United States. In contrast, homicide rates in general can vary dramatically from one geographic region to another in the United States.

Gastil (1971) and later Doerner (1975), explaining the consistently higher murder rates in the southern states, concluded that a regional subculture of violence exists in this area. Blau and Blau (1982), controlling for income ine- quality, found, however, that poverty and southern location were not related to homicide rates, and that the number of blacks in the community was a poor prediction of violence. This lack of consensus regarding a regional subculture of violence is pervasive among current researchers. Unlike homicides in general, where blacks are responsible for over 50 percent of the deaths, serial murderers comprise only 10 percent of the offenders in our study. Since 1975, however, 21 percent of all reported offenders in this study were black.

Serial murderers are often portrayed by the media as killers who travel wan- tonly across the United States in search of victims. As noted earlier, Hickey (1986) created a mobility classification typology for serial murderers and iden- tified three distinct serial killer types (pp. 76–77). The first is place-specific offenders or those who murder within their own homes, place of employment, institutions, or other specific sites. John Wayne Gacy, Jr. murdered 33 young males in his home spanning nearly a seven-year period. The second type is the local serial killer who remains within a certain state or urbanized area to seek out victims. In 1986 Michael D. Terry confessed to killing six male street prostitutes all of whom he encountered within a fourteen square mile area of downtown Atlanta. Finally, the traveling serial murderer is distinguished by his or her acts of homicide while traveling through or relocating to other areas in the United States. Randall B. Woodfield, also known as the "I–5 Killer," is believed to have murdered as many as 13 victims while he traveled the 800- mile stretch of freeway through Washington, Oregon, and California.

By utilizing these typologies to analyze our victim data we found that overall, 36 percent were killed in a specific place while 29–32 percent were murdered by offenders identified as local killers (Table 3.4). The traveling killers accounted for 32–35 percent of the victims. From these data we noted that the majority of serial killers (71 percent) operated in a specific place or general urbanized area but did not travel into other states. By grouping these two mobility typologies we found that 65–68 percent of all our victims were killed by men and women who generally stayed close to home. Since 1975, our data indicate a shift in mobility, with those who travel out of state declining to 23 percent and place- specific offenders also declining to 19 percent. Conversely, those offenders classified as local killers increased dramatically to 58 percent. One explanation for these changes may be related to the increase in urbanization. With nearly three-fourths of the U.S. population distributed among large urban areas such as Los Angeles, New York, and Chicago, offenders are able to maintain ano- nymity and also have access to a large pool of victims.

Place-specific offenders have also decreased in part due to the methods of killing. Poisons such as arsenic and cyanide once commonly used by women to

Table 3.4

Victims of Serial Murder in the United States by Mobility Classification, 1795–1988

Mobility Classification Of Killers	Percent of Victims (N=1483-2161)	No. of Cases	Percent of Offenders (N=203)	Average # Victims per Offender	Average # Victims Per Case
Total	100	159	100	7-11	9-14
Traveling	32-35	46	28	10-16	10-16
Local	29-32	70	45	5-7	7-9
Place Specific	36	43	27	10-14	12-18

Table 3.5

Percentage of Offenders Murdering Family, Acquaintances, and Strangers in the United States, 1795–1988

	Male Offenders (N=169)	Female Offenders (N=34)	Total (N=203)
Family only	3%	26%	7%
At least one family member	10	50	17
Acquaintances only	5	0	4
At least one acquaintance	25	38	27
Strangers only	68	29	62
At least one stranger	89	56	84

kill their families and friends are now more easily detected. Consequently, between 1975 and 1988 the number of victims killed by place-specific offenders in this study declined from 36 percent overall to 16–19 percent. The percentage of victims killed by local offenders between 1975 and 1988 rose sharply from 29–32 percent to 49–51 percent. The change in the percentage of victims killed by traveling offenders during this timespan was negligible. In short, since 1975 we found that approximately the same percentage (65–70 percent) of all victims were killed by offenders who carried out their murders in one state but the majority of these homicides were done by the local-type killer.

Two major homicide studies by Wolfgang (1958), and Pokorny (1965) found that victims of homicides were almost equally divided between being killed in the home or in areas outside the home. By comparison, serial murder victims were more likely to be killed away from their homes, suggesting that they may be vulnerable in areas of the community where contact is more readily accessible by their assailants.

In comparing the three mobility groups in Table 3.4, we notice that place-specific cases were the least common but responsible for the greatest percentage of homicides and having the greatest average number of victims per offender and per case. These findings contradict the general belief that serial killers are primarily offenders who travel across the United States, murdering as they go. According to these data, perhaps a greater area of concern should be focused on serial killing in hospitals, nursing homes, and private residences.

A commonly held notion about serial murder is that offenders have a tendency to operate in pairs or groups, making the abduction and/or killing of a victim an easier task for the offender. Of the 203 offenders surveyed, 37 percent appeared to have at least one partner in committing their homicides. Of all offenders who started killing since 1975, 35 percent were found with at least one partner. Similarly, the percentage of all victims killed by these "team" offenders between 1975 and 1978 was 25–31 percent. Although team-type offenders in this study appear to have increased, the majority of offenders apprehended tended to commit their murders alone.

Another important issue concerns the types of victims serial killers single out. One of the most common beliefs surrounding serial killing is that the offender often develops a pattern in his or her modus operandi. To a great extent the offender's behavior is directly related to the type of victim selected. For homicides in general, victimologists agree that sometimes the offender and victim are "partners in crime" or at least that the victim precipitates his own demise. Many domestic disputes which lead to fatalities are often initiated by the victim. Karmen (1984) refers to this notion of shared responsibility as "victim blaming" (pp. 94–98). Homicides in general often contain this element especially because of the prior relationship of the victim to the offender. In the Wolfgang (1958) study and Pokorny's (1965) Cleveland study, a replication of Wolfgang's work, the findings showed a similar pattern. In both studies those directly involved in the homicide were usually family relatives or close friends. A common as-

Figure 3.2
Frequency of Offenders Reporting Killing at Least One Family Member,
Acquaintance, or Stranger in the United States, 1795–1988

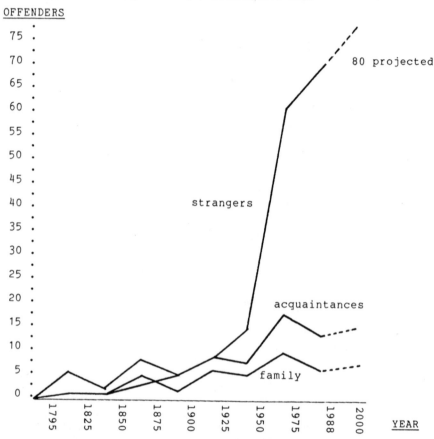

sumption, however, is that victims of serial murder are killed primarily by strangers. Of the three categories of victims—family, acquaintances, and strangers—Figure 3.2 indicates that stranger-to-stranger serial homicides markedly increased between 1950 and 1974. According to these data, the number of offenders killing at least one stranger can be projected to steadily increase by the year 2000, in comparison with the 1950–75 data.

As stranger-to-stranger homicides appeared to continue on a steady rise, acquaintance and family serial killings declined in our study group. We may speculate a slight resurgence of offenders killing one or more acquaintances or one or more family members by the year 2000 due to increased media attention. Their gains are expected to be relatively small, however, in comparison with stranger-to-stranger homicides.

To further illustrate this apparent rise in stranger-to-stranger serial murder, offenders were surveyed regarding preferences toward strangers, acquaintances, or family members as victims. Historically, 7 percent of offenders were found to murder family members only, with female offenders most likely to do so. Only 4 percent of all offenders targeted acquaintances only and they were all males. In contrast, 62 percent killed strangers only, male offenders again most likely to do so.

Table 3.5 indicates that combined, at least 44 percent of all offenders in this study killed one or more acquaintances or one or more family members, although the trend continued to lean toward increased stranger-to-stranger homicide. Since 1975 only 3 percent of offenders were found to have killed family members only and only 8 percent killed at least one family member. There were no offenders believed to have killed acquaintances only and of those murdering at least one acquaintance, only 18 percent had done so between 1975 and 1988. By contrast, those offenders murdering strangers only increased sharply to 75 percent and overall, 96 percent had killed at least one stranger.

Various reasons can be offered for such a dramatic trend. Killing strangers is probably perceived by most offenders as the safest target in terms of avoiding detection. The anonymity and thrill derived by seeking out unsuspecting strangers certainly must attract many (Leyton, 1986). Perhaps even more importantly, offenders can much more easily view the stranger as an object and thereby dehumanize his victim. Upon his capture one offender confessed that he did not want to know his victims' names or anything about them, and if they did give their name he would quickly forget it. Another factor influencing victim selection is the degree of power and control the offender is able to exert. Serial killers rarely seek out those who are as physically or intellectually capable as themselves. Instead, by either randomly or carefully targeting victims, serial killers mentally and/or physically stalk their prey. As strangers seem to be the primary target, offenders were also surveyed as to the specific type of stranger-victim they most commonly murdered.

While many of the categories under the heading of "stranger" in Table 3.6 are not mutually exclusive, they do represent the types of strangers reported in our study. Thus, "young women alone" in category one may also fit into the category of "hitch-hikers" or "people walking on streets." "Young women alone, including female college students and prostitutes," was the most commonly noted stranger-victim category. The second category of "children: young boys, young girls" was also frequently noted as desirable victims. Combined, these two categories comprised most of the stranger-victim serial murders.

When offenders murdered acquaintances, "friends and neighbors" appeared to be the most common victims although they were followed closely by "children: young girls, young boys." With the addition of "women alone including waitresses and prostitutes," these first three categories represent the majority of the acquaintance-victims. In the family grouping, offenders were most likely to kill their own children, husbands, or wives although several other family relations were represented. The most salient factor among the groupings of strangers,

Table 3.6
Rank Order of Types of Victims Sought Out by Serial Murderers

STRANGERS

1. Young women alone including female college students and prostitutes
2. Children: young boys young girls
3. Travelers including hitchhikers
4. People in homes including entire families
5. Hospital patients including the handicapped
6. Business people including store-owners and landlords
7. People walking on streets/in stores
8. Older women alone
9. Police officers
10. Employees
11. Derelicts/transients
12. People responding to newspaper ads
13. Racial killings

ACQUAINTANCES

1. Friends and neighbors
2. Children: young boys and young girls
3. Women alone including waitresses, prostitutes
4. Adult males
5. People in authority including landlords, employers, guards
6. Members of one's own group, i.e., gangs and inmates
7. Patients

FAMILY

1. Own children
2. Husbands
3. Wives
4. Inlaws
5. Other relatives, i.e., nephews, nieces, uncles
6. Mother of the offender
7. Siblings
8. Grandparents

acquaintances, and family members was that most of the victims were women and children. Whatever the specific motives of the killers were, they chose to act out their aggressions upon the weak, helpless, and powerless. Males certainly were not exempt from victimization but they were in the minority. This contrasts with homicides in general: in 1986 about 75 percent of the approximately 20,000 murder victims were male. In addition, the typical murder victim is also over-represented by racial and ethnic minorities. The opposite is true of victims surveyed in this study, in which the majority of victims and offenders were caucasian.

Offenders in this study did not overwhelmingly target a specific age group. For example, in Table 3.7 only 6 percent of offenders murdered "children only" and 2 percent specifically targeted teens. Young and middle-aged adults were the most likely targets but less than half of all offenders killed "adults only." Overall, 12 percent of offenders killed "elderly victims only." While we might expect a substantial percentage of offenders to kill at least one child or teenager, the number of offenders (18 percent) killing at least one elderly person was much higher than anticipated. Very few offenders killed victims in all age groups, but of all combinations of victim relatedness, offenders were most likely to kill teens and children together. Since 1975, the data indicate a shift in some of the trends, which may be a foreboding of things to come. The percentage of offenders killing "children or teens only" declined to only 2 percent in the children's category and increased by 2 percent in the teen category. An increase, however, was noted in offenders specifically targeting adults. Offenders were much more

Table 3.7
Percentage of Offenders Murdering Specific Victim-Age Categories*

Age Range of Victims	Percent of Offenders
Only:	
Children	6
Teens	2
Adults	43
Elderly	12
At Least One:	
Child	29
Teen	30
Adult	70
Elderly	18
Combinations:	
Teens/Children	54
Adults & Children	16
Adults & Teens	22
All Age Groups	8

* N=202 Except for Elderly: N=196

likely since 1975 to target the 'elderly only' (21 percent) than compared with the overall trend of 12 percent. Similarly, since 1975 trends changed little for offenders killing at least one child or teen. By contrast, the overall trend in the serial killing of at least one or more elderly person had risen from 18 to 29 percent since 1975. This noticeable rise in the serial killing of the elderly may indicate a continued increase in such crime as the U.S. population continues to get older. The increase in nursing homes and the rising demand for home care of the elderly may attract individuals wishing to fulfill an "angel of death" fantasy. This fantasy includes offenders who for some reason nurture hatred for the elderly, believe in mercy killing, derive pleasure from watching unsuspecting, powerless individuals die, or simply wish to be recognized as someone of importance. In one instance, an orderly confessed to poisoning patients so that when they stopped breathing he could be the first on the scene to save them. Unfortunately, in his quest to be a hero, several patients died. In another case, Donald Harvey, who worked as a nurse's aide in Ohio, was arrested in 1987 and pled guilty to the deaths of 54–58 people, almost all hospital patients and many of them elderly.

Offenders were described earlier as being more likely to target women and children than males. Table 3.8 supports this claim that, in general, serial killers have victimized females consistently more than males, but nearly half of all offenders surveyed killed both males and females. Over two-thirds of offenders murdered at least one female adult and one-fourth killed at least one female teen.

Table 3.8
Percentage of Offenders Murdering Specific Victim-Sex Categories

Sex of Victims	Percent of Offenders
Only:[1]	
Females	31
Males	21
Both	48
At Least One:[2]	
Female Adult	69
Male Adult	59
Both	40
At Least One:[3]	
Female Teen	24
Male Teen	16
Both	4
At Least One:[4]	
Female Child	21
Male Child	21
Both	10

1. N= 199
2. N= 199
3. N= 200
4. N= 198

An equal number of offenders killed at least one female or one male child. Since 1975 offenders have increasingly selected at "least one female victim" whether they were adults (79 percent) or teens (30 percent). Conversely, offenders were consistently less likely to kill "one or more males" whether they were adults (54 percent) or teens (13 percent). The decline by offenders killing at least one male or female child was equal (17 percent). Although the change was small it may indicate a trend toward female adults as the most suitable target for offenders. Overall, since 1975, 37 percent of offenders killed "females only" while those offenders targeting "males only" declined to 11 percent. This shift may in part be due to the increasing accessibility men have to women as they become more visible in the workplace and institutions of higher education.

A final consideration regarding the etiology and demographics of serial murder victimization focuses on the concept of facilitation, or the degree to which victims make themselves accessible or vulnerable to attack. Wolfgang (1958) in his noted Philadelphia study examined the notion of "victim-precipitated" homicide. He observed that some victims are catalysts to a fatal attack by either rendering the first blow or a threatening gesture. Among Wolfgang's several conclusions, he found that the victim was often the husband of the offender, had been drinking,

Table 3.9
Degree of Victim Facilitation in Serial Murder Cases in the United States,
1795–1988

Facilitation	No. of Victims	Percent of Victims	Percent of Cases	No. of Victims Per Case
High	233- 327	16	17	9-13
Low	1023-1561	72-75	78	9-13
Combination	161- 193	9-12	5	20-24
Total	1417-2081	100%	100%	--

Based on 150 cases, 194 offenders.

and had reported a history of assaultive behavior. He concluded that the victim himself may be one of the critical precipitating causes of his/her own death (pp. 245, 264). In addition, Reiss (1980) studied victim-prone individuals and found they were more likely to experience a common form of victimization than to be subject to two different criminal acts. McDonald (1970) observed that victim-prone people have acquired particular attitudes and lifestyles that increase their vulnerability. Wolfgang (1958) noted that the characteristics of homicide victims in many instances resembled those of their assailants. Who became the offender and who became the victim often was determined more by chance than by any other factor. He noted that few women committed murder and that most were responding to the violent behavior of males. The Philadelphia study also revealed that most murders were intraracial: blacks killing blacks and whites killing whites.

The victims of serial murder, as discussed earlier, appear to be increasingly falling prey to strangers. Unlike homicides in general, in which the victim often knows the offender and provocation plays an important role in the killing, culpability for victims of serial murder may be best determined by the degree of facilitation created by the victim. High facilitation was defined in this study as the degree to which the victim had placed him/herself in a vulnerable situation. For example, hitchhiking can place the driver or passenger of a vehicle in a highly facilitative position for killing. Low facilitation was defined as sharing little or no responsibility for the victimization: for example, a child abducted by a stranger while playing in his yard, a patient poisoned to death during a hospital stay, or a woman abducted from a shopping mall during business hours. Usually these types of victims are completely unsuspecting of any imminent danger.

Offenders were examined with regard to the methods used to select victims, and in turn victims were examined as to their lifestyles, type of employment, and location at the time of abduction and/or killing. The overall trend indicated that 16 percent of victims in this research were highly facilitative in their own deaths (see Table 3.9). Some were hitchhiking, others worked as prostitutes, and still others placed themselves in one way or another at the mercy of strangers. Three-fourths of all victims were generally in the "right place at the right time" yet still became a homicide statistic. In some cases, offenders selected victims from categories of both high and low facilitation. Since 1975 a slight decrease was noted in both categories of facilitation, including a 6 percent increase in combinations of high and low. Whether this reflects a trend in offender versatility, a statistical aberration, or simply problems in consistently defining and measuring facilitation over time will require further exploration.

CONCLUSION

While this research substantiates the contention of those claiming that our society has experienced a dramatic emergence of serial killing, others may argue such claims to be the product of vague definitions, variations in reporting, the omnipresence of high-tech media, or a statistical artifact. Of greater concern than the extent of serial murder is its reality. The pervasiveness of serial murder is unlikely ever to challenge that of domestic homicides. What does seem to be increasingly apparent is that we are confronted with a phenomenon for which we have little explanation or ability to deter. The risk of victimization in our general population appears to be extremely small yet there are those who are at greater risk as a result of their age, sex, place of residence, or lifestyle. The fact that relatively few individuals are victims of serial murderers should in no way alter our concern for the victim or the dynamics of victimization.

The etiology of victimization should be of concern to researchers who wish to enhance their explanatory abilities for criminal behavior. Victim profiling can be an effective tool in understanding causation as well as in providing direction for deterrence. Victims in this study, except for California, exhibited little regionality. Increasingly, they were targets of offenders who operated locally in areas of higher populations. Unlike homicides in general, in which the victim often knows his attacker, serial murder was usually in the form of stranger-to-stranger violence. Young women and children were at greatest risk of victimization, especially those who were alone or could be isolated. In terms of age groups, offenders appeared to kill young adults in greater proportion, yet in recent years the elderly were frequently selected as victims. Most victims did not facilitate their deaths as a result of their lifestyles, although in recent years an increasing number of victims appeared to place themselves at risk.

REFERENCES

Blau, J. R. and P. M. Blau. (1982). "The Cost of Inequality: Metropolitan Structure and Violent Crime." *American Sociological Review, 47*, February, 114–29.

Doerner, W. G. (1975). "A Regional Analysis of Homicide Rates in the United States." *Criminology, 13*, May, 90–101.

Egger, S. A. (1986). "Utility of the Case Study Approach to Serial Murder Research."

Paper presented at the 1986 annual meetings of the American Society of Criminology, Atlanta, Georgia.

———. (1985). "Serial Murder and the Law Enforcement Response." Unpublished
dissertation, College of Criminal Justice, Sam Houston State University, Huntsville, Texas.

Eitzen, D. S. and D. A. Timmer. (1985). *Criminology.* New York: John Wiley and Sons.

Federal Bureau of Investigation, U.S. Department of Justice. (1985). *Crime in the U.S.:
Uniform Crime Reports, 1984.* Washington, DC: U.S. Government Printing Office.

Gastil, R. D. (1971). "Homicide and a Regional Culture of Violence." *American Sociological Review, 36,* June, 412–27.

Glaser, B. G. and Anselm Strauss. (1967). *The Discovery of Grounded Theory: Strategies
for Qualitative Research.* Chicago: Aldine.

Hewitt, J. D. (1988). "The Victim-Offender Relationship in Convicted Homicide Cases:
1960–1984." *Journal of Criminal Justice, 16* (1), 25–34.

Hickey, E. (1986). "The Female Serial Murderer." *Journal of Police and Criminal
Psychology, 2*(2) October.

Holmes, R. M. and J. DeBurger (1988). *Serial Murder.* Newbury Park, CA: Sage Publications.

Jenkins, P. (1988). "Myth and Murder: The Serial Killer Panic of 1983–5." In *Criminal
Justice Research Bulletin, 3*(11).

Karmen, A. (1984). *Crime Victims.* Monterey, CA: Brooks/Cole Publishing Company.

Levin, J. and J. A. Fox. (1985). *Mass Murder.* New York: Plenum Press.

Leyton, E. (1986). *Hunting Humans.* Toronto: McClelland and Stewart Limited.

McDonald, W. (1970). "The Victim: A Social Psychological Study of Criminal Victimization." Unpublished doctoral dissertation, Ann Arbor, Michigan, University
Microfilms.

Pokorny, A. D. (1965). "A Comparison of Homicides in Two Cities." *Journal of Criminal Law, Criminology and Police Science, 56,* December, 479–87.

Reiss, A. Jr. (1980). "Victim Proneness in Repeat Victimization by Type of Crime."
In Stephen Fineberg and Albert Reiss, Jr. (eds.), *Indicators of Crime and Criminal
Justice: Quantitative Studies.* Washington, DC: U.S. Department of Justice,
pp. 41–54.

Wolfgang, M. E. (1958). *Patterns in Criminal Homicide.* Philadelphia: University of
Pennsylvania Press.

4

Dissociation, Psychopathy, and the Serial Murderer

HAROLD VETTER

The psychopath may indeed be the perverted and dangerous front-
runner of a new kind of personality which could become the central
expression of human nature before the twentieth century is over.
Norman Mailer, "The White Negro,"
in *Voices of Dissent* (1958)

To many, a person who commits a series of heinous, apparently senseless, murders *must* be "out of his mind." The exact nature of the "mental illness" is not especially important, but the more bizarre the murders, the more convincing is the self-evident proposition that they are the work of someone who is "mad."

Criminal law deals with incompetence and insanity, not with mental illness. People charged with criminal offenses are not competent to stand trial if they can neither understand the nature of the charges against them nor participate in their own defense. With regard to insanity, the courts require that a judgment of insanity be based on specific criteria, for example, the capacity to distinguish between right and wrong and to be aware of the consequences of one's actions. Thus, a paranoid schizophrenic who murders a public official in the belief that he is carrying out a divine order to destroy an emissary of Satan, would probably be found NGRI ("not guilty by reason of insanity") because the nature of the disorder made it impossible for him to understand that killing is wrong. Anyone who does not share the paranoid person's delusional system is apt to find such motives incomprehensible.

Serial murderers also pose a problem of comprehensibility. Although they are unlikely to exhibit signs of psychosis, their crimes do not appear to be based on any motives that make sense to the average person. Indeed, some serial murderers have committed crimes that are so far outside the bounds of human experience that the perpetrators seem almost to belong to a different species. Consider Lawrence Bittaker, who was sentenced to death for kidnapping and murdering five teenage girls. According to the account in *Time* (Andersen, 1983):

he and a partner raped and sodomized four of them first for hours and days at a time, sometimes in front of a camera. But that is not all. He tortured some of the girls—pliers on the nipples, icepicks in ears—and tape-recorded the screams. But that is not all. The last victim was strangled with a coat hanger, her genitals mutilated, and her body tossed on a lawn so that he could watch the horror of its recovery. (p. 39)

Bittaker's prosecutor coined the term "mutants from Hell" for Bittaker and his partner.

Implicating the infernal regions as a source of motivation for human malignancy is not particularly new; neither is the tendency to interpret moral failure as illness. Serial murderers are almost routinely characterized in media accounts and much of the legal literature as "psychopaths" or "sociopaths." Both of these terms were superseded by the diagnostic category "antisocial personality disorder" when the American Psychiatric Association carried out the second revision of its *Diagnostic and statistical manual of mental disorders* in 1968 (DSM-II). The older term "psychopath" had been in use for more than a century, but both the term and concept of psychopath have been wrapped in controversy since their inception.

One of the questions that criminologists consider themselves entitled to raise is whether we make any real gains in understanding the psychological and motivational dynamics of people like Bittaker, Henry Lee Lucas, Kenneth Bianchi, and Ted Bundy by using psychiatric terms such as "antisocial personality disorder," rather than expressions like "mutant from Hell." If these serial murderers are "sick," what is the exact nature of their "illness"?

THE HILLSIDE STRANGLER

In the case of Kenneth Bianchi (the so-called "Hillside Strangler"), the motive for the murders he committed—as a lone perpetrator and in partnership with his cousin, Angelo Buono—was sexual gratification. There are parallels between Bianchi and Theodore "Ted" Bundy, who was recently executed in Florida. Bianchi and Bundy exhibited perverse needs to obtain sexual gratification by inflicting pain and mutilation on their victims. Nevertheless, both Bianchi and Bundy had periods in their lives during which they were able to achieve sexual gratification through conventional channels, according to Bianchi's common law wife and Bundy's live-in girlfriend, the pseudonymous "Liz Kendall."

Bianchi was diagnosed "antisocial personality disorder 301.70," a diagnosis which requires that at least 3 of 12 criteria be met prior to the age of 15 years. His history indicated that he (1) persistently lied from an early age; (2) had school grades that were consistently below his estimated intellectual ability; and (3) chronically violated rules at home and at school.

The antisocial personality disorder diagnosis further requires at least 4 of 9 manifestations of the disorder after the age of 18 years. In Bianchi's case, he displayed (1) an inability to maintain consistent work behavior; (2) failure to accept social norms with respect to lawful behavior; (3) an inability to maintain an enduring attachment to a sexual partner; and (4) a failure to honor financial obligations. Also required for diagnosis is a pattern of continuous antisocial behavior in which the rights of others are violated. Finally, the diagnosis of antisocial personality disorder requires that the behavior noted cannot be attributed to severe mental retardation, schizophrenia, or manic episode (American Psychiatric Association, *Diagnostic and statistical manual*, DSM-II, 1980).

Documentation that Bianchi was appropriately diagnosed antisocial personality disorder does not provide an explanation for the murders he committed. In addition to the manifestations required for the primary diagnosis, Bianchi exhibited signs of a psychosexual disorder, classified by the DSM-III as "sexual sadism 302.84." This disorder is seen as rarely leading to murder. Individuals identified as sexual sadists may find fantasized sadomasochistic activity sexually arousing or satisfying. It is, presumably the combination of antisocial personality disorder and sexual sadism that creates the potentiality for acting out sexually sadistic impulses, that is, the commission of serial murders.

According to Martin Orne, one of the several psychiatrists who interviewed Bianchi rather extensively (Orne, Dinges, and Orne, 1984):

Though the pattern of Kenneth Bianchi's psychopathic behavior goes back many years, the sexual psychopathy was manifested overtly for apparently only a relatively short period of his life. What were the factors that could have transmitted the impulse into overt action? We may speculate that the relationship with an older male [Bianchi's cousin Angelo Buono] with whom he carried out a number of illegal activities, most particularly the running of juvenile prostitutes in Los Angeles, and who shared a similar sexual perversion, may have played a crucial role in causing Mr. Bianchi to actually commit a series of sexually motivated murders. Further, given the profound ambivalence toward his mother, it also seems likely that the stress from living with his common-law wife during her pregnancy in Los Angeles (as she was becoming a mother) and his negative response to the mother of the baby in Bellingham, essentially eliminated sexual relations with his common-law-wife. However, his heightened ambivalence toward women was not expressed as overt aggressive behavior toward either his common-law-wife or his mother; rather, it contributed to the transformation of his perverted sexual impulses into acts of murder. Thus, we believe that while no single diagnosis is fully adequate to explain Kenneth Bianchi's behavior, the two combined aspects of the DSM-III diagnosis, *along with situational factors*, resulted in the multiple murders, though not in multiple personality. (pp. 163–64, emphasis added)

Orne rejected the diagnosis of multiple personality for Bianchi and claimed that he was a clever malingerer. Watkins (1984), on the other hand, claimed strong evidence in support of the diagnosis of multiple personality, based on test results, analysis of handwriting specimens, and extensive interviews, many of them with Bianchi under hypnosis.

In order to meet minimal diagnostic criteria for the diagnosis of multiple personality, a number of features must be present:

1. The essential feature is the existence within the individual of two or more distinct personalities, each of which is dominant at a particular time.
2. Each personality is a fully integrated and complex unit with unique memories, behavior patterns, and social relationships that determine the nature of the individual's acts when that personality is dominant (DSM-III, p. 237).

Typically, the predominant personality is not aware of the other personalities; consequently, reports of unaccounted-for gaps in memory (amnesic periods) are characteristic. Watkins (1984) maintains that Bianchi's behavior conformed closely to these criteria.

As Wulach (1983) has pointed out, criticisms concerning the reliability and validity of an established diagnostic nomenclature are of particular concern when the consequences of diagnosis can mean the difference between liberty and imprisonment—or execution—as they do throughout the U.S. criminal justice system: "Indeed, regular and frequent use of diagnostic evaluations occurs in determining questions of insanity, incompetency, diminished responsibility, probation, parole, and sentence length" (p. 330).

Even a cursory examination of the criteria used in arriving at a diagnosis of antisocial personality disorder according to the DSM-III raises serious questions about the use of this profile in a forensic setting. Wulach notes that it is easy to construct hypothetical case histories of individuals who would satisfy three of the childhood manifestations and four of the adult criteria but would hardly be considered antisocial by most clinicians.

The Bianchi case both underscores the problems of serial murder research and highlights the limitations of DSM-III and the later 1987 revision of the DSM-III nosology as a basis for attempting to understand the motivational dynamics of serial murderers. Given the circumstances under which Orne's analysis of Bianchi took place—a forensic setting in which the diagnosis of multiple personality might have had significant implications for Bianchi's defense—it is difficult to see what alternative was available to Orne, other than the diagnosis of antisocial personality.

Once the prosecution expert witnesses had been led by the weight of the clinical evidence to reject the diagnosis of multiple personality for Bianchi, further professional interest in the case tended to dissipate. This seems a rather unfortunate, but perfectly understandable, consequence of the forensic nature of the setting. Unfortunately, it leaves unanswered and unexplored a number of intriguing issues that clinicians and criminologists might find worthwhile exploring at greater length. In the absence of a full-blown multiple personality, did Bianchi show any other indications of being subject to dissociative states and processes? Watkins claimed that he did. If such indications were present, what form might they have taken? The same question might be raised with regard to other serial murderers who have been apprehended, convicted, and incarcerated.

An even more provocative question is the possible relationship between dissociative states and processes and the antisocial personality. As I shall try to show in the later section of this discussion, most of this clinical area is almost completely unexplored.

PSYCHOPATHOLOGY AND DISSOCIATIVE PHENOMENA

Dissociation—the lack of integration of thoughts, feelings, and experiences into the stream of consciousness—has been viewed as both a normal process and a psychophysiological mechanism that is involved in the psychopathology of certain mental disorders. The creation of the dissociative disorders category in the DSM-III (1980), together with other developments in psychiatry, has led to an increased interest in the nature of dissociation and its role in specific symptoms and syndromes.

The DSM-III identifies five dissociative disorders: psychogenic amnesia, psychogenic fugue states, depersonalization syndrome, multiple personality disorder, and atypical dissociative disorder. Additional forms of dissociative phenomena such as hypnoid states, abreaction, possession syndromes, the Ganser syndrome, and out-of-body experiences have been described in the clinical literature for well over a century (Cocores, Santa, and Patel, 1980; Ellenberger, 1970; Putnam, 1985).

The contribution of dissociation to the psychopathology of other psychiatric conditions such as post-traumatic stress disorder (PTSD) (Blank, 1985; Bliss, 1983; Kolb, 1985), eating disorders (Pettinati, Horne, and Staats, 1985), and phobic disorders (Frankel and Orne, 1976) has been recently documented. Dissociative symptoms, primarily feeling of depersonalization and/or derealization, are common in psychiatric patients as a group, irrespective of diagnosis (Brauer, Harrow, and Tucker, 1970; Cattell, 1972; Fliess, Gurland, and Goldberg, 1975; Tucker, Harrow, and Zuinlan, 1973).

A strong linkage between the development of dissociative symptoms and traumatic experiences has been documented to occur following a wide variety of traumatic situations including: combat (Fisher, 1945; Grinker and Spiegel, 1943; Sargent and Slater, 1941; Torrie, 1944); concentration camp internment (Bettelheim, 1979; Dor-Shav, 1978; Jacobson, 1977; Krystal, 1969); incest; and several other forms of trauma (Putnam, 1985). Brief depersonalization syndromes have been identified as a frequent response to life-threatening experiences in normal people (Fullerton et al., 1981; Noyes and Kletti, 1977; Noyes et al., 1977). Mild transient feelings of depersonalization and derealization appear also to be a normal experience which is particularly common during adolescence (Dixon, 1963; Myers and Grant, 1970). The overall subject ranges from 8.5 to 70 percent depending on the definitions, methodology, and age of the sample population (Dixon, 1963; Harper, 1969; Myers and Grant, 1970; Roberts, 1960; Sedman, 1966).

It must be pointed out that the nature, extent, and clinical significance of dissociative states and processes are matters of continuing controversy in psychiatry and psychology. The DSM-III dissociative disorders account for less than 2 percent of psychiatrically diagnosed behavior disorders formerly identified as neuroses (Coleman, Butcher, and Carson, 1980); and adequately documented cases of multiple personality, despite the popularity of this syndrome in fiction, television, and the movies, are infrequent enough to raise serious doubts among psychiatrists and psychologists about the validity of this diagnosis.

Because multiple personality phenomena can be induced experimentally, the question has been raised whether the cases reported by therapists are, in fact, artificial creations produced inadvertently by suggestion. Berman (1975), for example, has noted that "there are good reasons for doubting the tales of split personalities: the therapists' intense involvement with their patients; their own belief in the reality of splitting; the use of hypnosis and other methods of suggestion" (p. 78).

The potential relevance of dissociative processes to the dynamics and etiology of certain types of criminal behavior has received little attention from criminologists, for reasons that are not difficult to discover. In a system of criminal jurisprudence that assigns focal importance to the role of volition in behavior, there is an understandable lack of interest in a type of behavior that appears to provide ways of avoiding stress while gratifying needs in a manner that permits the individual to deny personal responsibility for his or her unacceptable conduct. Lipton's (1943) famous case of Sara and Maude K. details the development of a dissociated personality (Maude) who permitted Sara to gratify her sexual desires by engaging in promiscuous sexual relations without conscious knowledge and thus without guilt feelings. Apparently, Sara reverted to Maude whenever her guilt feelings over her own previous promiscuity became too intense and self-devaluing.

When apprehended in Texas in late October 1986, a drifter named David Martin Long confessed to the hatchet murders of three women, one of them a blind invalid, and asked to be executed by lethal injection, "like they do to animals." He told the police, "I've got something inside my head that clicks sometimes. It just goes off." He said that the murders of the three women— and of two men he had killed earlier in California, in unrelated incidents—had not bothered him much: "It's just like watching a movie or something" (*Tampa Tribune*, October 27, 1986, p. 3A).

Criminal justice authorities would probably tend to dismiss such comments as self-serving in the interests of denying guilt for these criminal actions. However, it is difficult to reconcile this interpretation with the fact that Long not only didn't seek to deny his guilt, but actually sought to be punished. He said, "I'm criminal. I thought I'd get better, but it appears to be getting worse and I'm pretty much ready to call it a day with my demented personality. I realize what I did is wrong. I don't belong in this society. I never have." Long had no plans to secure legal counsel. "Texas has proven itself to be both humane and sensible in the disposal of guys like me."

To a psychiatrist or psychologist, comments such as those made by Long would suggest the presence of a dissociative state or process. Even the use of the movie analogy is a familiar one in the reported dissociative phenomenon called depersonalization, which often occurs in normal persons under severe stress.

In *The Phantom Prince* (1985), Liz Kendall recollects that on a rafting trip, "Ted [Bundy] was quiet as we drifted slowly, daydreaming . . . when suddenly, and without warning, Ted lunged at me, put his hands on my shoulders and pushed me into the river. I looked up at Ted and our eyes locked. His face had gone blank, as though he was not there at all."

Dissociation and Psychopathy: The Mephisto Syndrome

A psychologist (Rieber) and psychiatrist (Green) have made a thorough attempt to explore the role played by dissociation in the dynamics of antisocial personality disorders. In their analysis of the "psychopathy of everyday life," Rieber and Green (1988) have chosen to use the term "psychopath" in preference to the antisocial personality disorder because of its wider range of connotations in ordinary usage. They are concerned with a whole continuum of behavior ranging from what might be called "normal psychopathy" (or "pseudo-psychopathy") all the way to the horrific extreme represented by the antisocial personality or "true psychopath," where we are likely to find the serial murderer.

Cleckley, in *The Mask of Sanity* (1941), pointed out that each of us possesses in rudimentary degree the distinctively psychopathic capacity *not* to respond to the salient moral or social requirements of a situation. A gang of unruly twelve-year olds cutting up during a school outing to Carnegie Hall to hear Mozart is behaving psychopathically, as are all of us when we momentarily break ranks with our conscience to laugh at what we otherwise hold in the highest reverence. Neither is such a capacity intrinsically bad. To paraphrase a point made by Cleckley, were it not for this ability to break ranks with our conscience occasionally, we would all be in danger of turning into pompous monsters of self-righteousness.

Having said this much, it is important for us to acquaint ourselves with the extreme pole of the continuum represented by the "true psychopath." This term indicates something more than a tendency to care only about others as a means to one's own self-centered aims; it indicates a *lack of capacity* to do otherwise. The true psychopath, as Rieber and Green view him, is lost to humanity, utterly incapable of human concern and involvement with others, except at the most superficial and exploitive level.

The authors distinguish between the true psychopath and the career criminal, at least as an ideal type. (There is plainly overlap.) The career criminal relies on superior strength and cunning to gain wealth; he feeds his ego on the fear he evokes and on his own ability to get things done outside the encumbrances of the law. Nevertheless, such people are quite capable of feeling empathy and concern for their immediate families and partners in crime. They rely on the support of others and are capable of erecting and adhering to quite formal procedures for inclusion within the peer group. They are concerned with winning admiration and praise from their criminal partners and they speak in derogatory and contemptuous terms of their victims. In short, they manifest salient characteristics of group identification and group loyalty. The true psychopath, by contrast, is typically a "bust" even as a member of an organized criminal ring; he cannot be relied on, he makes unnecessary trouble, and though he may be useful for carrying out specific acts of an unusually unseemly nature, there is no question of obtaining his long-term loyalty. When trouble arises, the psychopath is the first to go, something which career criminals understand and for which they typically plan expeditious means. (New York City police are still investigating the murder in a mid-town Manhattan restaurant of one Jonathan Schiff, wheeler-dealer and con man extraordinaire; the further the investigation proceeds into the incredible trail of bribery, extortion, and swindles that is this man's sole legacy, the harder it has become to fix a motive for his death. Seemingly everyone who ever knew Schiff, including career criminals and ordinary businessmen, had something to gain by killing him.)

The DSM-III declares that although people who exhibit the antisocial personality disorder may show a stereotypically normal mental status, most frequently there are signs of personal distress, including complaints of tension and/or depression, an inability to tolerate boredom, and the conviction of the hostility of others (which, to be sure, is a predictable consequence of their behavior). The interpersonal difficulties these people experience and the discordant moods they suffer persist far into mid-life and beyond, even though their more flagrantly antisocial behavior—especially assaultiveness—typically diminishes by the time they pass 45 or 50 years of age. Invariably there is a markedly impaired capacity to sustain any kind of lasting close relationship with family, friends, or sexual partners. Such individuals, in fact, generally cannot become independent, self-supporting adults outside of persistent criminal activity and the penal system. However, some who warrant this diagnosis are able to achieve some degree of political or economic success—the "adaptive psychopaths"—and to outward appearances, their day-to-day functioning is not characterized by the impulsivity, hostility, and general chaos that typify the general syndrome.

The problem of the ''adaptive psychopath'' is especially elusive, since such people come to psychiatric attention late and only after they have run seriously afoul of the law. And an indeterminate number of them, an ''elite'' subgroup, have simply never been caught; therefore, they have never been seen psychiatrically. Accordingly, it is impossible to achieve a clear picture of how they functioned during their period of ostensibly normal adjustment. Apparently, whether by virtue of superior endowment or because their survival was facilitated by adopting an outwardly compliant facade, their educational development was substantially less hampered than is typically the case. Bundy, the notorious serial killer recently executed in Florida, had attended law school and had become active in politics in California. His career as a prolific serial murderer was incomprehensible to many who knew him during this phase of his life, although even then he was considered to have a hair-trigger temper. While the enigma of the ''adaptive psychopath'' remains largely unsolved, such people still show certain hallmarks of the general syndrome, most specifically a search for thrill-seeking through dangerous behavior, an attitude of omnipotence typically expressed in a feeling that they will never get caught, and a dissociative capacity that, among other things, enables them to demarcate periods of frankly antisocial behavior from their ''normal'' periods.

THE MEPHISTO SYNDROME

In their attempt to identify the salient characteristics of the psychopathic syndrome, Rieber and Green (1988) emphasize their belief that the underlying cognitive, conative, and emotional processes they describe are far from unique to the psychopath. Instead, they perceive these processes to represent gross exaggerations of tendencies found in everyone. Even in their pathologically exaggerated form, they are not unique to the psychopath. For example, the kind and quality of dissociative processes exhibited by the psychopath can also be found in multiple personality.

What is unique to the psychopath, in the authors' view, is the specific combination of these processes; it is the combination that discriminates true psychopathy from other syndromes.

Rieber and Green begin at the level of discriminating characterological traits and subsequently work their way down to the underlying processes. Four salient characteristics—thrill-seeking, pathological glibness, antisocial pursuit of power, and absence of guilt—distinguish the true psychopath.

Thrill-seeking

True psychopaths habitually rush in where angels fear to tread. The more dangerous an undertaking, the more irresistible it becomes. This behavior cannot merely be classified as impulsive, since it often entails planning and, in a surprisingly large number of instances, the cooperation of an accomplice. But such planning as does occur fails to mitigate the element of danger. There is some evidence to suggest that psychopaths have unusually high thresholds for perceptual stimulation. Certainly, their overt behavior suggests that only in situations of threat and danger do they feel truly alive. The world of predictable cause and effect, of instrumental acts and expectable rewards, has no emotional meaning for them. They can grasp that this humdrum, predictable, and boring world exists, but they cannot relate to it. The adaptive psychopath has taken this to a paradoxical extreme: he can go about his routine activities precisely because he has turned them into a dangerous charade of passing for normal while in his off-hours he lives an entirely different life. Much of what has been observed of the psychopath's inability to learn from experience needs to be related to this characteristic. Life would be much less dangerous—and much less fun for the psychopath—if he really allowed himself to learn and thus to know the altogether likely consequences of his behavior. The true psychopath prefers an open-ended world: whether he takes off in his car cross-country, with no planned destination or time of arrival, or merely says something outrageous and shocking in conversation, he is looking to create situations of ambiguity and potential danger.

We might pause here to distinguish psychopathic thrill-seeking from the pursuit of excitement that normal people use to offset boredom. On a continuum of thrills, one might rate tennis relatively low and ice-hockey, with its sanctioned violence, rather high. But for the true psychopath, even ice-hockey is boring—too many rules. Psychopathic thrill-seeking consists of breaking the rules, whatever they might be. At a poker table, the psychopath does not merely want to win; he wants to cheat—and get away with it. Rieber and Green describe the psychopath as performing a Mephisto Waltz on the tightrope of danger.

Pathological Glibness

The psychopath speaks well—colorfully, persuasively, and volubly—about himself and his past, although only minimally about the future. What is said, however, has little discernible relation to facts. There is, in Cleckley's term, a "semantic dementia." Cleckley's point was that the ordinary emotional demands of a situation make no impression on the psychopath; like rowdy schoolboys at a concert, they behave as if the accepted meanings of a situation simply were not there. But the same dissociation is also manifest in their speech. Words have become detached from meaning and serve, instead, as a means of placating an enemy or fleecing an unwary victim. By the same token, they do not allow themselves to be moved by words and concepts that are valued by their fellow citizens. Consider the psychopath's response who was asked by an exasperated interviewer, "Don't you have any compassion?" The interviewer was told, "it's in the dictionary, between 'shit' and 'sucker.' "

Antisocial Pursuit of Power

(Not only are psychopaths extremely sensitive to power relations and intent upon securing maximum power for themselves, they also seem hell-bent on using that power for destructive ends.) Only in paranoid states and in the attitudes of career criminals can a comparable fusion of antisocial trends with the power drive be found. It is as though, for the psychopath, power can only be experienced in the context of victimization. If the psychopath is to be strong, someone else must suffer. There is no such thing in the psychopathic universe as the merely weak: whoever is weak is also a sucker, someone who begs to be exploited.

When inmates seized control of the New Mexico State Penitentiary in 1980, they murdered and mutilated selected victims. Afterward, one of the suspected ringleaders was interrogated at length. While being careful to avoid self-incrimination, he made it clear that the victims of the riot "didn't understand morality" (sic!). He also made it clear that he and his cronies ran the prison, anyway, and that apart from the freedom to leave, they enjoyed every advantage they had on the outside. The prisoners, given room to maneuver by legal reforms designed to safeguard their rights, had in effect created a psychopathic universe in which the strong preyed on the weak in the name of "morality."

The fusion of the power drive with antisocial trends in the psychopath need not always be so bloodthirsty (violence per se is not a distinguishing trait of the syndrome). Consider the young man who explained that he stole cars because it was the only thing he was good at—and everyone needs to be good at something.

Absence of Guilt

Psychopaths are aware that certain people at certain times will bring punitive sanctions against them. Accordingly, they are skilled in evasion and rationalization. Some, who are gifted histrionically, can even feign remorse. (But they do not *feel*. The absence of guilt is essential to the syndrome, for guilt, besides being a consequence of certain acts in normal people, is also a powerful deterrent against the commission of those same acts in the future.) The psychopath is undeterred. Indeed, those very characteristics that, to another person, would portend guilt as a consequence, to the psychopath portend the excitement of danger. Moreover, when the absence of guilt is investigated clinically, one discovers a general poverty of affective relations. The young man in the example above who stole cars could distinguish only two feelings in himself: boredom and excitement. All other feelings were for suckers.

(The combination of the four characteristics—thrill-seeking, superficial glibness, antisocial pursuit of power, and absence of guilt—constitutes what Rieber and Green have dubbed the Mephisto Syndrome.) As they point out, it is difficult to resist the impression that the true psychopath is a personification of the demonic. Since time immemorial, mankind has outlined in figures of the demonic an inherently human capacity to fuse despair and drive discharge in an antisocial posture. The devil has been important to man as a personification of what, as an intrinsically social creature, he cannot afford to be. But it is precisely the inhibiting sense of being intrinsically social that psychopaths lack. They are not social, only superficially gregarious; not considerate, merely polite; not self-respecting, just vain; not loyal, only servile—and down deep, they are quite shallow. Hence, the observed homologies with the figures of the demonic: the psychopath is free to be what ordinary man does not dare to be. For the ordinary person, the figure of the devil is always experienced as a projection, as something outside the ego. For the psychopath, the demonic is a way of life. Just as the devil has evolved through the centuries and has, in the process of the evolution, acquired a whole host of representations, ranging from the truly bestial to the philosophic troublemaker of George Burns's portrayal in *Oh God, You Devil!*, so too can the presenting facade of the psychopath range from the grotesquely animalistic to the sweet-talking confidence man.

THE CENTRALITY OF DISSOCIATION

We ordinarily conceive of dissociation as an hysterical trait. In this context, (dissociation refers to the tendency of individuals to separate, or dissociate, their "real" selves from their "public" selves.) Such people histrionically alter their public presentations to create a succession of socially acceptable images or facades.(Dissociation thus serves as a mechanism for distracting others from the unpleasant realities that may constitute the "real" self.) And it can reach the point, so spectacularly manifest in multiple personality, where it constitutes a self-distracting process so powerful that it utterly prevents the individual from experiencing and/or integrating painful thoughts or emotions. At a less severe level of disturbance, the charming, dramatic, or even seductive facade of the histrionic personality prevents him or her from dwelling on the inadequacies that he or she may possess, inadequacies that nonetheless are available to conscious-ness if the histrionic is sufficiently motivated to deal with them.

With the psychopath, dissociation reaches an even deeper level; paradoxically, it is also more readily put at the service of the pathologically inflated ego. Where the histrionic splits off the "bad me" from the "good me," to use Sullivan's terminology, the psychopath's internal split seems to take place at an even more basic level, that of the "me" and the "not me." In a double sense, in both fantasy and reality, there is nothing that is "not me" for the psychopath. There is no limit to the grandiosity of their fantasy; similarly, there is no limit to what they might do. And, given that "me" and "not me" form a continuum of meaning, with each necessary as a semantic counterpole to the other, the inability of the psychopath to arrive at a "not me" self-structure results in a corresponding inability to arrive at a stable sense of "me" as well. To avoid misunderstanding, let us make clear that though we speak of a stable self-structure, we do not conceive of the self as an entity, but rather as a system of interlocking processes that link the individual to the social milieu.

Paradoxically, the deficit in the psychopath's self-structure or self-concept at this most elemental level is coupled with a greater capacity for the techniques of dissociation at the higher level of "good me" and "bad me." Whereas for the multiple personality, and for the hysteric generally, dissociation is primarily as unconscious process—this is the beauty of it, that it primarily works outside of awareness—for the hysteric generally, dissociation primarily works outside of awareness. For the psychopath there is a definite ego-involvement in it, at least insofar as social judgments are concerned. The psychopath is constantly on the lookout for ways of distracting the interviewer, rationalizing his behavior, or deflecting the blame. He shows both foresight and perceptiveness in forestalling any confrontation with the "bad me"—he knows what he is doing.

We must be careful not to confuse levels here: because at the level of the "bad me" the psychopath manifests a degree of conscious control over his self-presentation does not mean that he can desist from this behavior. Indeed, the contrary is true; the deeper dissociation is utterly uncontrolled and this makes it practically impossible for the psychopath to do anything else but con at the level of social valuations. The same is true of the kind of rationalizations and trumped-up emotions on which the psychopath relies. True, at this point, there is a level of conscious ego involvement in these techniques, but this is a pathologically inflated ego we are talking about here, further, an ego that has lost the ability to produce either genuine reasons or genuine feelings. The psychopath's grandiosity may take him in, but it ought not take us in. He has lost the ability not to con people; he is a slave to this behavior. What appears to be the ultimate freedom is actually bondage.

The psychopath, in short, cannot turn off the dissociative tendency. This sometimes wreaks diagnostic havoc in courtroom proceedings. During the trial of Bianchi, the defense brought forth evidence suggesting that he was a multiple personality and that the crimes of "the Hillside strangler" were done by a second self outside of Bianchi's control. In support of this contention, evidence derived from the use of hypnosis was also brought in. In a celebrated battle of rival experts, Martin Orne won the case for the prosecution by arguing that Bianchi had faked being a multiple personality—the police searching his home found numerous psychological texts that might have helped Bianchi do this—and that he had faked hypnosis as well. With regard to the outcome, there can be little quarrel with Orne's strategy, but in our view he could have gone much further. For Bianchi was not just a malingerer; he was also faking being normal, faking consulting with the defense attorney, and faking under cross-examination. This man could only con people; there existed no counterpole of an inwardly valid set of truths that would allow one to say that he had faked one thing and not everything else.

If we hope to make progress in understanding the psychopath, we must understand which psychological processes are essential to the syndrome and which are peripheral. And in teasing out the etiology of the essential processes, we must be willing to cut across the walls of established diagnostic entities to observe whether or not the same or similar psychological factors obtain for any particular process regardless of diagnostic designation. Take the issue of dissociation. It is clear that a profound reliance on dissociation is an essential hallmark of the psychopathic disorder. (Indeed, we would argue that together with an abnormally high psychological threshold for stimulation—manifest in thrill-seeking—and a profoundly disturbed relation to issues of power and dominance, dissociation constitutes part of the distinguishing triad of traits basic to this syndrome.) But when we compare the degree and quality of dissociative processes in the psychopath with the degree and quality of the same processes in other syndromes, do we arrive at generally valid psychological principles? Do we learn anything about etiologically significant environmental variables? These are questions worth pursuing. There is some evidence to suggest that the dissociation typical of multiple personality originates in the context of severe physical and/or sexual abuse in childhood. It is also clear that some psychopaths come from comparable home situations. Nonetheless, it is clear that the psychopathy syndrome, though it overlaps with multiple personality in respect to dissociation as a constituent mechanism, basically constitutes an inherently different response of the developing personality. Thus, we may well ask what other factors besides physical and/or sexual abuse must be present to produce the particular outcome of psychopathic dissociation. In the multiple egos of the developing child who has not yet left the magical stage, and thus is readily prepared to imagine himself as more than one person, we have the fundamental level of dissociative capacity. Faced with traumatic physical or sexual abuse, the child at this stage readily defends himself with the thought that the abuse happened to someone else; this imagined "someone else" then becomes the nucleus of a second personality. Children who have a high innate dissociative capacity do this readily; children with a low innate capacity have to work at it. It seems likely, therefore, that traumatic physical or sexual abuse is instrumental in heightening the child's capacity for and reliance on the mechanism of dissociation. What has to happen in psychopathic development, however, is for this heightened capacity to attach itself to the child's own antisocial behavior; currently, it is not at all clear how this comes about. It is quite possible that the link to antisocial behavior occurs somewhat later in childhood and that differential associative networks, of the sort Sutherland described, play an instrumental role.

Here let us observe that psychopaths have significant social relationships, relationships that are important in the maintenance of the disorder. Fritz Redl and David Wineman discovered this to their chagrin when they set up a residential facility for antisocial youths. As they report in *Children Who Hate* (1951), they were initially surprised and pleased to see their charges banding together into tight-knit groups—until they discovered that the group functioned as a means of perpetuating pathology and resisting the demands of the therapeutic milieu. Redl and Wineman report in vivid clinical detail that the children were masters at using the group as a means of maintaining their essential ego deficits. The same reliance on interpersonal relations can also be seen in the adult psychopath, even in the most profoundly disturbed. Thus, in a majority of cases, serial killers have been found to have employed right along the services of an accomplice. And when they can be got to confess to the accomplice's existence, they invariably turn the tables on him—he not only killed, but mutilated the corpse, they say, he's really sick. In this way, they excuse their own behavior by dispersing its significance onto others. Henry Lee Lucas, for example, decried his accomplice's alleged cannibalism. The accomplice, like the juvenile gang, protects the psychopath from a confrontation with his deficits through differential association. In this way, the innate dissociative capacity becomes more closely linked with antisocial trends.

This, then, in large overview is our portrait of the psychopath. The essential psychological mechanisms appear to be thrill-seeking, dissociation, and a profound disturbance in the relationship to issues of power and dominance evident in a grandiose delusional belief in the exceptional nature of the self. Of these three traits, dissociation in all its myriad forms—psychopathic glibness, absence of guilt, semantic dementia—is the most readily observable, but all three are necessary to constitute the syndrome. (Obviously, they interact. Dissociative mechanisms subserve both thrill-seeking and grandiosity. By the same token grandiosity becomes a rationale for thrill-seeking and an organizer of dissociative mechanisms. The techniques of rationalization rely on the dissociation of affect and the concomitant semantic dementia; so, too, does the absence of guilt, and so forth.) In the exercise of these psychological mechanisms, moreover, psychopaths rely on select interpersonal relations as both social insulators and as preferred social instigators to further psychopathy.

Dissociation and the Serial Murderer

Egger (1986) has observed that serial murder research is "rapidly becoming repetitive rather than cumulative" (p. 4). Part of the problem, as we have already seen, arises from the near-impossibility of conducting research in a forensic setting in which the judicial processing of the accused killer takes precedence over any other considerations. In the case of Bianchi, neither Orne or Watkins were able to approach their task of plumbing the psychic depths of the "Hillside Strangler" within a context of detachment and objectivity. Neither does the problem end, by any means, with the adjudication and conviction of the accused, for occupants on death row, with very few exceptions, are extremely reticent to engage in any lengthy interaction with researchers on the grounds that anything they disclose may jeopardize ongoing appeals.

Of almost equal importance, perhaps, is the lack of a conceptual frame of reference for approaching the convicted serial murder in confinement. The DSM-III is essentially a taxonomy or classification system based on descriptive features that meet certain criteria of reliability, if not validity, among clinicians. At best, they can only provide researchers with departure points for their investigations. This is especially true for the study of dissociation in syndromes other than the dissociative disorders category of the DSM-III.

The Dissociative Experiences Scale (DES)

Bernstein and Putnam (1986) have devised a dissociation scale that could provide the serial murder researcher with an instrument that might lead to the systematic collection of valuable data from serial murderers who are presently in custody. The Dissociative Experiences Scale (DES) was developed to offer a means of reality-measuring dissociation in normal and clinical populations. Scale items were developed, using clinical data and interviews, that involved memory loss and consultation with experts in dissociation. The scale that resulted is a 28-item self-report questionnaire, which contains such items as:

- Some people have the experience of finding themselves in a place and have no idea how they got there.
- Some people sometimes have the experience of feeling as though they are standing next to themselves or watching themselves do something and they actually see themselves as if they were looking at another person.
- Some people find that in one situation they may act so differently compared to another situation that they feel almost as if they were two different people.

In their original study, the authors asked subjects to indicate how often they had undergone the experiences described by the scale items by placing a mark on a horizontal line between values of 0 and 100 percent. In addition, demographic data (age, sex, occupation, and educational level) were collected so that the connection between these variables and the scale scores could be examined. The mean of all item scores ranges from 0 to 100 and is called the DES score.

The scale was administered to between 10 and 39 subjects in each of the following populations: normal adults, late adolescent college students, and persons suffering from alcoholism, agoraphobia, phobic-anxious disorders, posttraumatic stress disorders, schizophrenia, and multiple personality disorder.

The authors report that the DES is internally consistent and yields scores that are stable over time. In addition, the scale shows good criterion-and construct-validity. It is able to differentiate between subjects with and without clinical diagnoses of a dissociative disorder. Multiple personality disorder patients obtained the highest group median scale score, scoring higher than all other groups. This finding is consistent with the characterization of multiple personality disorder as the most severe of the dissociative disorders.

As we have already seen, spontaneous utterances that strongly suggest the presence of dissociative processes abound in the published material on serial murderers. Admittedly, this is sketchy and anecdotal evidence, but it is typical of the circumstances that characterize the opening phase of any worthwhile investigation. If a start has to be made somewhere, the use of the Bernstein-Putnam DES may well represent such a beginning.

REFERENCES

American Psychiatric Association. (1968). *Diagnostic and statistical manual of mental disorders*, (2nd edn.). Washington, DC: American Psychiatric Association.

———. (1980). *Diagnostic and statistical manual of mental disorders*, (3rd edn.). Washington, DC: American Psychiatric Association.

———. (1987). *Diagnostic and statistical manual of mental disorders*, (3rd edn. revised). Washington, DC: American Psychiatric Association.

Andersen, K. (1983). "An eye for an eye." *Time*, January 24, 28–39.

Berman, E. (1975). "Tested and documented split personality: Veronica and Nelly." *Psychology Today*, 9(4), 78–81.

Bernstein, E. M and Putnam, F. W. (1986). "Development, reliability, and validity of a dissociation scale." *Journal of Nervous and Mental Disease*, 174, 727–35.

Bettelheim, B. (1979). "The individual and mass behavior in extreme situations." In B. Bettelheim, *Surviving and other essays*. New York: Harcourt.

Blank, A. S. (1985). "The unconscious flashback to the war in Vietnam veterans: Clinical mystery, legal defense, and community problem." In S. M. Sonnenberg, A. S. Blank, and J. A. Talbott (eds.), *The trauma of war: Stress and recovery in Vietnam veterans*. Washington, DC: American Psychiatric Press.

Bliss, E. L. (1983). "Multiple personalities, related disorders, and hypnosis." *American Journal of Clinical Hypnosis*, 26, 114–23.

Bliss, E. L. and Larson, E. M. (1977). "Sexual criminality and hypnotizability." *Journal of Nervous and Mental Disease, 173*, (9), 522–26.

Brauer, R., Harrow, M., and Tucker, G. J. (1970). "Depersonalization phenomena in psychiatric patients." *British Journal of Psychiatry*, 117, 509–15.

Cattell, J. P. (1972). "Depersonalization phenomena." In S. Arieti (ed.), *American handbook of psychiatry*. New York: Basic Books.

Cleckley, H. (1941). *The mask of sanity*. St. Louis: C. V. Moley Co.

Cocores, J., Santa, W., and Patel, M. (1980). "The Ganser syndrome: Evidence suggesting its classification as a dissociative disorder." *International Journal of Psychiatric Medicine*, 14, 47–56.

Coleman, J. C., Butcher, J. N., and Carson, R. C. (1980). *Abnormal psychology and modern life*. Glenview, IL: Scott Foresman.

Confer, W. N. and Ables, B. S. (1983). *Multiple personality: Etiology, diagnosis, and treatment*. New York: Human Sciences Press.

Dixon, J. C. (1963). "Depersonalization phenomena in a sample population of college students." *British Journal of Psychiatry*, 109, 371–75.

Dor-Shav, K. N. (1978). "On the long-range effects of concentration camp internment on Nazi victims: 35 years later." *Journal of Consulting Clinical Psychology*, 46, 1–11.

Egger, S. A. (1986). "Utility of the case study approach to serial murder research." Paper presented at the American Society of Criminology annual meeting in Atlanta, Georgia, November.

————. (1989). "Serial murder." In W. C. Bailey (ed.), *The encyclopedia of police science*. New York: Garland Publishing Company, pp. 578–81.

Ellenberger, H. F. (1970). *The discovery of the unconscious: The history and evolution of dynamic psychiatry*. New York: Basic Books.

Fisher, C. (1945). "Amnesic states in war neuroses: The psychogenesis of fugues." *Psychoanalysis Quarterly*, 14, 437–68.

Fliess, J. L., Gurland B. J., and Goldberg, K. (1975). "Independence of depersonalization-derealization." Journal of Consulting Clinical Psychology, 43, 110–11.

Frankel, F. H. and Orne, M. T. (1976). "Hypnotizability and phobic behavior." *Archives of General Psychiatry*, 33, 1259–61.

Fullerton, D. T. et al. (1981). "Psychiatric disorders in patients with spinal cord injuries." Archives of General Psychiatry 38, 1369–71.

Greaves, G. B. (1980). "Multiple personality: 165 years after Mary Reynolds." *Journal of Nervous and Mental Disorders*, 168, 577–96.

Grinker, R. T. and Spiegel, J. P. (1943). *War neuroses in North Africa*. New York: Josiah Macy, Jr. Foundation.

Hale, N. G. (ed.) (1975). *Morton Prince. Psychotherapy and multiple personality: Selected essays*. Cambridge: Harvard University Press.

Harper, M. (1969). "Deja vu and depersonalization in normal subjects." *Australian and New Zealand Journal of Psychiatry*, 3, 67–74.

Hilgard, E. R. (1977). *Divided consciousness: Multiple controls in human thought and action*. New York:Wiley and Sons.

Hollingshead, A. B. (1957). *Two-factor index of social position*. Unpublished manuscript.

Howe, E. G. (1984). "Psychiatric evaluation of offenders who commit crimes while experiencing dissociative states." *Law and Human Behavior*, 8, 253–82.

Jacobson, E. (1977). "Depersonalization." *Journal of American Psychoanalysis Association*, 7, 581–609.

Kendall, E. (1981). *The phantom prince: My Life with Ted Bundy*. Seattle: Madrona Publishers.

Kolb, L. C. (1985). "The place of narcosynthesis in the treatment of chronic and delayed-stress reactions of war." In S. M. Sonnenberg, A. S. Blank, and J. A. Talbott (eds.), *The trauma of war: Stress and recovery in Vietnam veterans*. Washington: DC: American Psychiatric Press.

Krystal, H. (1969). *Massive psychic trauma*. New York: International Universities Press.

Lipton, S. (1943). "Dissociated personality: A case report." *Psychiatric Quarterly*, 17, 35–36.

Ludwig, A. M. (1983). "The psychobiological functions of dissociation." *American Journal of Clinical Hypnosis*, 26, 93–99.

McKellar, P. (1977). "Autonomy, imagery, and dissociation." *Journal of Mental Imagery*, 1, 93–108.

Meares, R. and Grose, D. (1978). "On depersonalization in adolescence." *British Journal of Medical Psychology*, 51, 335–42.

Murphy, G. (1947). *Personality: A biosocial approach to origins and structure*. New York: Harper & Row.

Myers, D. and Grant, G. (1970). "A study of depersonalization in students." *British Journal of Psychiatry*, 121, 59–65.

Nemiah, J. C. (1981). "Dissociative disorders." In A. M. Freedman and H. I. Kaplan (eds.), *Comprehensive textbook of psychiatry* (3rd edn.). Baltimore: Williams & Wilkins.

Noyes, R. and Kletti, R. (1977). "Depersonalization in response to life-threatening danger." *Psychiatry*, 18, 375–84.

Noyes R., Hoenk, P. R., and Kupperman, B. A. (1977). "Depersonalization in accident victims and psychiatric patients." *Journal of Nervous and Mental Disorders*, 164, 401–407.

Oborne, D. J. and Clarke, M. J. (1975). "Questionnaire surveys of passenger comfort." *Applied Ergonomics*, 6.2, 97–103.

Oppenheim, A. N. (1966). *Questionnaire design and attitude measurement*. New York: Basic Books.

Orne, M. T., Dinges, D. F., and Orne, E. C. (1984). "On the differential diagnosis of multiple personality in the forensic context." *International Journal of Clinical Hypnosis*, 32, 118–69.

Parikh, D., Sheth, A., and Apte, J. (1981). "Depersonalization." *Journal of Postgraduate medicine*, 27, 226–30.

Pettinati, H. M., Horne, R. L., and Staats J. M. (1985). "Hypnotizability in patients with anorexia nervosa and bulimia." *Archives of General Psychiatry*, 42, 1014–16.

Prince, M. (1909). "Psychological principles and field of psychotherapy." In Hale, N. G. (ed.) (1975), *Morton Prince. Psychotherapy and multiple personality: Selected essays*. Cambridge: Harvard University Press.

Putnam., F. W. (1985). "Dissociation as a response to extreme trauma." In R. P. Kluft (ed.), *The childhood antecedents of multiple personality*. Washington, D.C.: American Psychiatric Press.

Putnam, F. W. et al. (1986). "The clinical phenomenology of multiple personality disorder: 100 recent cases." *Journal of Clinical Psychiatry*, in press.

Redl, F. and Wineman, D. (1951). *Children who hate*. New York: Free Press.

Remington, M. et al. (1979). "Comparative reliability of categorical and analogue rating scales in the assessment of psychiatric symptomatology." *Psychological Medicine*, 9, 765–70.

Rendon, M. (1973). "The dissociation of dissociation." *International Journal of Social Psychiatry*, 19, 240–43.

Rieber, R. W., and Green, M. R. (1988). *The psychopathy of everyday life*. Unpublished manuscript, New York.

Roberts, W. (1960). "Normal and abnormal depersonalization." *Journal of Mental Science*, 106, 478–93.

Sargent, W. and Slater, E. (1941). "Amnesic syndromes in war." *Proceeding of the Royal Society of Medicine*, 34, 757–64.

Sedman, G. (1966). "Depersonalization in a group of normal subjects." *British Journal of Psychiatry*, 112, 907–12.

Sedman, G. and Reed, G. F. (1963). "Depersonalization phenomena in obsessional personalities in depression," *British Journal of Psychiatry*, 109, 376–79.

Simon, R. I. (1977). "Type A, AB, B murderers: Their relationship to the victims and to the criminal justice system." *Bulletin of the American Academy of Psychiatry and Law*, 5, 344–62.

"Something in my head . . . clicks." (October 27, 1986). *Tampa Tribune*, p. 3A.

Spiegel, D. (1984). "Multiple personality as a post-traumatic stress disorder." *Psychiatric Clinicians of North America*, 7, 101–10.

Spiegel, H. (1963). "The dissociation-association continuum." *Journal of Nervous and Mental Disorders*, 136, 374–78.

Taylor, E. (1982). *William James on exceptional mental states: The 1896 Lowell lectures*. New York: Scribners.

Taylor, W. S. and Martin, M. F. (1944). "Multiple personality." *Journal of Abnormal Social Psychology*, 39, 281–300.

Torrie, A. (1944). "Psychosomatic casualties in the Middle East." *Lancet*, 29, 139–43.

Tucker, G. J., Harrow, M., and Zuinlan, D. (1973). "Depersonalization, dysphoria and thought disturbances." *American Journal of Psychiatry*, 130, 702–706.

Watkins, J. G. (1984). "The Bianchi (L.A. Hillside Stranger) case: Sociopath or multiple personality?" *International Journal of Clinical and Experimental Hypnosis*, 32 67–101.

West, L. J. (1967). "Dissociative reaction." In A. M. Freedman and H. I. Kaplan (eds.), *Comprehensive textbook of psychiatry* (2nd edn.). Baltimore: Williams & Wilkins.

White, R. W. and Shevach, B. J. (1942). "Hypnosis and the concept of dissociation." *Journal of Abnormal Social Psychology*, 37, 309–28

Wulach, J. S. (1983). "Diagnosis the DSM-III antisocial personality disorder." *Professional Psychology: Research and Practices*, 14, 330–40.

II

Those Who Kill, and Kill, and Kill, and Eventually Are Caught

The three chapters in this section provide the reader with the diversity of the serial murder phenomenon. In the first chapter Richard Doney describes the aftermath of the Yorkshire Ripper investigation and the strong pressures brought to bear upon the Home Office of the United Kingdom to develop a more effective response to future Rippers in order to identify and apprehend them with a great deal more speed. The Byford Report, a commissioned report of the problems and errors of the Yorkshire Ripper investigation and the apprehension of Peter Sutcliffe in January 1981, is summarized for the reader. This report has never been made public but a number of recommendations included in it have been implemented by British police agencies with the help of the Home Office.

Doney describes how the methods used to manage the Yorkshire Ripper investigation began to falter under the volume of information that was collected. Following this investigation and the presentation of the Byford Report recommendations, new standardized methods, both manual and computerized, have been implemented in every police force in the United Kingdom. The result of this effort has been the Home Office Large Major Enquiry System, a standardized investigative computer system specifically designed to support criminal investigation.

David Ford, a sociologist, was placed in a unique position for a university professor. He was selected to work as an active member of the Central Indiana Multiagency Investigative Team investigating a series of gay murders in and around the Indianapolis, Indiana area. In Chapter 6, Ford discusses various key aspects of this team's investigative strategy, including its search for information on both suspects and victims. Ford analyzes the impact of problems facing the team and describes its successes and failures. Further, the critical need for an expeditious application of a victimological analysis in the earliest stages of a serial murder investigation is examined.

The chapter on Henry Lee Lucas is a summary of information about one of the most controversial of this nation's contemporary serial killers. This controversy that surrounds Lucas stems primarily from charges of a hoax from exploiting politicians and journalists as a result of Lucas's recanting of all of his confessions to murder. Despite his ten criminal convictions for murder, not including the conviction for killing his mother, and the fact that Lucas has been recently indicted for two murders in Florida, the Lucas case will undoubtedly fade into criminal history with this controversy unresolved.

For law enforcement agencies in 27 states in this country, however, this controversy was long ago resolved. For these agencies still hold Lucas as their primary and, in most cases, only suspect in over 160 homicides. These homicide cases will remain officially open but as a practical manner have been resolved from a criminal investigative perspective. These agencies remain convinced that Lucas is their man. Homicide detectives in these agencies and their colleagues in agencies throughout the country remain convinced that Lucas killed in excess of 100 people and is one of the most prolific serial killers in recent history.

Lucas, possibly more infamous for his recantation of his numerous confessions than for the over 100 victims that law enforcement attribute to him, is examined from a number of different background dimensions. In Chapter 7, Egger summarizes and highlights over 40 hours of interviews with Lucas, supplemented with official records and investigative reports from numerous law enforcement agencies. Egger provides no causal propositions regarding the behavior of Lucas, as idiographic research does not produce a "bottom line." Further, the allegations by journalists and politicians that the confessions made by Lucas were a hoax are analyzed and, for the most part, discounted.

5

The Aftermath of the Yorkshire Ripper: The Response of the United Kingdom Police Service

RICHARD H. DONEY

The term "major crime investigation" is commonly used in the United Kingdom (UK) to group those crimes which are offenses against the person resulting in death or serious injury. Examples of these offenses are organized crime (such as involving the Mafia, the Chinese Triads, and other similar groups) or commercial crime (such as business frauds and insider trading). However, in an age of increasing violence, many of these other types of serious crime are precursors to murder and it is true to say that the techniques described in this chapter are being applied successfully to the investigation of these other types of serious crime. Finally, it is worth noting that while the concept of serial murder is understood in the United Kingdom, its occurrence there is rare as compared with the United States. The Yorkshire Ripper (Peter Sutcliffe) was an extreme rarity and there is no evidence that there are any undetected serial murders on the Ripper scale. In the United Kingdom, the clear-up rate for murders, attempted murders, and manslaughter is more than 90 percent, with there being about 700 cases of homicide a year.

SCOTLAND YARD AND SHERLOCK HOLMES

Throughout the world, Scotland Yard, officially the headquarters of the (London) Metropolitan Police, has earned itself an enviable reputation as a center of excellence for crime investigation (Howe, 1965). Over the years, this reputation has been reinforced on film, television, and in books. It is possible that the reputation of its detective ability may even have put fear into offenders and thus prevented some crimes from occurring (Home Office, 1938).

On the freelance side, Sherlock Holmes, the fictional character invented by Sir Arthur Conan Doyle, "dealt" with some 60 cases during his career, often assisting Scotland Yard (Eyles, 1986). Even today, his adventures command a loyal following. With his partner Dr. Watson, Holmes established a substantial reputation for solving cases through his ability to notice obscure clues and through the power of his deductive logic. Without wishing to detract from Holmes's abilities, it is perhaps interesting to note that nearly always the victim and killer were known to each other, a situation rather simpler than the stranger-to-stranger relationships which characterise serial killings.

The Man from the Yard

In years gone by, the organisation of police forces in the United Kingdom was rather different from that which exists today (Critchley, 1967). Before World War II, there were approximately four times as many forces as there are today and this meant that many of the smaller forces had a limited capability and experience in dealing with protracted, complicated investigations. The Home Office made arrangements that allowed these smaller forces to call on the (free) services of Scotland Yard although in reality the number of such cases in a year was usually fewer than ten (Prothero, 1931). Scotland Yard would typically send two experienced detectives, one a chief inspector or superintendent who would lead the investigation and the other a sergeant who brought with him a "box of tricks." This box was essentially a rudimentary paper-based system for organising the information that the investigation collected. Over the years, this system was copied by many provincial (i.e., outside London) forces and so a measure of uniformity grew up. As experience and procedures became more sophisticated, the "murder room," as it was known, increased in importance as the administrative center of the investigation and became known as the incident room.

Reorganisation of Police Forces in the United Kingdom

Until the 1960s there were many small town and county forces, a structure similar to that which exists in the United States today. By 1960 there were 125 forces in England and Wales and 33 in Scotland. At that time, a Royal Commission on the Police (1960) was set up to review all aspects of police organisation and its reports led to the Police Act of 1964 (Stead, 1985). Following this Act and a reorganisation of local government in 1972, the number of forces settled at 52 (43 in England and Wales, 8 in Scotland, and 1 in Northern Ireland), the boundaries of each being coterminous with the top tier of local government. This resulted in an average force strength of 2,000–2,500 officers, the largest being the (London) Metropolitan Police (2,700) and the smallest, Dumfries and Galloway in Scotland (333). This compares with over 12,000 forces in the United

States averaging 39 officers (Federal Bureau of Investigation, 1985) and begins to suggest why there are differences of approach between the United Kingdom and the United States in cases involving two or more forces. It is perhaps interesting to note how much greater is the disparity in the number of forces (1:230), compared with a population ratio of 1:4 and a land area ratio of 1:40 (Diagram Group, 1980).

The chief constables of UK forces are responsible to statutory Police Authorities, which in England and Wales are composed of (elected) members of the local council and nominated members of the local judiciary (known as magistrates). The composition is slightly different in Scotland. Unlike in the United States, chief constables are not elected and are not answerable to Police Authorities for their decisions on how their area is to be policed. Funding of police forces is provided by central and local government approximately equally.

As far as major crime investigation is concerned, the effect of this reorganisation was to produce investigative units that were now sufficiently large to have enough experience to be able to sustain their own complex investigations. Subsequently, the "man from Scotland Yard" faded from the provincial scene.

EARLY RESEARCH INTO THE USE OF COMPUTERS

The Role of the Home Office

The Home Office is one of the oldest and most senior departments of British government and its history can be traced back to 1782. The head of the department, the Home Secretary, ranks alongside the Chancellor of the Exchequer and the Foreign Secretary in importance. The Home Office has a broad sweep of responsibilities, far wider than many equivalent ministries in other Western nations. Its major responsibilities include the prison service; immigration, nationality, and passports; criminal justice; broadcasting; equal opportunities; fire and emergency planning; and in particular, the police.

For the fire, prison, and police services, the Home Office provides a central source of research and development and spends approximately £4 million ($7.2 million) each year in support of this activity. The Scientific Research and Development Branch (SRDB) is at the center of this research and employs about 110 scientists and engineers.

1974–80 Experiments

In 1974 SRDB (in fact, its predecessor the Police Scientific Development Branch) started the Major Incident Project, a programme of work aimed at finding out how computers and associated technology could be used to support major crime investigations (Peace and Barrington, 1985). More specifically, this meant support to the incident room, the administrative centre of the investigation where all the information received was collated, stored, and analysed. Initial work involved surveying a number of incident rooms to see the procedures used and to assess the numbers of documents such as statements and actions (leads) handled. This work gave a useful indication of the way in which computers could be used to support incident rooms and indeed a number of ad hoc trials were set up. In the end, though, it became clear that the technology available in the late 1970s was the limiting factor. In 1980 the Home Office decided to stop the various trials and attack the problem head-on by devising a computer system that would supplant the manual procedures rather than augment them. Of course, by this time the Yorkshire Ripper was engaged in his career.

Technology Problems

What had been learned from the experiments of the 1970s about the technology required? The volume of information that required processing was substantial by any standards and demanded systems that at least as far as the police service was concerned, were too large and too expensive compared with their existing investment in data processing. The result was that practical systems which could be devised tended to be underpowered and could not adequately meet police needs. This technological limitation was about to change with the fortuitous appearance in the early 1980s of powerful microprocessors and the consequential improvement in computer price/performance ratios.

The MIRIAM Experiment

The next stage was a project known as MIRIAM (Peace and Barrington, 1985). This acronym stood for Major Incident Room Index and Action Management and reflected the dual requirement for indexing information and for managing the work of detectives pursuing enquiries in the field. The system also provided free text retrieval, that is, the ability to search for the occurrence of specific words in textual documents. There had been continuing debate over the relative merits of indexing and free text retrieval but in MIRIAM these were viewed as complementary rather than mutually exclusive. Essex police (a force bordering London) volunteered to be the test site for the MIRIAM project.

Suppliers of computer systems were invited to bid for the work and the contract was awarded in December 1981 to Honeywell Information Systems (now known as Honeywell Bull) to develop and install the system. The finished system became operational in July 1983. The system was given a trial run using information from old investigations and this gave a good simulation of real life, apart from the pressure. There was little the project team could do about a real incident but wait. It was only a few weeks before there was a near-fatal stabbing of a young hairdresser and the system was at last able to show how much more efficient (and indeed pleasant) a computerized incident room could be.

MIRIAM had three major components: (1) indexing; (2) action and document management; and (3) a typing service/free text retrieval.

1. *Indexing.* A number of standard indexes were maintained—name, address, vehicle, telephone, category (which allowed the creation of indexes of specific interest), and sequence of events (which ordered items of information by time of occurrence). In addition to comprehensive methods of searching the information held in the index records, the system also had the important feature of making operators search existing records before creating a new one. This was seen as a way of avoiding the possibility of duplicate records. Each index record also had a list of cross-references. Documentary cross-references showed, for example, the source of any information such as a statement number. Index-to-index cross-references showed relationships between people and objects; for example, the owner of a vehicle, or a husband and wife.

2. *Action and document management.* Actions (individual tasks given to detectives) and documents were monitored in their various states. For example, actions could be "raised," then "allocated," and finally "completed." Documents passed through a similar process to ensure that none was lost in the system. This management information was used to monitor the flow of work and allowed measures to be taken when backlogs began to appear.

3. *Typing service/free text retrieval.* This service allowed all documents to be word-processed and thus provided a "no-cost" data entry method for the free text retrieval part of MIRIAM. As mentioned earlier, this facility was seen as complementary to the indexes and provided a safety net behind the structured indexes should pieces of unindexed information acquire an unforeseen significance.

All the time this work was going on, the Yorkshire Ripper was in custody and had been since February 1981. As will be seen later, the consequences of the Ripper investigation brought tremendous pressure on the researchers to complete their work and devise the definitive system. As a result, the MIRIAM experiment had a relatively short life but was largely successful, with many of its features being incorporated in the successor system HOLMES.

THE YORKSHIRE RIPPER CASE AND ITS CONSEQUENCES

Description of the Case

Peter William Sutcliffe was born in 1946 in the Yorkshire town of Bingley. He grew up in the area and married his wife Sonia in 1974 (Cross, 1981; Pithers et al., 1981). Eleven months later, in July 1975, Sutcliffe carried out the first of the 20 attacks for which he was eventually tried. The first recorded pointers to his future activities came in 1969 when he was arrested for carrying a hammer and was subsequently convicted of going equipped for theft. In the same year, he was accused of attacking a woman in the red-light district of Bradford with a weighted sock but no charges were brought.

It is not known whether Sutcliffe was responsible for any later attacks on women involving the use of a blunt instrument until 1975, when he tried to kill two women and then managed to kill a third, Wilma McCann, in Leeds in October. His usual weapon, the hammer, was used in each attack. As the police began to suspect that the same person was responsible for the attacks, the name "Yorkshire Ripper" came into popular usage in newspapers and on television. The name alluded to Jack the Ripper, a serial killer in the time of Queen Victoria, and indicated similarities in damage done to the victims' bodies. In November 1975 another woman, Jane Harrison, was murdered in Preston. This attack was of major significance as later related events were to set the police on lines of enquiry that were to prove fruitless.

By March 1978 Sutcliffe had killed eight women and attempted to kill five more. Then came two letters claiming to be from the Ripper. By March 1979 when he killed once more, a further letter arrived, followed by a tape recording in June. The three letters and the tape had been posted in Sunderland, in the northeast of England, and this fact together with the accent of the voice on the tape led those in charge of the investigation to believe that the murderer came from that area. The letters appeared to show that the author knew details about the earlier Harrison killing that had not been made public, and the police thought that the author could well be the Yorkshire Ripper. Forensic tests showed that the person who had licked the envelopes had a relatively rare blood group which was the same as that identified from semen found on Harrison's body. Sutcliffe has the same blood group but, as was found out later, is a "non-secretor" which means that his saliva does not contain substances that allow blood group identification. Sutcliffe was never charged with the Harrison murder and, to this day, no one really knows how the letters and tape fit into the case. A massive publicity campaign was mounted to identify the author of the letters and the tape, and the whole country hoped that somebody would recognise something and give that vital clue.

Another important line of enquiry concerned a five-pound note which had been found in the handbag of Jean Jordan, who was killed in Manchester in October 1977. As the note was new, the police hoped to discover through whose hands it had passed. By diligent detective work, they established a list of firms that could have received the note as part of batch; one of these firms employed Sutcliffe and he was eventually interviewed. However, the police had no reason to suspect him any more than the other 8,300 possible recipients of the note. Indeed, he had a near-perfect alibi although this was later found to be flawed.

Sutcliffe was eventually caught in January 1981 as he sat in a car with a prostitute whom two uniformed officers had decided to arrest for soliciting. The registration plates of Sutcliffe's car proved to be false. This led to a chain of events that culminated in his tools being recovered and his confessing that he was indeed the Yorkshire Ripper (see Table 5.1 for a chronology of the case).

From 1975 on Sutcliffe was interviewed by the police on nine occasions. This was later to prove a major source of criticism of the handling of the investigation. The interest and pressure from the media and the public had been intense throughout the investigation and, at one point, the Home Secretary had to answer

Table 5.1

A Chronology of the Yorkshire Ripper Case

	1975	
5 Jul		attempted murder of Anna Rogulsky at Keighley
15 Aug		attempted murder of Olive Smelt at Halifax
30 Oct		murder of Wilma McCann at Leeds
	1976	
20 Jan		murder of Emily Jackson at Leeds
9 May		attempted murder of Marcella Claxton at Leeds
	1977	
6 Feb		murder of Irene Richardson at Leeds
24 Apr		murder of Patricia Atkinson at Bradford
26 Jun		murder of Jayne MacDonald at Leeds
10 Jul		attempted murder of Maureen Long at Bradford
1 Oct		murder of Jean Jordan at Manchester
14 Dec		attempted murder of Marilyn Moore at Leeds
	1978	
21 Jan		murder of Yvonne Pearson at Bradford
31 Jan		murder of Helen Rytka at Huddersfield
Mar		letters "from the Ripper"
16 May		murder of Vera Millward at Manchester
	1979	
Mar		letter "from the Ripper"
4 Apr		murder of Josephine Whitaker at Halifax
Jun		tape recording "from the Ripper"
2 Sep		murder of Barbara Leach at Bradford
	1980	
20 Aug		murder of Marguerite Walls at Leeds
24 Sep		attempted murder of Upadya Bandara at Leeds
5 Nov		attempted murder of Theresa Sykes at Huddersfield
17 Nov		murder of Jacqueline Hill at Leeds
	1981	
2 Jan		Sutcliffe arrested

questions about the case in the House of Commons. It is still difficult to appreciate the weight carried by the team on an investigation unprecedented in its size, but some simple statistics help: there were 268,000 names in the nominal index, 21,000 people were interviewed in connection with just one particular line of enquiry, 115,000 actions were raised, 31,000 separate statements were taken, at times between 500 and 1,000 letters were received daily from the public, 5.4 million vehicle registration numbers were recorded, 250 detectives were involved full-time for more than three years, and the whole investigation absorbed some 5 million hours of police time at an estimated cost of £4 million ($7.2 million) (Pithers et al., 1981 Byford, 1984).

Contemporary Serial Cases

Serial killers are not unknown in the United Kingdom (Jenkins, 1988) but none has had the impact of the Yorkshire Ripper, probably because they were less well publicized. Donald Neilson (the "Black Panther") achieved some notoriety during 1974–75 shortly before Sutcliffe embarked on his career (Hawkes, 1978). Neilson was a robber who murdered four sub-postmasters and injured several others. He subsequently kidnapped Lesley Whittle, the teenage daughter of a well-off family, and murdered her by leaving her in a culvert.

Dennis Nilsen was rather a different type of serial killer whose 15 victims (1979–83) tended to be transients and homosexuals (Lisners, 1983). In some ways, Nilsen is the closest approximation to the U.S. killer John Wayne Gacy in that his victims came from a group of people whose absence might not be noticed for a time or whose movements were difficult to trace. However, Nilsen's distinguishing feature was that he would kill his victims at his own home and dispose of the body in situ. This came to light when a drainage engineer was called to investigate a blockage and discovered some grisly remains.

Difficulties Caused by Size

The Ripper investigation was in many ways unprecedented as far as the UK police service was concerned. There have been other killers whose "score" approximated to that of Sutcliffe but none has had such an effect on the public and the media. Here was a killer apparently selecting women at random in a small area of England who was able to taunt his police pursuers with letters and a tape recording. Three police forces were directly involved, with West Yorkshire bearing the brunt, and it cannot be surprising that in view of the statistics given earlier, the paper administration systems that had evolved over many years were found to be incompatible and not designed to cope with the volume of information that was forthcoming. A final illustrative statistic is that the paper records at one point weighed 24 tons, requiring a move within the building in which they were housed because of concerns over the building's structural integrity. Some of these practical problems led to detectives in the field not being aware of the investigation's up-to-date knowledge when they went, say, to interview a potential suspect. The effect was to frustrate the work of both senior and junior detectives.

The Byford Review

Once Sutcliffe had been caught, it was almost inevitable that there would be a review of the investigation so that lessons could be learned for the future. Lawrence Byford, who was at that time Her Majesty's Inspector of Constabulary for the region which included West Yorkshire, was appointed by the Home Secretary in May 1981 to lead this review. Her Majesty's Inspectorate of Constabulary is staffed by retired chief constables who are each responsible under the Police Act of 1964 for inspecting the eight or so forces within their region. The chief inspector of constabulary (which Byford later became) reports to the senior Home Office official in charge of the Police Department.

Byford's review team consisted of two deputy and two assistant chief constables, other senior officers, and a leading forensic scientist. The review team reported in December 1981. Byford himself said that any police errors and mistakes that his review might comment upon had to be set against a background of professional pressure that was unprecedented in a recent crime investigation in the United Kingdom (Byford, 1984). There were many positive outcomes to the review and some of these are detailed later. At the top level, the Association of Chief Police Officers (ACPO) set up a Working Group on Major Crime Investigation (Peace and Barrington, 1985) which was to act as the driving force for developing and implementing the review's proposals. This Working Group, which represented the interests of chief officers, detectives, and researchers, first met in June 1982 and continues to meet today.

Lessons Learned

The key lessons that Byford (1984) concluded had to be learned were as follows:

- standardisation of procedures
- computerisation of records
- training of senior investigating officers
- appointment of an advisory team
- use of specialist and scientific support

The Working Group was asked to "examine all aspects of the management and investigation of major crime, particularly those of a multi-force nature, and to make recommendations." It saw its first task as the creation of a standard national manual system as this would mitigate the difficulties encountered on multi-force investigations. Members of the Home Office MIRIAM project team were invited to join the group and work was started on the manual system. Proposals were discussed in detail, which members took back to their own forces for further consultation. This cyclical process was repeated until the "Standardised Administrative Procedures'' were agreed. These procedures were accepted by the ACPO in January 1983. The Working Group then devised a tiered training programme, based on national, regional, and local teams to enable the procedures to be taken into use on January 1, 1984. The first lesson had been learned.

Computerisation was proceeding apace with the MIRIAM experiment and later in this chapter the emergence of the HOLMES system is explained in some detail.

The Ripper case emphasised the need for overall coordination among several forces involved in an investigation and the role of the senior investigating officer was established. This officer was seen as someone of assistant chief constable rank who had the necessary executive authority to take charge of a lengthy and complex serial type of case. A training course was developed at the Police Staff College at Bramshill to cover techniques that senior detectives would not normally need for routine investigations. The extension of the standard procedures and the HOLMES system into "routine" murder and other serious crime investigations has meant that a version of the course is now offered to all senior detectives of the rank of superintendent and above.

The concept of an advisory team was seen as a way of helping a hard-pressed senior detective and his colleagues, particularly when an investigation was stalled. It was hoped that fresh minds being brought to bear in a spirit of helpful cooperation might assist in keeping the investigation properly focused.

In commenting on specialist support, Byford identified a problem parallel to one already encountered in the police organisation: the number of forensic scientists involved (10) offered the possibility of things being overlooked through extended lines of communication. Byford proposed that a scientific adviser be appointed to suggest possible scientific courses of action and to be responsible for making them happen rather than just liaising between the investigation and the forensic laboratories.

Interim Arrangements

Mention has already been made of the contract for MIRIAM being awarded in December 1981 and of the need for a period of development and subsequent evaluation. The time scale for this seemed rather lengthy to a police service that had to digest the Ripper case and was awaiting the Byford review. The practical difficulty for the Home Office was in trying to anticipate the outcome of MIRIAM before the system existed. In response to police demands, it established the "Interim Arrangements," the procedures that the police service was to follow if it wanted to use computers on major investigations before MIRIAM was assessed. Systems based on free text retrieval were at one stage thought to be the way forward but the experiments that were carried out showed that structured indexing could not be entirely abandoned.

Then, in the summer of 1981, some articles in computer journals claimed that the Yorkshire Ripper could have been caught with the aid of a microcomputer which in one instance was cited as costing as little as £3,000 ($5,400). As the MIRIAM system was costing £666,000 ($1,200,000), it is not surprising that questions were asked about the correctness of the Home Office's plans. There is no doubt that even now, with a massive increase in price/performance ratio, a £3,000 microcomputer would never be able to provide the range of features considered necessary for a major incident room. At the time (1981) microcomputers were still a novelty and their capabilities were not widely understood. Nevertheless, it was felt that a microcomputer might be able to provide a system under the Interim Arrangements.

Eventually, a commercial indexing software package, AutoIndex, was selected for trial and in January 1982, training commenced with the prototype system in anticipation of its use in a live investigation. This latter event happened in July 1982 and by June 1983 the system had been sufficiently enhanced and proved that it could be presented to the police service as fit for operational use. By this time, multi-user microcomputer systems were much more common and suitable systems could be purchased for about £30,000 ($54,000). As with the later HOLMES system, standards were enforced for data entry and a national training scheme was developed. The Home Office provided an emulation of the AutoIndex package on the Police National Computer and this gave an "upwards growth path" that could be used by a force at the point when an investigation began to outgrow its own AutoIndex microcomputer system. This point was normally considered to be at about 10,000 AutoIndex records. In the end, some 18 forces took advantage of AutoIndex but all of these systems have now been supplanted by HOLMES.

THE HOLMES SYSTEM

Design

It had been intended that the MIRIAM system would be evaluated over a twelve-month period which was due to finish in the summer of 1984. This period was felt necessary to ensure that the system's effect on major crime investigations was thoroughly understood before it was taken into widespread use throughout the United Kingdom. However, the police service was well aware of the recommendations of the Byford review and was well aware of the help that computerization could bring because of its exposure to MIRIAM and the Interim Arrangements. As a result, the police service was keen to see an end to the research which many felt had gone on too long. In early 1984 the Home Office and ACPO agreed to review all the work that had gone before and to devise the specification for the definitive system which became know as HOLMES (Home Office Large Major Enquiry System).

The project team wanted the MIRIAM system reviewed by experienced detectives who had not been directly involved with the development and thus a group was set up under the chairmanship of a senior officer who had acted as an outside expert during the Ripper investigation. This group consisted of detectives from a variety of ranks and with a broad range of experience. The group first met in April 1984 and by August of that year the first release of the HOLMES specification was completed (Eagle et al., 1988).

Development

The definition of the HOLMES system was in itself a major undertaking but another equally important consideration was to establish just how the actual system would be built. Quite rightly, most computer users, including police officers, do not concern themselves with the technical issues of system development but this can sometimes lead to expectations which cannot be met. In the case of HOLMES, many officers thought that it would be provided as another application on the Police National Computer, this being a system provided by the Home Office servicing every police force and holding information on matters such as stolen vehicles, vehicle owners, and convictions. It was very quickly apparent to the Home Office that the size of a HOLMES system that would meet the national demand would be cost-prohibitive or at least such that at a time when the government was seeking to curb public expenditure, a request for additional funding would be rejected.

Nevertheless, the police service demanded HOLMES as it still felt vulnerable should another Ripper-type enquiry occur. The solution devised by the Home Office was to invite the computer industry to develop the system at its own cost with the almost guaranteed prospect of UK sales and the possibility of overseas sales. The systems themselves were to be purchased by individual police forces, sized according to their own projected usage. The Home Office planned to control the development through a scheme of certification; each supplier's system would be tested thoroughly by the Home Office to ensure conformity with the specification and chief constables would be advised by the Home Office to use only systems that had been certified.

An important consequence of there being several system models manifested itself in the area of linking incidents (i.e., the computer aspects of a serial investigation). Computer standards for exchanging data were (and still are) emerging and fragile and it was therefore not possible to contemplate joining individual systems electronically. The only practical solution was to specify a format for magnetic tape so that all linked databases could be moved onto a common machine. The drawback has proved to be that this transfer process takes time when detectives would like it to be instantaneous.

The general development arrangements seemed attractive to the industry and initially more than 50 companies requested copies of the specification. The size of the UK market clearly would not allow this number of suppliers to make a return on their investment (typically 10–15 work years) and in the end, four companies, all of whom were existing suppliers to the police market, felt it worthwhile to press on with their development.

Implementation

One consequence of systems being purchased locally was that the advantages of economy of scale were no longer available. In particular, it would be difficult for individual forces to decide how large their systems should be. The occurrence of murders is unpredictable and it is perfectly possible for a long quiet period to be followed by several murders within a period of a few weeks. In addition, forces were also not immune from restrictions on public expenditure and would have competing bids.

In the earlier stages of development, it was not clear whether forces, particularly the smaller ones, would be able to justify the cost of the complete system. Following discussions with the police service, the HOLMES system was divided into three modules similar to the three parts of MIRIAM (indexing, action and document management, and a typing service/free text retrieval). The idea was that forces could purchase modules in combinations (one, one and two, or all three) according to their operational needs and the size of their purse. However, because the competitive market systems have been cheaper than originally estimated virtually all forces have bought complete systems. Variations arise in the size of the systems both in terms of the number of concurrent incidents that can be handled and the size of each incident.

As has been mentioned, the issue of standardization across forces was a key part of the strategy resulting from the Byford review. Having devised a way of getting standard systems developed, the Home Office and ACPO agreed that standards should also be set for the way in which operators used the system. A National Training Team was created, comprised at its peak of 12 police officers experienced in incident room procedures. This team was at the top of a tiered scheme of training whereby the national team would train each force's trainers, who would in turn train the staff needed by each force. The national team devised a complete course that lasted four weeks and the complete package of course notes and training database was given to each force for its own use. Additionally, a manual of ''Rules and Conventions'' was created which dictated data entry standards so as to enforce further the concept of standardisation. These standards covered such things as abbreviations for addresses (e.g., Rd for Road, Av for Avenue). They are now in their second edition as the opportunity has been taken to incorporate suggestions from forces who have by now gained experience in the use of HOLMES.

The maintenance of these various standards is vital in ensuring that the problems encountered on the Ripper investigation do not recur. By fostering the concept of a community of HOLMES users through annual seminars, a regular newsletter, and the availability of a three-officer Holmes Support Group at the Home Office, it has been possible to sustain a commitment to standardisation.

Problems and Benefits

No system is perfect and HOLMES is no exception. Because of the scope and power of the system there is a tendency to use all of its features on every investigation. In a fast-moving investigation generating large amounts of information, this can impose a heavy workload on the operators, leading to backlogs and even shortcutting. The specification for the system does not set limits or allow variations for incidents of different size and thus the overhead of running the system is the same for small incidents as it is for large ones. It is tempting to devise a trimmed-down version of the procedures but a difficulty can arise when an incident suddenly grows in complexity because, perhaps, it is seen to be part of a series. This possibility is unpredictable. The pressure of workload described earlier also leads to a reduction in researching, that is, using the power of the system to look actively for clues.

The system costs money just like any substantial system; in the United Kingdom typical systems cost £200,000 ($360,000) but this amount varies according to the budgeted number and size of concurrent incidents in a particular force. The system is complex and operators require initial training lasting several weeks. Furthermore, they need to practice their skills and in smaller forces where the number of incidents is small, this means regular refresher training. Many forces have taken to using the system for other crimes as a way of maintaining operator skills.

Considering that HOLMES has caused a major change in the way in which a major crime investigation is administered, it has been absorbed into the detective process with remarkably few difficulties. The subjective view is that it has been well received by detectives who perceive it to be a considerable advance. The administration of investigations has been much improved and incident rooms are much calmer and less chaotic places in which to work. The outside enquiry teams are also better served now because they can be provided with all the relevant information that the investigation currently holds when, say, they go to interview a suspect. The designers of the system never intended that Holmes by itself would detect crimes and there is no evidence of it doing so. However, there is evidence that by organizing the running of the investigation, detections have happened sooner and with less wasted effort.

Overall, this application has forged a unity among UK police forces that has not been seen before with other applications. There is an expectation that future applications will benefit in the same way.

FUTURE RESEARCH

Investigation Procedures

The introduction of the Standardised Administrative Procedures and the HOLMES system has without doubt provided detectives in the United Kingdom with a practical methodology that substantially reduces the risk of an investigation being compromised by "information overload." But in an age when information management is a growth industry, is this enough? Or is it now time to expand the research horizons and look at activities across the whole investigation rather than just within the incident room?

Those who have been involved in a difficult investigation will have little doubt about the stress imposed on the senior detectives as they are forced to select courses of action whose outcome is uncertain while all the time being subjected to the scrutiny of the media. In many ways, there are parallels with managers in the commercial world who have to make decisions on courses of action that will affect their company's future well-being and thus it might be possible to transport modern decisionmaking techniques into the investigative process. More obviously, the detective manager has responsibility for disposing of substantial amounts of the organization's resources and so any method that can help to identify unproductive lines of enquiry must be worth exploring.

This responsibility has led to the development of a research strategy covering three distinct areas: (1) strategic management—providing better information to detective managers to help them make more informed decisions about the direction of an enquiry; (2) analysis of information—integrating modern methods of analysing information (such as Criminal Intelligence Analysis) into the structure of incident rooms presently defined by the standardized procedures; and (3) volume productivity—reducing the clerical effort required to enter information into the system by use of new technology. This strategy is intended to build on the success so far achieved and generally to enhance the productivity of major crime investigation; productivity in this context means reducing the time it takes to identify an offender while minimizing the effort required to do so.

Application of New Technology

The research outlined above should produce many useful techniques but almost inevitably some of these will require the application of technology and in particular, computers. The computer industry is at present investing heavily in artificial intelligence, that is, a range of computing techniques that try to embody various aspects of human behaviour in computers. The more obvious examples are robotics, natural language understanding, and expert systems. How would any of these techniques help? One problem described above concerns the volume of work that has to pass through an incident room. By providing modern powerful work stations that improve the way in which humans and computers interact, it should be possible to automate partially the process of transcribing the raw free text into the annotated index records that are currently created by indexers. As there are more indexers than any other job function, an improvement in their efficiency would conserve substantial resources.

The need to research more aggressively the information collected is also an area in which technology could help. Another area of artificial intelligence is "expert systems" (Hart, 1988), that is, systems that have been taught how an expert in a particular field weighs up items of information and then makes a decision or draws a conclusion. These rules are often unwritten and difficult to tease out of the expert, but imagine the possibility of a machine being able to look through a mass of information and pull out things worth further review by using the same rules that a detective would use.

Finally, improved graphics might allow the criminal intelligence analysis process to become automated, both by reducing the drudgery of producing the various charts and by creating charts directly from a database rather than having a human transcribe the information first.

Linking of Crimes

As was described at the beginning of this chapter, the occurrence of serial killers in the United Kingdom is rare. However, other serious offences such as rape often are part of a series, quite possibly unidentified, and any techniques developed would be useful in investigating these other crimes. The term "linkage blindness" (Egger, 1984) has been coined to describe the situation in the United States in which the sheer number of police forces inevitably makes it difficult to circulate information that might be of mutual benefit. In the United Kingdom such blindness does not really exist for a number of reasons: there are fewer forces, the country is smaller, the various television and newspaper organisations operate on a national rather than local basis, and so generally news travels faster. Of course, homicide is also not as commonplace as in the United States and so this type of offence attracts a great deal of attention.

It is often said that two questions spring to a detective's mind when faced with a new case: what has happened like this before? And whom do we know who could have done this? Answers to these questions will identify serial offenders and can also identify occurrences of different offenders using a similar modus operandi. Although not helpful in detecting serial offenders, this second possibility might be put to good use in describing characteristics of unidentified offenders. There are systems in both the United Kingdom and United States that store information about cases for comparison; crime pattern analysis is an application on the UK Police National Computer which holds a limited amount of detail on a few types of more serious offence. The VICAP system run by the FBI (Howlett et al., 1986) is very similar in concept and attempts to capture far more information about a wide range of individual cases. However, both systems have the disadvantage of being "voluntary"; that is, the quality and completeness of their databases is dependent on individual police forces supplying the necessary information. In the case of VICAP particularly, it is easy to see that the number of forces in the United States must make it difficult for the system to function as an identifier of serial offences.

There is the possibility then that this type of database could serve a dual purpose: to identify the activities of a serial offender, and to use statistical information to build up the characteristics of different types of crime (even though they involve many offenders). This second aspect is already being researched actively in the United Kingdom for certain types of murders and there is evidence that characteristics can be evinced in relation to, for example, the residence of the offender and his likely previous convictions. This latter point is of particular value as the process of calling for lists of people with specific previous convictions and then eliminating them from the enquiry is painstaking and likely to be very costly. The inference so far is that previous convictions might be for minor assault or dishonesty rather than for more serious offences such as murder (to repeat: serial killings are rare in the United Kingdom). Overall then, this research could establish the likely outcome and cost of different lines of enquiry. In passing, it is interesting to speculate whether, having established the characteristics of some types of offence, it would be possible to determine if there were any anomalous features of old undetected cases.

If these ideas prove to be of value to detectives, how best then to make them available? Expert systems have been described earlier and there is the intriguing possibility that an expert system that could be left to wander through the mass of information held on a HOLMES or VICAP database might be able to identify associations that would be of great interest to a detective. However, this is very much in the future.

CONCLUSIONS

This chapter has explained how the police service in the United Kingdom has been able to rationalise and standardise the way in which it investigates major crime. Efforts to achieve this lasted many years, but it was the investigation into the Yorkshire Ripper that had a galvanising effect and produced the will within the police service and the Home Office to achieve a result. This circumstance is not unusual; stressful times, particularly war, have often produced major advances in science and technology very quickly. As a consequence, the UK police service is now well placed to cope with large and complex investigations. No one would want to claim that there will be no problems in the future but at least there is now agreement on the way to approach the problem of detecting the offence. The phenomenon of "linkage blindness" does not appear to be a problem in the United Kingdom because the relatively small number of forces and their large size makes cooperation and interchange of information commonplace.

As for the future, it is important to note that the systems so far developed are targeted at the handling and control of information. Further work is needed to be targeted at improving the analysis of information and at providing decision support to detective managers. Technology has a part to play in delivering new types of systems that can "think" like humans and provide a powerful modern version of the old-time Scotland Yard sergeant's "box of tricks."

REFERENCES

Byford, Sir Lawrence. (1984, September 28). "Lessons to be learned." *Police Review*, 1870–71.

Critchley, T. A. (1967). *A history of police in England and Wales 900–1966*. London: Constable.

Cross, R. (1981). *The Yorkshire ripper*. New York: Dell.

Diagram Group. (1980). *The book of comparisons*. London: Sidgwick and Jackson.

Eagle, R. W., William, K. C., Mylam, H. M., Wilkinson, R. A., and Oldfield, R. W. (1988). *HOLMES application design specification*. London: Home Office.

Egger, Steven A. (1984). "A working definition of serial murder and the reduction of linkage blindness." *Journal of Police Science and Administration, 12*, 348–57.

Eyles, A. (1986). *Sherlock Holmes: A centenary celebration*. London: John Murray.

Federal Bureau of Investigation. (1985). *Uniform crime reports for the United States*. Washington, DC: Department of Justice.

Hart, A. (1986). *Expert systems: An introduction for managers*. London: Kogan Page.

Hawkes, H. (1978). *The capture of the Black Panther*. London: Harrap.

Home Office. (1938). *Report of the departmental committee on detective work and procedure*. London: Her Majesty's Stationery Office.

Howe, Sir Ronald. (1965). *The story of Scotland Yard*. London: Arthur Baker.

Howlett, J. B. et al. (1986). "The violent criminal apprehension program—VICAP: A progress report." *FBI Law Enforcement Bulletin, 55*, 14–22.

Jenkins, P. (1988). "Serial murder in England 1940–1985." *Journal of Criminal Justice, 16*, 1–15.

Lisners, J. (1983). *House of Horrors*. London: Corgi.

Peace, D.M.S.P. and Barrington, R. C. (1985). "HOLMES: The development of a computerised crime investigation system." *The Police Journal, 58*, 207–23.

Pithers, Malcolm et al. (1981, May 23). Weekend Guardian. *The Guardian*, p. 9–11.

Prothero, Margaret. (1931). *The history of the criminal investigation department at Scotland Yard from earliest times until today*. London: Herbert Jenkins.

Royal Commission on the Police. (1960). *Interim Report, Cmd 1222*. London: Her Majesty's Stationery Office.

———. (1962). *Interim Report, Cmd 1728*. London: Her Majesty's Stationery Office.

Stead, P. J. (1985). *The police of Britain*. New York: Macmillan.

6

Investigating Serial Murder: The Case of Indiana's "Gay Murders"

DAVID A. FORD

This chapter describes an investigation into a series of seemingly related murders committed in central Indiana between 1980 and 1983. Each of eight original victims had some relationship to the gay community of Indianapolis. Most were male prostitutes commonly known as "street hustlers." The investigation involved a cooperative effort by representatives from over ten city, county, state, and federal law enforcement agencies, as well as civilian social scientists and a forensic pathologist, organized as a task force called CIMIT—Central Indiana Multiagency Investigative Team. CIMIT ultimately assisted the investigation of at least 25 unsolved murders in Indiana and bordering states.

CIMIT's efforts took different directions as investigators came to believe that, despite victim and crime scene similarities, more than one killer was responsible for the several crimes. Primary attention focused on a suspect thought to have murdered two of the original eight victims; the remaining deaths required more general attention and review as an alternate string of unsolved murders. To its credit, the task force succeeded in identifying Larry Eyler, an alleged serial killer eventually convicted of murdering a young man in Chicago. Yet when CIMIT was effectively disbanded ten months after it was formed, most of the central Indiana murders remained unsolved.

The experience of CIMIT points to perplexing aspects of serial murder that defy traditional investigative approaches. Drawing on the author's observations as a civilian task force member, this chapter examines some of those issues, suggesting in particular the value of a victimological approach to the investigation of serial murder with its consideration of who is targeted for victimization, how they come to be at risk, and what surviving victims and targeted victims can offer to the interpretation of information about possible suspects. The chapter concludes with a discussion of problems faced by CIMIT and lessons learned for both investigation and research into serial murder.

SERIAL MURDER: A SEQUENCE OF UNSOLVED HOMICIDES

The key feature of so-called "serial murders" is that several similar killings remain unsolved long enough for a sequence of crimes to become obvious. That the crimes are not solved sooner testifies to both the cunning of the killer and the limitations of investigative assumptions and strategies. Who can say how many potential serial killers are caught after their first victims? A killer who preys on acquaintances, for example, is likely to be detected long before he has created a string of deaths labeled serial murder. And might not our assumptions about the nature of a serial killer's activity preclude his being recognized or defined as such? We find it difficult to believe that the same killer would stab a young boy in one jurisdiction, shoot a man in another, and strangle a woman in a third. Our understanding of the serial murderer is skewed by selective observation of the nature of serial murder and of who perpetrates such crime.[1]

Investigative Approaches to Serial Murders

In some respects, serial murders should be easier to solve than one-time stranger-on-stranger homicides. Multiple crimes yield multiple crime scenes with more evidence, more information on motives, and a greater chance of detection by witnesses. Multiple crimes also imply a higher chance of killer contacts with targeted victims who were not victimized or who survived attempted murder. But unless investigators are oriented toward the possibility of a serial crime spree, they are likely either to ignore or to be lackadaisical in pursuing leads that have no obvious relevance to the crime. Thus, apart from the need for routinely thorough initial investigations likely to detect serial killers before they repeat, law enforcement must consider new investigative emphases when faced with an apparent serial crime.

The Basic Investigation

Homicide investigators typically begin their search for information to identify suspects in two steps. First, they examine a crime scene for evidence of victim circumstances immediately prior to death, including clues as to the nature of the victim's relationship to his or her killer and killer motives (see, for example, O'Hara, 1980, and Geberth, 1983). Then they attempt to find and interview witnesses with the hope that witness testimony will yield the identity of a perpetrator along with motives for his crime. Detectives generally begin looking for suspects among victim acquaintances who might be motivated to kill. In practice, it is not unusual for investigators to direct their witness interviews toward finding known suspects without considering aspects of the victim's activities or lifestyle that might point to suspects unknown to family and friends.[2]

An investigator must go well beyond these basic steps in searching for a typical serial killer who has already defied detection by the time his sequence of murders is apparent. He may be mobile. His victims are usually strangers or he lacks established personal relationships with his victims. His crimes appear motiveless. Some known serial killers are social isolates. They have no friends to talk to or confide in. Others lead dual lives such that their friends "would never believe" they could kill. In many cases, investigators must also seek information from jurisdictions other than their own. This sometimes means dealing with people and situations for which they are unprepared, as well as having to cooperate with other police agencies.[3] Together, these issues create difficulties in generating information to identify a serial crime spree and to detect the criminals.

VICAP and Criminal Profiling

Serial killers are obviously adept at eluding immediate detection. The number of unsolved serial killings attests to the lack of information needed to identify the murderers. In the hope of discovering more of these offenders, the FBI's Violent Criminal Apprehension Program (VICAP) seeks to generate comparative data on unsolved cases by analyzing information from several jurisdictions (Howlett et al., 1986; NCAVC, 1985). By bridging the information gap across jurisdictions, VICAP attempts to optimize the use of evidence from unsolved murders, especially evidence from crime scenes. It seeks ultimately to describe the types of victims targeted for predation and to construct a profile of the likely killer (Brooks et al., 1987, 1988; Douglas and Burgess, 1986; NCAVC, 1985).

The VICAP effort should prove valuable in revealing geographically scattered serial crimes. By uncovering evidence of a serial crime spree, VICAP helps to bring information from each separate investigation to bear on all other related investigations. Detailed victimological commonalities, for example, can help focus the investigative effort devoted to each separate killing, as described below. Such victim data should also prove useful in understanding the activities of the serial predator. Beyond that, however, the criminal profile provides little useful information to the crime investigator. It holds promise for helping detectives understand motives of murderers driven by fantasy to victimize strangers (Ressler and Burgess, 1985a, b), but it is too unreliable to be promoted as an investigative tool (Levin and Fox, 1985, p. 176). Moreover, a criminal profile is unlikely to point to new sources of information and may even foreclose the pursuit of fruitful leads. As discussed below, it may also serve to confine attention to a single killer when several are preying on the same types of victims. Nevertheless, suspect information is critical to the solution of a case; victims are a key source for actual descriptions of suspect characteristics.

The VICAP effort is limited to the degree that its information is only as good as the detail provided by local investigative agencies. Should a police department give incorrect, incomplete, or worse, no information on relevant cases, VICAP loses its potential to assist. But whatever its shortcomings, VICAP is an important advance toward systematic investigation and management of murder data. It is especially significant for utilizing victim data in guiding investigative effort. And by collecting victim data, VICAP holds promise for using information generated through forensic investigations for social scientific inquiry on serial crime.

A Victimological Emphasis

Victimology examines victims' contributions to their own victimization by evaluating the risk associated with the role of the victim in the crime setting (see, for example, Karmen, 1984, p. 26; and Schafer, 1977, p. 3). One need not dwell on criminal motives to explain interpersonal crime. Instead, one can take as given an offender predisposed to crime and proceed to analyze patterns of victim behaviors accounting for their victimization.

By directing investigative attention to victims and victim-offender relationships, one can first identify a set of prospective victims targeted by a serial killer. Among the targeted victims are likely to be survivors of criminals who prey on those victims and perhaps survivors of the killer himself. Analysis of targeted victim networks yields insight into the victim's role in the crime setting and thus the risk of victimization. That insight helps to predict a killer's patterning of activities to increase opportunities for victim encounters. It permits inferences about the decisionmaking process underlying the selection of crimes and victims. Finally, information extracted from targeted victim networks will call attention to additional suspects, including copycats, who may in fact be responsible for some of the murders.

An applied victimological approach begins with the assumption that a killer is at large seeking targeted victims. Investigative strategy develops from an analysis of factors linking the killer to his victims and of activities placing those victims at risk. It should proceed with five sets of general tasks, each oriented toward assembling information on victim social characteristics and circumstances: identify a category or type of victim; delineate victim social networks; identify personal factors affecting risk; describe situational factors affecting risk; and identify routine victim activities and expected behaviors related to contact with and risk of victimization by a serial predator.

Victim categories are defined by the social roles and status characteristics by which people are categorized in everyday life. Those targeted might include, for example, gays or prostitutes, or those fitting such a detailed description as "young brunette women who part their hair down the middle." Beyond such broad characterization, a victimological analysis will seek to identify particular personal factors—generally, personal interests—underlying a lifestyle with risk. Drug dependence, for example, may drive risk-taking behavior while impairing judgment to the point at which a prospective victim is targeted. A willingness to take risks for money or sex may similarly increase the vulnerability of targeted victims. It should be noted, however, that a victim need only be perceived as a particular type with special interests for the chance of his victimization to increase. A predator's perception will be shaped by both actual characteristics and those inferred from factors such as where a victim hangs out and with whom. CIMIT presumed that a killer was preying on hustlers, some of which made contacts with tricks by hitchhiking (see Humphreys, 1975, p. 161). It was understood that unwitting hitchhikers were at risk if mistaken for hustlers.

The social networks with which one is identified will generally help define categories and interests discussed above. They may also reveal mutual acquaintances (i.e., social links) of victims and killers as by Milgram's (1967) "small world" phenomenon. They are key to understanding victim activities, including especially, deviance. While deviant street networks can sometimes reduce risk through surveillance and protection, risk is often high at the outset by virtue of their deviant activities (Cohen, 1980). Routine activities (generally associated with personal interests and identification with particular networks) enable a predator to arrange contact with targeted victims and to shape expectations for interaction.[4] Finally, the situational context within which network interaction and routine activities occur is critical to understanding ultimate risk. If a predator targets victims in a location at which contact is likely to be witnessed, the chance of detection will increase. An analysis of the ecology of possible contact settings can help to narrow the focus of investigation to promising areas for locating witnesses, including surviving victims.

THE GAY MURDERS AND CIMIT

In May 1983 officers from law enforcement agencies around central Indiana met to exchange information on what appeared to be a string of gay-related murders. Police in a rural county adjoining Indianapolis had found the body of a 22-year-old white male who had been stabbed to death near Interstate 70 and buried in a shallow grave. His wrists showed signs of having been bound, and his jeans were pulled to his ankles. The crime scene was strikingly similar to that of a victim found less than five months earlier and 20 miles west along I 70. He too had been bound, stabbed to death, and buried with his jeans pulled below his waist.

The gay community had by then already become alarmed by the unsolved murders of gays from Indianapolis whose bodies were found north of the city (see Figure 6.1). Table 6.1 displays the similarities among the original victims as presented to the police and public. The first was a 15-year-old white street hustler murdered in June 1980. His nude body was found in a ditch in a county north of Indianapolis. The youth was known to hang out in downtown Indian-

Figure 6.1
Map Showing Locations of Bodies in the Gay-Related Murders Investigated by CIMIT

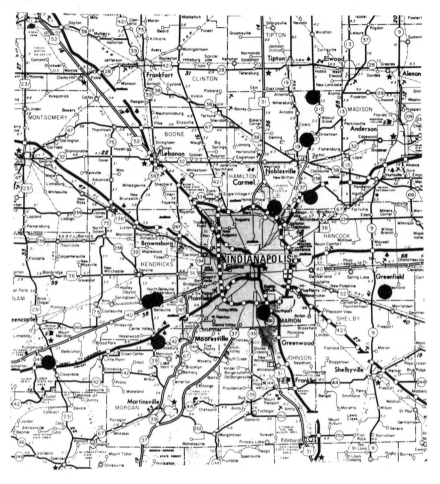

apolis areas frequented by men looking for hustlers. A second gay victim was found strangled to death in his bedroom on August 10, 1981. He was not known to be a hustler. His murder resembled other occasional homosexual killings investigated by police over the years. It did not arouse special attention. But two more murders of street hustlers in June and October 1982, along with the suspicious death of another young man in July 1982, moved an irate gay community to demand aggressive police action. The June victim, a white 22-year-old, was found by the side of a country road, clothed but missing his shoes and

Table 6.1
The Original CIMIT Victims

Victim #	Race	Age	Missing: date	from	Remains found: date	area	Cause of death	Hustler	Clothing missing
1	W	15	6/11/80	Indianapolis	6/16/80	rural	?	yes	nude
2	W	25	8/08/81	Indianapolis	8/10/81	(home)	strangled	?(gay)	nude
3	W	26	6/01/82	Indianapolis	6/02/82	rural	?	yes	yes
4	W	23	7/17/82	Indianapolis	7/21/82	rural	?	yes	yes
5	B	14	10/02/82	Indianapolis	10/03/82	rural	strangled	yes	yes
6	W	21	12/22/82	Indianapolis	12/28/82	rural	stabbed	yes	yes
7	W	22	5/07/83	Indianapolis	5/09/83	rural	stabbed	yes	yes
8	W	22	5/29/83	Indianapolis	6/05/83	rural	strangled	no	yes

one sock. Though treated as a murder, his cause of death is unknown. The July victim, a white 23-year-old, eventually proved to be another Indianapolis hustler with indeterminate cause of death. His shirtless body was found floating in a creek by a bridge from which it appeared to have been dropped. The October victim was a black 14-year-old. He had been strangled, and, like the first victim, his body was abandoned in a ditch north of Indianapolis.

Although all of the victims lived in and frequented areas within the city limits, there was no evidence that they had been killed in the Indianapolis Police Department's (IPD) patrol area. IPD had no jurisdiction over these cases. And despite the similarities pointed out by members of the gay community, the cases were being handled separately by each of three other police agencies normally responsible for homicide investigations where the bodies were found. But the need for a single, coordinated investigation could not be ignored by the time a fifth victim, the first of the hustlers murdered along I–70, was found in December 1982. Early in 1983, IPD took the lead in assigning two detectives to assist with coordinating information generated in Indianapolis. Their intent, in part, was to act as a catalyst for others' investigations.

Concern over a serial murder spree had first been raised with police in December 1982 by Dr. John Pless, the forensic pathologist who conducted the autopsy on the sixth victim. Pless also performed the autopsy on a young man found eviscerated north of Terre Haute the same week. This victim had no known ties to gays, but the wounds on both bodies were so similar that the likelihood of a common killer could not be ignored. Pless immediately informed the state police, although it was not until the central Indiana effort was underway six months later that the Terre Haute victim was added to the list of similar victims.

With the various agencies in agreement on the need for a more tightly coordinated investigation following the May 1983 meeting, yet another victim, a 22-year-old, white, middle-class male was strangled to death and dumped in a stream by a country road. He had been reported missing a week earlier on the eve of the Indianapolis 500 auto race. Although it has never been established that he was gay, police felt that they had sufficient evidence of at least a casual association with the gay community to view him as the eighth victim in the series of gay-related murders.

The Central Indiana Multiagency Investigative Team—CIMIT—was formally in place two weeks later. From the outset, the task force split its efforts between the pursuit of leads on previously identified suspects and the less-focused search for additional victim information for victimological analysis.

Suspect Profiles

CIMIT investigators sought assistance from the FBI. They provided federal agents with basic information on three of the cases with known causes of death. In turn, they were presented with two criminal profiles based on the presumption that two independent killers were responsible. In each of the cases reviewed, the police had already identified specific suspects bearing some physical resemblance to the profiles.

The first profile characterized the killer of the 14-year-old black youth last seen hustling downtown. The FBI described the murderer as a middle-class, 45-year-old, married man who does not sleep with his wife. He was said to be overweight from a comfortable life consistent with his good job. He was supposed to be sexually attracted to children, but ashamed of it.

The second profile described a murderer presumed to have killed the two I 70 stabbing victims. He was said to be a white male in his late twenties or early thirties intent on proving his manhood while he repressed his homosexuality. He was supposed to be a muscular, beer-drinking laborer who frequents redneck bars:

But he is in a homosexual panic, always afraid someone will think he's homosexual, ready to defend himself at the slightest mention that he may be one. As a result, he has an outward hatred for gays.

And he kills what he hates the most.

(*Indianapolis Star*, June 12, 1983)

Identified Suspects

Police today feel that the black victim was murdered by a local businessman. He was investigated by a grand jury, but refused to testify. He made an argument for immunity which was ultimately thrown out by the U.S. Supreme Court, yet he was not prosecuted. At the time in question, the suspect was slightly overweight for a man in his fifties. He was very affluent. He was separated from his wife. Indeed, he was typical of scores of men who cruise downtown Indianapolis looking for commercial sex.

The profile of the knife-wielding killer similarly bears only superficial resemblance to the suspect eventually arrested—an apparent serial murderer who worked part-time as a painter and liquor store clerk. He is strong, as was expected given his ability to overpower strong young men. However, his strength derived from weightlifting more than work. Most significantly, he is gay, well-integrated into one segment of the gay community which enjoys macho appearances and, sometimes, rough sex. He has neither hidden his homosexuality nor revealed unusual signs of guilt or anxiety to friends and family.

That suspect, Larry Eyler, has since been arrested, convicted, and sentenced to death for the murder of a Chicago youth. He was one of the first suspects considered in the investigation. A police officer from western Indiana recalled having investigated Eyler a year earlier when he had been accused of drugging an adolescent boy, beating him, and leaving him for dead. Suspicion grew when a former friend called the CIMIT hotline to suggest that police look at Eyler because he was known to be violent. In fact, some four years earlier the state police had investigated Eyler for stabbing a man in a sexual encounter. CIMIT placed Eyler under periodic surveillance; his friends and known acquaintances were interviewed, and he was eventually connected by circumstantial evidence to murders in Illinois and western Indiana. CIMIT issued a notice to police agencies alerting them to Eyler as a suspect in the gay murders and requesting information on possible prior contact with Eyler.

By chance, on September 30, 1983, Eyler was detained and interrogated in northern Indiana after a state trooper noticed his pickup truck parked along Interstate 65. The truck was pulling away when the trooper stopped it to investigate. Eyler was driving, accompanied by a young man. As he questioned them, the trooper was not aware of who Eyler was. He only knew that the two men claimed to have stopped to relieve themselves down an embankment. When the trooper radioed for registration and warrant information, a dispatcher recognized Eyler's name and alerted the trooper. The officer handcuffed Eyler and transported him to the nearby state police post for questioning. Eyler gave permission for the police to search his truck and personal effects. He was questioned and released some five hours later without charges.

Evidence from Eyler's truck supported probable cause for police to obtain subpoenas for telephone and credit records showing a pattern of travel between Terre Haute, Indianapolis, northern Indiana, the Chicago area, and southern Wisconsin—areas in which young men had been stabbed to death and buried in shallow graves (see Figure 6.2). An analysis of his boots later revealed that they had been soaked with human blood matching that of a victim found stabbed to death near Waukegan, Illinois. Armed with this evidence, police in Lake County, Illinois, arrested Eyler for the murder of the Waukegan man. But he was released six months later after a judge ruled that his detention in Indiana without charges was improper (see Keppel, 1989). Consequently, under the exclusionary rule, all evidence gathered on the basis of his statements and the search of his truck was inadmissible for later trials.

Figure 6.2
Map Locating Body Remains of Suspected Serial Murder Victims and Travel Routes Frequented by Convicted Killer Larry Eyler

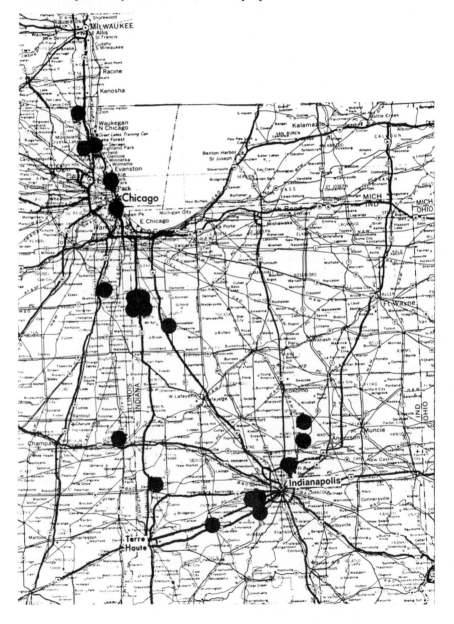

In August 1984, Eyler was seen hauling suspicious trash bags from his Chicago apartment. A curious janitor moved them to make room for other garbage. He noticed something dripping from one bag. Looking inside, he found severed body parts—the remains of a young street hustler murdered by Eyler. Eyler was arrested, tried and found guilty of the murder, and sentenced to death.

Ironically, although it was the Indiana task force that first brought Eyler to the attention of Illinois authorities, he has never been formally charged for any of the Indiana killings. Neither has he been charged in any of at least 11 other murders he is strongly suspected of committing (see Table 6.2). None of the central Indiana killings ever yielded information sufficient to arrest Eyler. In fact, of the original eight murders, Eyler is a strong suspect in only two and a plausible suspect in three others.

Although no one apart from the businessman has ever been formally processed as a suspect for any of the eight killings, it is unlikely that Eyler killed the remainder. Police believe there were other killers involved. What is it about this set of victims that makes them targets for murder? And what can an understanding of the targeted group contribute to investigations?

Victimology of the Gay Murders

A typical serial killer may be characterized as a sociopath desirous of a particular type or social category of victim (see, for example, descriptions in Egger, 1984; Holmes & DeBurger, 1985, 1988; and Levin and Fox, 1985, p. 71). He preys on those whose activities bring them to his attention. The killer's desire is often normal, socially expected, or even approved (Leyton, 1986). His victims enact routines consistent with their social definitions, routines that one can learn and observe—routines that facilitate the hunt for victims of a given type. Some attract potential killers by their actions. Prostitutes, for example, overtly solicit attention from and avail themselves to strangers. They are doubly vulnerable insofar as society provides derogatory and demeaning labels to identify them as deserving of "punishment" for their deviance.

Victims and criminals act together within what von Hentig (1979) called, a "duet frame of crime"—a predator-prey interaction: "In a sense the victim shapes and moulds the criminal . . . They work upon each other profoundly and continually, even before the moment of disaster. To know one we must be acquainted with the complementary partner" (pp. 384–85). Victimization is explained through opportunities for violence. In contrast to a traditional criminological approach focusing on the perpetrator, victimology takes as given the perpetrator's propensity to kill and then focuses on the lifestyle of the victim and the circumstances under which the crime unfolds. It looks at cases of young men who were literally in the wrong place at the wrong time.[5]

Violence is an ever-present risk to those who adopt extra-legal careers and lifestyles. Involvement in gambling, drugs, stolen property, and prostitution, to name a few, usually involve financial transactions enforced by the threat of

Table 6.2
Suspected Eyler Victims

Victim	Race	Age	Missing: date	from	Remains found: date	county	Cause of death	Eyler suspect
A	W	15	6/11/80	Indianapolis	6/16/80	rural	?	weak
B	W	26	6/01/82	Indianapolis	6/02/82	Marion, IN	?	weak
C	W	23	7/17/82	Indianapolis	7/21/82	Hamilton, IN	?	weak
D	W	19	10/23/82	Chicago	12/25/82	Kankakee, IL	stabbed	weak
E	W	26	12/25/82	Chicago	12/25/82	Lake, IN	?	weak
F	W	23	12/19/82	Terre Haute	12/28/82	Vermillion, IN	stabbed	strong
G	W	21	12/22/82	Indianapolis	12/28/82	Putnam, IN	stabbed	strong
H	W	26	10/31/82		3/04/83	Vermillion, IL	stabbed	weak
I	W	28	4/07/83	Chicago	4/08/83	Lake, IL	stabbed	strong
J	W	15	2/01/83	Chicago	4/13/83	Lake, IL	stabbed	strong
K	W	22	5/07/83	Indianapolis	5/09/83	Hendricks, IN	stabbed	strong
L	B	18		Chicago	5/09/83	Cook, IL	stabbed	weak
M	W	28	8/03/83	Chicago	8/31/83	Lake, IL	stabbed	strong
N					10/15/83	Jasper, IN	?	weak
O	W	19	3/03/83	Chicago	10/18/83	Newton, IN	stabbed	strong
P	W	23	3/07/83	Chicago	10/18/83	Newton, IN	stabbed	strong
Q	W				10/18/83	Newton, IN	stabbed	strong
R	B				10/19/83	Newton, IN	stabbed	strong
S	W	18	3/21/83	Indianapolis	12/07/83	Hendricks, IN	stabbed	strong
T	W				12/07/83	Hendricks, IN	stabbed	strong
U	W	20	12/25/82	Chicago	5/07/84	Lake, IL	stabbed	strong
V	W	16	8/20/84	Chicago	8/21/84	Cook, IL	stabbed	convctd

violence to deter normative transgressions (e.g., Humphreys, 1975, p. 47). Each is a category of crime with at least two offenders motivated by complementary interests including a mutual interest in avoiding detection. Thus, under society's legal sanctions, all such crimes entail risk to all parties involved.

Within the "duet frame," alternative victim roles may carry differing degrees of risk affected in part by alternative criminal types. This has been noted in previous studies of male prostitutes (see Reiss, 1961; Ross, 1959). Each of the various types of hustlers runs some risk of violence as an occupational hazard.

The risk may be endemic to prostitution and not unique to male hustlers. But the risk of violence may vary in both nature and likelihood according to the type of role assumed. Street hustlers run the greatest risk of violent victimization. Other types of hustlers have lower degrees of risk. Bar hustlers and call boys, for example, may have less to fear in the way of violence from their tricks because both they and their tricks may be known to others. In the event of serious violence a perpetrator would likely be detected.

The Indianapolis victims known to be street hustlers exposed themselves to extraordinary risk by accepting rides (especially by hitchhiking) from their tricks. The visibility of their interaction to witnesses was minimal, the driver was advantaged by luring victims to his domain, and the driver could quickly travel some distance beyond their contact point to the ultimate crime scene without untoward protest from his victim. Individually, these cases left little concrete information for police action. Together, they provided a pattern of victim-offender contacts in which some witnesses and survivors played a part.

Victimological Analysis in the CIMIT Investigation

CIMIT began its investigation by organizing information on each victim for comparison with other victims and for matching with suspects. An associate's chart constructed for each victim formed the core of an analysis of victim social networks.[6] Each chart was derived from information provided by the victim's family, friends, and acquaintances. Associates who had not been interviewed by the original detectives were sought to be certain that information on the victim and his activities was available from each person on his chart. An effort was then made to discover those deviant street networks in which he participated to reveal possible links with other victims and with suspects. This entailed additional interviews with informants from those networks who may or may not have been previously identified as an associate of either a victim or a suspect. Additional information on the networks was obtained from direct observation of areas frequented by the victims. A tour of the streets worked by hustlers gave insight into the ecology of the hunting ground, the opportunities for interaction between killer and prey, and the timing of such encounters. Interviews with hustlers provided detail on the susceptibility of certain victims to potential predators. The task force thus learned details of victim activities likely to put them at risk of victimization, for example, taunting gays or tricks, indiscriminate drinking or drug usage (including willingness to take different kinds of substances), hitchhiking to procure tricks, and willingness to play at bondage.

Once victim-types were identified, members of their street networks were able to point to suspects and suspect associates, including some acquainted with Eyler's deviant side. None of the street hustlers interviewed could link themselves directly to Eyler, but they did link to Eyler friends, including at least one who claimed his life had been threatened by Eyler over jealousy in a gay love triangle.

That same associate was able to provide useful insight into gays' interactions with hustlers, with "rough sex," "outdoor sex," and with patterns of drinking and drug usage. His cooperation helped to make sense of some crime scene evidence and of some of Eyler's driving locales.

Eyler and His Victims

A critical task under a victimological approach is to locate "survivors" among the pool of prospective victims; that is, to find anyone who may have had contact with a suspect and who may have been victimized in a manner similar to those killed, yet who survived. Several street hustlers reported suspects who had raped and/or severely beaten them, though not Eyler. To date, no one can say for certain that those suspects were responsible for any of the killings not attributed to Eyler. As it happened, several survivors of Eyler's violence did come forward, though not from the extended networks associated with Indianapolis victims.

Eyler's surviving victims gave critical information on his interaction with victims prior to killing them. Police believe his modus operandi involved looking for hustler-hitchhikers who might be amenable to his advances for sexual favors. He offered a targeted victim a $100 bill if he would consent to letting Eyler tie him up for sexual gratification. Eyler also offered beer either laced with drugs or in addition to drugs. The combination of beer and drugs no doubt disabled a victim to the point at which he would not resist and could easily be overpowered. The victim was partially disrobed, bound, and perhaps sexually violated before Eyler allegedly stabbed him to death. It is the reports of survivors in conjunction with what is known of those he killed that led CIMIT investigators to conclude that most of the original central Indiana victims were not killed by Eyler.

SUCCESS AND FAILURE IN THE CIMIT EFFORT

CIMIT proved to be an effective, grassroots effort to mobilize a multi-agency investigation. It succeeded in identifying an apparent serial killer and in developing information that ultimately contributed to his indictment for murder. But the murder for which Eyler was convicted involved a relatively straightforward investigation independent of the task force. CIMIT's efforts were nullified when police failed to charge him with any crime on September 30, 1983. One can only wonder how many lives might have been spared with a more expeditious investigation. But then one must also wonder whether a more expeditious investigation was possible in the face of problems confronting CIMIT.

Organizational Problems

The Multi-agency Investigative Team (MAIT) manual (Brooks et al., 1988) points to the significance of multi-agency task force problems as impediments to successful serial murder investigations. CIMIT organizers were attentive to most of the critical issues in structuring the task force. Two sets of organizational problems, however, may have had negative effects on the quality of the CIMIT effort. The first concerns the impact of initial, non-task force investigations on subsequent multi-agency efforts. The second concerns personnel qualifications and management.

CIMIT faced inevitable difficulties in beginning a multi-agency investigation on the heels of previously initiated single-agency investigations. Local detectives had already spent time on their cases. When CIMIT became involved, it examined the files expecting to find thorough basic work. Instead, it found some cases with such serious problems as contaminated crime scenes and post mortem examinations performed by unqualified personnel. Some files lacked formal statements from important witnesses, and in some cases such witnesses were never interviewed. Crime scene and evidence processing could not be redone. Interviews could be redone, but not without accepting the unreliability of statements given months after the crime. This is not to fault the original detectives. It was obvious that some of the rural detectives first assigned to the cases needed assistance. They generally had little homicide experience. They definitely had little experience with the Indianapolis gay community and hustling scene. And they were subject to competing investigative priorities by their employing agencies.

The second set of organizational problems includes those stemming from task force reviews of initial investigations, those dealing with selection and assignment of personnel, and those reflecting interagency competition and jealousy. Together, these constituted problems of management imposed on CIMIT for which the idealism of team commitment provided an inadequate solution (cf. Brooks et al., 1988, p. 9).

CIMIT promised to save the several participating agencies duplications of effort while relieving their detectives of the burden of a long-distance investigation in Indianapolis. But by its involvement, CIMIT challenged the competence of the original detectives. As one might expect, although CIMIT was defined as a group to assist original detectives, some of those detectives clearly resented CIMIT's "taking over" their work, especially when CIMIT found shortcomings in their efforts. On the other hand, some of the original detectives were assigned full-time to the task force. They had an opportunity to dedicate themselves to solving their cases in cooperation with others. But this posed additional management problems. First, it made it awkward for the task force commander to assign a task to detectives who should have previously done it without prodding. It was especially awkward when the assignments were perceived as redoing work already completed in the original investigation. To save face, the solution was to downplay the importance of the task as if one would not have expected it to have been completed before. But no task should be approached with the attitude that it is unimportant.

Brooks et al. (1988) argue that "the MAIT approach provides broader access to qualified personnel" (p. 9). This may be true in theory, but in practice it is hard to conceive of a police department giving up its best detectives to a long-term investigation of murders that may not have occurred within its jurisdiction. CIMIT included some detectives assigned by their agencies for reasons other than having worked on one of the cases. It was obvious that participating police departments did not give up their best detectives. They detailed some for whom they had little use otherwise. Of course, individual agencies are reluctant to assign highly qualified homicide investigators to a task force when to do so would compromise work on their usual murder caseloads. CIMIT found itself with many inexperienced homicide investigators.

The CIMIT commander was called on to lead these officers as a team, free of distraction from employing agencies. They were to be singularly committed to solving the murders. But could he reasonably expect detectives from other agencies to take orders or directives from him? For the most part, he could. In fact, he found few complaints with his work assignments, although he also found that when some detectives left the office they could not be relied on to vigorously pursue their assignments. It is not clear whether that was due to traditional work habits or resentment over a cross-agency command structure.

Finally, interagency cooperation, in general, is difficult to maintain when activities are outside usual organizational reward and authority structures. Jealousies are especially likely when task force detectives sense that a police agency other than their own is getting undue publicity or credit for their work. Jealousy among departments is more than an emotional response rooted in loyalty to one's employer. Departments and individual detectives invest a great deal of time and effort in their investigations. Naturally, they want due credit. Individuals on multi-agency task forces have special concerns for credit given that they have sometimes forsaken opportunities for rewards and advancement in their employing agency to cooperate with other agencies. These detectives need to be recognized as members of a team whose collective efforts merit rewards to individuals from their employing agencies.

When detectives cannot expect such recognition, they are likely to withhold information, to make individual contact with the press, and to use the press as a vehicle for self-aggrandizement, sometimes at the expense of the investigation. CIMIT experienced each of these outcomes.

Did these problems jeopardize the investigation? Probably not. With attention on Eyler, the work was focused and well coordinated. But the problems did hinder the investigation of non-Eyler cases from moving much beyond the original work.

Relations with the Gay Community

CIMIT encountered special problems in obtaining information on both suspects and victims associated with the gay community. Important witnesses concealed that part of their life such that family and friends were of less value in providing relevant information. Those who patronized the prostitute victims, for example, had much to lose in coming forward. Indeed, some acknowledged that the death of street hustlers was not an event worth sacrificing one's reputation over.

Police have long hassled gays and male prostitutes with both arrests and extra-legal harassment. The legacy of those practices was not lost on gays who found themselves terrorized by the thought of a murdering predator while dependent on traditional predators to protect them. Many did not trust the police and did not believe the police could be serious in wanting to investigate extant murders.

With many people holding this belief, CIMIT had problems in soliciting information from the gay community. There is no doubt that gays could contribute to the investigation. Some gay leaders, who expressed concern over the murders months before police acknowledged a problem, took the lead in setting up a hotline of their own and offered to serve as intermediaries for tips. Some even contacted victims' families in a search for evidence. They were clearly dissatisfied with the efforts of the original case detectives. Establishing CIMIT met some of the gays' concerns. But the perceived inertia of earlier police efforts perpetuated distrust and threatened to foreclose information sources.

Consequently, the police made a special effort to solicit information. CIMIT established a hotline to accept anonymous calls and printed cards to be distributed in the gay community and through the network of targeted victims on the streets. Arrangements were made for anyone with information who was reluctant to meet the police to make preliminary police contacts through non-police task force members.

With publicity over the formation of CIMIT, police received many tips on suspects, including Eyler. Information on Eyler was especially notable because of his having been a suspect in a near murder of a young teenager the year before (see above). But interviews with Eyler associates were largely unproductive, in part because the obvious associates resented police investigation of a gay and they presumably did not share that side of Eyler's lifestyle which brought him to the victims of his crimes.[7]

CIMIT found itself caught in the politics of the gay community and the competition for leadership. While the police were being attacked for insensitivity and inaction by one faction, they were meeting regularly with informants in gay bars and among street hustlers committed to offering every assistance they could within the constraints of anonymity demanded by many members of the community.

Misinformation abounded because of ideological support for the notion that a hater of gays or a self-hater with gay tendencies was on the loose. This was reinforced not only by the FBI profile, but also by a leader of the gay community who proposed a psychological profile months before the police took serious notice of the pattern of killings. He also suggested that the killer must be a repressed gay. Ultimately, it was disquieting for gays to learn that the principal suspect, Eyler, was by all accounts comfortable with his homosexuality.[8]

LESSONS LEARNED

Eyler was identified by information garnered through tips and earlier criminal investigations. Once named as a suspect, a case against him was developed through rigorous traditional investigative techniques. Inferences about which victims he killed and which ones may have been killed by others were derived, in part, by tracking Eyler's activities, and in part from a victimological analysis. One cannot say for certain that he did not kill others, but his capture served to effectively close the investigation of the original CIMIT cases. It was felt that investigators had exhausted all leads for solving the remaining cases. And by the time Eyler was apprehended, no new killings had come to light.

CIMIT concluded its work with murders still unsolved. Notwithstanding the effort that led to Eyler's detection, the lack of closure in the original CIMIT cases leaves questions as to how investigative effort might have been redirected for greater success. Task force commander Jerry Campbell has concluded that an important lesson for future investigations is to pay more attention to victims at the outset; that is, to systematically exhaust victimological data to increase the odds of identifying a suspect, or at least to make sense of his activities, while searching for survivors.

Victimological data are too important to be ignored early in an investigation, regardless of suspect information. Serial murder involves more than patterned deaths. It is the culmination of a pattern of confrontation and assault. Detectives need to anticipate a killer's moves by observing pick-up points and by frequenting those areas where surviving victims are most likely to be found. It is important to keep in mind, too, that a positive police presence in risk-sites can have a preventive effect serving to protect targeted victims while encouraging their participation in surveillance and communication with the task force. One cannot expect deviants to seek out police with relevant information. Police must cultivate informants among deviant street networks.

This is not to suggest that suspect leads should have lower priority. On the contrary, suspects must be aggressively pursued, but with a caveat. Intriguing descriptions of crime scene similarities and psychological profiles threaten to foreclose investigation of suspects who deviate from expectations. The reification of speculative data stands to divert attention from such possible cases as those with series of similar victims with multiple killers as well as from those involving a single killer using varied modi operandi. There can be no doubt that police run a risk of ignoring preventable crimes when they ignore suspects who do not meet our understanding of a serial killer type.

Police and prosecutors sometimes forget that murders are worth investigating, even when there is little hope for winning a conviction in court. Not only are victims' families entitled to the peace of mind in knowing what happened, but the community must be protected from violent predators who are likely to continue killing as long as they are not pursued. This should be no less true when the community of targeted victims is unpopular or unsavory to the larger community.

Would a decision to arrest Eyler on a weak case have protected others and saved lives? Who can say for certain? But in retrospect, it is obvious that had Eyler been arrested outright for an early murder, police would have taken him out of circulation while gaining lawful access to the very evidence ultimately lost following his detention in northern Indiana.

Finally, criminologists depend on law enforcement data to study serial murder. New ideas are only as good as those data. To ensure valid and reliable data for their studies, researchers need to address the practical problems faced by investigators seeking information to solve murders (cf. Egger, 1984). They must certainly evaluate more carefully the scope of any explanations grounded in case studies. And in general, just as a detective must resist the appeal of unreliable speculation, researchers must be attentive to the common pitfalls of social inquiry as they proceed to chart new territory using data accumulated through selective observation.

NOTES

The author gratefully acknowledges the helpful exchanges of ideas and information with Sgt. Joseph Hein of the Cook County Sheriff's Police, Detective Daniel Colin of the Lake County Sheriff's Department, and Dr. John Pless, forensic pathologist at the Indiana University Medical Center. Linda Haas and Wendy Ford offered valuable suggestions for improving this manuscript. Special thanks are due Homicide Lieutenant Jerry Campbell of the Indianapolis Police Department who contributed essential insight and information on the CIMIT investigation.

1. One celebrated serial killer, Edward Kemper III, used multiple methods in killing both kin and strangers. He was incarcerated in a mental institution for killing his grandparents when he was 17 years old. But his potential as a serial offender was not recognized either by his psychiatrists or by his police friends when, upon his release, he embarked on his murderous spree. See Leyton (1986) for a synthesis of accounts on Kemper.

2. Investigations textbooks simply do not emphasize the utility of such victimological evidence. For example, Geberth's (1983) discussion of victims is incidental to describing information needed for profiling rather than to directing active investigative work. Still, experienced detectives intuit the significance of such factors, particularly when they are familiar with deviant lifestyles and street activities.

3. CIMIT was a grassroots effort to organize multiple agencies and supporting consultants in a unified investigation. Its organizational problems and solutions are not unique. Today, similar efforts may be guided by the MAIT manual (Brooks et al., 1988) developed to assist police agencies facing the need for a multi-agency task force to investigate serial crime.

4. It may be, too, that deviations from expected routine activities also place targeted victims at greater risk. This may be true, for example, when a hustler works an unprotected gay cruising circuit or a gay bar.

5. The case of serial killer Dean Corll has victimological parallels with the set of murders described here, despite the CIMIT presumption of multiple predators (see Nettler, 1982, p. 142).

6. An associates chart is a sociogram centered on the victim with lines radiating to all known associates even vaguely relevant to the case. The associates are themselves linked by lines depicting their interrelationships. Known suspects should be included with whatever links can be drawn to associate them with the victim. The chart may also include organizations, locations, and vehicles. CIMIT maintained a computer database to manage

its information, including especially, details on people and places connected to victim social networks.

7. When Eyler was first arrested for murder, some of his friends concluded that police were persecuting him for his homosexuality. They circulated an "Open Letter to the Gay Community" soliciting funds for his defense, arguing that "the police are not seeking to solve these horrendous crimes but to indict the gay 'lifestyle.' " Some of Eyler's friends are suspected of having knowledge of alleged murders, given early morning phone calls to their residences within hours of some killings.

8. Incredibly, an unidentified source associated with the Indiana investigation told reporters, "the information surfaced early on this guy. It was through the psychological profile that we were able to look at him for [the two victims]. All the facts on him fit the characteristics of the profile to a 'T.' " Unfortunately, in the Indianapolis cases, the profile may have led some detectives to avoid seeking evidence and information from sources most useful to the investigation, namely other gays and gay haunts.

REFERENCES

Brooks, P. R., Devine, M. J., Green, T. J., Hart, B. L., and Moore, M. D. (1987). "Serial murder: A criminal justice response." *The Police Chief, 54*, 37–45.

———. (1988) *Multi-agency investigative team manual*. Washington, DC: U.S. Department of Justice.

Cohen, B. (1980). *Deviant street networks*. Lexington, MA: Lexington Books.

Douglas, J. E. and Burgess, A. E. (1986). "Criminal profiling: A viable investigative tool against violent crime." *FBI Law Enforcement Bulletin, 55*, 9–13.

Egger, S. A. (1984). "A working definition of serial murder and the reduction of linkage blindness." *Journal of Police Science and Administration, 12*, 348–57.

Geberth, V. J. (1983). *Practical homicide investigation*. New York: Elsevier.

Holmes, R. M. and DeBurger, J. E. (1985). "Profiles in terror: The serial murderer." *Federal Probation, 49*, 29–34.

———. (1988). *Serial murder (Studies in crime, law and justice*, vol. 2). Newbury Park, CA: Sage.

Howlett, J. B., Haufland, K. A., and Ressler, R. K. (1986). "The Violent Criminal Apprehension Program—VICAP: A progress report." *FBI Law Enforcement Bulletin, 55*, 14–22.

Humphreys, L. (1975). *Tearoom trade*. New York: Aldine.

Indianapolis Star, June 12, 1983.

Karmen, A. (1984). *Crime victims: An introduction to victimology*. Monterey, CA: Brooks/Cole.

Keppler, R. D. (1989). *Serial murder: Future implications for police investigations*. Cincinnati: Anderson Publishing.

Levin, J. and Fox, J. A. (1985). *Mass murder*. New York: Plenum.

Leyton, E. (1986). *Compulsive killers*. New York: New York University Press.

Milgram, S. (1967). "The small world problem." *Psychology Today, 1*, 61–67.

National Center for the Analysis of Violent Crime. (1985). *VICAP crime report*. Quantico, VA: Federal Bureau of Investigation.

Nettler, G. (1982). *Killing one another*. Cincinnati: Anderson.

O'Hara, C. E. (1980). *Fundamentals of criminal investigation* (5th edn). Springfield, IL: Charles C. Thomas.

Reiss, A. J. (1961) "The social integration of queers and peers." *Social Problems, 9*, 102–20.

Ressler, R. K. and Burgess, A. W. (1985a) "The split reality of murder." *FBI Law Enforcement Bulletin, 54*, 7–11.

———. (1985b). "Crime scene and profile characteristics of organized and disorganized murders." *FBI Law Enforcement Bulletin, 54*, 18–25.

Ross, H. L. (1959). "The 'hustler' in Chicago." *Journal of Student Research, 1*, 13–19.

Schafer, S. (1977). *Victimology: The victim and his criminal*. Reston, VA: Reston.

von Hentig, H. (1979). *The criminal and his victim*. New York: Schocken.

7

Henry Lee Lucas: Case Study of a Prolific Serial Killer

STEVEN A. EGGER

METHODOLOGICAL CONCERNS

This chapter presents a case study of a serial murderer. It is not the intent or purpose of the author to suggest that Henry Lee Lucas is representative of other serial murderers. Seeking knowledge of serial murder (a phenomenon about which social science knows very little) through a case study approach requires an exploratory effort concerned primarily with description verified through a variety of data sources. Katz argues that " statistical evidence of representativeness depends on restricting a depiction of qualitative richness in the experience of the people studied" (Emerson, 1983, p. 139). Such a restriction is disavowed.

No attempt has been made to control the research setting during the period of data collection on Lucas. Flexibility and fluctuation was considered necessary and frequently a requirement in order to conduct interviews or collect relevant data. The analytical field methods utilized made valuable substantive data out of Lucas's responses with verification, anticipated methodological criticisms of reactivity to the contrary.

In order to exploit the development of qualifications in substantive analysis categories or dimensions, coding specifications were not developed until months had passed and a number of interviews conducted. Specification at the onset would have been inconsistent with the modified grounded theoretical approach to this research effort.

While replicability of this research with other serial murderers is of concern to the author, the eclectic and creative nature of future research requires that the process and products are shaped from the data rather than from pre-specified theoretical frameworks. To meet this requirement, the author has tried to remain flexible throughout this effort. The dimensions utilized in presenting this case study should, however, facilitate the requisite comparisons of subjects paramount to better defining the phenomenon of serial murder and its eventual etiological explications.

Research Methodology

The research methodology utilized involved respondent and informant interviewing concurrent with the collection and analysis of a variety of formal and informal records and documents. A modified grounded theoretical framework was followed in interviews with the respondent, Lucas, and in the analysis of notes and electronic recordings. The respondent was the initial focus of the investigation from which questions were developed for informants and the direction of records and document analysis was determined. At later stages of the research, information tabulated and analyzed from multiple sources provided some structure to subsequent interviews with the respondent. Following each interview with the respondent, informant interviews were conducted and additional documents and data were collected in order to verify and in some cases bring into question the respondent's retrospection regarding the accuracy and efficacy of past events and acts as well as to broaden the researcher's understanding of the respondent's past and provide further direction to the research.

Audio-recordings were made of each interview with Lucas and in some instances video tapes were made. These recordings were supplemented with jotted notes on major points to capture the researcher's observations and perceptions of non-verbal cues and physical surroundings. All interviews, except for recent contacts with Lucas, were generally unstructured in character to enhance validity. Various behavioral dimensions, events and specific acts, once referred to by Lucas, were systematically referred to in later sessions to determine their reliability (see Klockars, 1974, p. 223).

Corroboration of specific violent acts that Lucas admitted committing relied primarily on official police crime reports which were documented in synopsis form and provided to the researcher by the Texas Rangers. First-hand corroborative interviews with law enforcement agencies in whose jurisdiction Lucas had committed these acts were limited to the southwest due to limited resources. Some interviews, however, were conducted of investigators from other geographic areas during their visit to Georgetown, Texas, to interview Lucas. The greatest problem confronted by the researcher in interaction with the law enforcement, academic, and media communities was the credibility of Lucas. His believability certainly defied reasonable expectations.

In order to counter and overcome the unbelievability of Lucas, a great deal of time was spent in documentation, first-hand observation, and analysis of the operation and administration of the Lucas Task Force at the Williamson County Jail in Georgetown, Texas. This effort included observing the instructions given to various law enforcement investigators by the task force prior to their interviews with Lucas as well as the investigators' interviews with Lucas.

The majority of documents that corroborate Lucas's testimony came directly and indirectly from official police records, psychological and psychiatric evaluations, or are the result of police investigations regarding his background. Hundreds of newspaper articles were also collected as secondary source material. These newspaper accounts were always treated as suspect and frequently found to be inaccurate in their details.

Ethnographers, life historians, and those conducting case histories on single criminal subjects are constantly warned by prison officials and other criminal justice professionals to beware of the "snow job" or "con job." Letkeman addresses this problem by stating, "I began on the premise of trust and I believe this expectation was met" (1973, p. 173). In the case of Lucas, validity checks through informant interviews, analysis of records and documents, and subsequent interviews covering the same material separated by lengthy periods of time were conducted to protect researcher gullibility. Further, a press for the truth gradually increased the dedication and sincerity of the researcher in the eyes of Lucas.

On the advice of individuals who had interviewed him earlier, the researcher was completely open with Lucas regarding the nature, extent, and objectives of the research effort. The fact that the results of the research would be documented and appear as part of a doctoral dissertation (Egger, 1985) was openly discussed and explained to Lucas. While this approach proved beneficial, Lucas's awareness of the researcher's criminal investigative experience also seemed to be instrumental in the rapport established.

The interviews with Lucas were reflexive in nature. No predetermined questions were used in the first seven hours of interviewing, although a directional pattern was not free from the researcher's mind during these first few months. Such patterns brought some indirect structure to each subsequent interview but specifically formulated questions were avoided. Questions were for the most part open-ended, with the researcher as an active listener, yet responsive and not passive. Hammersley and Atkinson (1983) advise that "a useful tactic is to make the question 'lead' in a direction opposite to that in which one expects the answer to be and thus avoid the danger of simply and misleadingly confirming one's expectations" (pp. 115–16). Such a technique was used frequently with Lucas.

Klockars (1974) intentionally put off interviewing his respondent about criminal conduct until rapport was established and he better understood how to interview the subject. Klockars attributes this technique to his success in obtaining trust and confidence. However, as Lucas seemed interested in the researcher's response to his heinous crimes, his criminal conduct was one of the major topics of the first interview.

Prior to the first interview with Lucas a list of potential informants to interview and data requirements was prepared. Once the interviews began, the list was modified and frequently expanded. Throughout the interview period with Lucas (June 5, 1984 to March 22, 1985), informant interviews were conducted and records and documents were collected. The results of these efforts become the "second sight" in determining how Lucas got from one point in his life to the next. While records and documents on Lucas were the primary source of this "second sight," recordings and research contributed by members of the press and electronic media were provided to the researcher. Informants located beyond the Texas area were not extensively interviewed but secondary source material from such informants was collected and proved very useful.

Documentary products or records provided the researcher with numerous analytical topics for process documentation and explication and were a valuable source of information. While records and documents from a variety of sources furnished a wealth of analytic and interpretative resources, all will not be specifically cited herein due to the confidentiality of some information and the anonymity promised to some of the sources.

A grounded theory of methodology (see Glaser and Strauss, 1967) was used in content and data analysis and greatly influenced the entire methodology of this ongoing research. During this research, the data collection activities were continually shaped and reshaped form analytical interpretations and discoveries. The process and products that began to emanate from this research effort were, as indicated above, shaped intentionally from the data rather than from preconceived, logically deduced theoretical frameworks. However, at the juncture of anticipating this preliminary draft, the researcher's intentions were modified. In order to facilitate further and similar research with other serial murderers a structure was sought that would not contaminate information collected but facilitate comparative future research. The typological literature was examined and dimensional categories developed by Gibbons (1965) were selected and modified. These dimensions are:

Background Dimensions
    social class
    family background
    peer group associations
    contact with defining agencies
Definitional Dimensions
    offense behavior
    interactional setting
    self-concept
    attitudes
    recall of events

It must be emphatically stressed that such a diversion from a pure grounded theory approach is not for the purpose of producing an actual etiological theory of serial murder. Too little is known of this phenomenon and a knowledge base is tentative and certainly preliminary. The use of dimensional categories is for the purpose of providing a logical and contextual presentation of the research. No causal propositions are intended at this stage.

As the informed criminologist will note, traditional quantitative canons of verification were not followed in this research. However, developing ideas and themes were checked with further specified data collection and systematic comparisons were made. Also, concurrent research at the macro level of the serial murder phenomenon has gone beyond the confines of the Lucas case and, where appropriate, specific similarities to or differences from other serial murderers were noted for further study.

The attempt to make sense of the social life of Henry Lee Lucas has itself been a process. It is for this reason that the final or complete interpretation of the data has not been made. The researcher as actor in this process must first better understand the role he has played. Idiographic research does not necessarily produce a "bottom line" and the role of the researcher is continuing.

Polsky (1967) argues that criminology needs information about crime from successful criminals. This argument may be technically out of context to the Lucas case since Polsky was providing a rationale for the observation of unincarcerated and therefore successful criminals. However, Lucas can certainly be considered to have been successful in eluding the law over a number of years while taking the lives of scores of people across this country.

The study of Lucas involved a number of methods. Triangulation is one method frequently suggested in the validation of data. Denzin (1978) concurs with Webb et al. (1966), who argue that "in the present stage of social research single method investigations are no longer appropriate" (Denzin, 1978, p. 28). Denzin further argues that "the combination of multiple methods in a single investigation [triangulation] will better enable the sociologist to forge valid causal factors" (pp. 28–29). The strategies of multiple triangulation have been utilized in this case study research so that eventually the data presented and the data from subsequent research will contribute to the development of valid propositions for theory construction.

SUMMARY LIFE HISTORY OF HENRY LEE LUCAS

Henry Lee Lucas was born on August 23, 1936, in Christianburg, Virginia. Lucas was the last of nine children born to Vyola Dison Wall Lucas. His family lived in a small two-room shack with dirt floors in the Craig section of Montgomery County, a poverty-ridden mountainous area of western Virginia. Lucas spent the first 14 years of his life living with four people: his mother, father, who was a double amputee, mother's live-in boy friend, and brother.

When he was approximately 6 years old, his left eye was injured when his brother accidentally stabbed him while cutting tree vines. When Lucas was 7, the eye was accidentally reinjured and had to be removed. Lucas was given an artificial glass eye.

In 1943, at age 7, Lucas entered Mt. Tabor School and remained in the first grade for three years. His eye accident and an apparent lack of interest or parental motivation contributed to his lack of achievement in school.

Lucas claims to have had a "terrible childhood." He talks of being forced to steal his own food, having to eat off the dirt floor instead of the table, receiving numerous severe beatings by his mother, being forced to watch his mother during sexual intercourse with many men (Lucas claims his mother was a prostitute), making bootleg liquor, and doing most of the work of the family. Both Lucas's parents were reportedly alcoholics and he began drinking shortly after starting school.

Lucas's father died of alcohol abuse and pneumonia in 1949. Lucas left home at age 14 after his father's funeral, never to return.

Lucas's first human victim was a 17-year-old girl whom he raped and strangled while she was waiting for a school bus near Harrisburg, Virginia, in 1951. He describes this killing as "just like shootin' a dog, really." His mother's boyfriend is alleged to have taught him how to have sex with dead animals. Lucas stated, "I would usually kill animals for sex. I had sex with them and eventually it got to where I went to human beings."

This first killing, which he attributes to his wanting to find out about sex with people, was described as follows: "I said to myself, 'can't leave her, she'll go tell the police and they'll come and arrest me. Ain't nobody around—I'll just strangle her.' So I strangled her and left her there on the bank." The girl's body was never found. Her disappearance was confirmed by law enforcement authorities 33 years after Lucas stated he killed her.

From New Year's day, 1952, to the day before his thirty-ninth birthday, Lucas spent over 70 percent of his life behind bars in some type of penal institution. He first spent a brief period in juvenile detention in Richmond, Virginia, and in March 1952 was committed to a training school for boys in Beaumont, Virginia, for breaking and entering and petty larceny. He escaped from this institution at least once before his release in September 1953.

Shortly after his release from the training school, Lucas was convicted of burglary in Richmond, Virginia, and was placed on probation. At the same time his mother was convicted of failing to make her son attend school. She received a suspended sentence. In June 1954, Lucas was convicted of breaking and entering and auto theft and was sentenced to four years in the Virginia State Prison at Richmond.

Lucas escaped from prison with another inmate while working on a road gang in May 1956. They stole a car and traveled to Ohio where they stole another car and drove to his half-sister's home in Techumseh, Michigan. He was arrested in Tecumseh the following month by the FBI and convicted in federal court of violating the Dyer Act, by transporting stolen motor vehicles in interstate commerce. After his incarceration in the Federal Reformatory at Chillicothe, Ohio, for 18 months, he was transferred back to the state prison in Richmond, Virginia, to complete his original sentence.

Lucas learned of his brother's death while in Virginia. His brother had been killed in a construction work accident in Tampa, Florida. Lucas petitioned the prison warden to attend his brother's funeral but was refused due to his escape record. He was discharged from the Virginia prison in September 1959.

Lucas claims he told Virginia prison authorities prior to his release that he would kill his mother if he was sent home. It was agreed that he would be paroled to Michigan and live with his half-sister in Tecumseh. Lucas's statement to prison authorities has not been confirmed.

On January 2, 1960, Lucas killed his mother in his half-sister's home in Tecumseh. He fled in a stolen car after the killing and traveled south. Two weeks later he was arrested by the Ohio state patrol while hitchhiking in Toledo, Ohio. Lucas stated that his mother's death was the result of an argument. He was planning to get married and his mother was against the marriage. She wanted him to return with her to Virginia. Lucas states she beat him with a broom and he struck her on the neck with a knife. Lucas claims he didn't kill her, but that she died of a heart attack.

Lucas was convicted of the second-degree murder of his mother and sentenced to 20–40 years of imprisonment. Lucas was incarcerated at the State Prison of Southern Michigan just outside Jackson, Michigan. He states he was involved in a number of violent altercations with other inmates, once requiring hospitalization and surgery due to a stab wound to the groin. There is no record of disciplinary actions taken against Lucas while in prison. He states that his primary work assignment while in prison was working as a clerk in the records office. This cannot be verified since some of his prison records were destroyed in a fire at the prison. Upon being admitted to the prison psychiatric clinic for the second time in June 1961, Lucas was transferred to the Ionia State Hospital in Ionia, Michigan. He remained at this mental hospital until February 1965. Reports from this hospital reveal the psychiatric staff considered him to be "potentially dangerous." He was released from prison on parole on June 30, 1970.

When learning of his impending parole from prison, Lucas states that he warned prison officials that he would kill if released. He claims to have killed four people the day he was released. The Texas Rangers-Williamson County Task Force (hereinafter referred to as the task force) have confirmed two homicides committed by Lucas between the time he left Jackson Prison and his next arrest. In August 1970, Lucas rammed a vehicle with the vehicle he was driving and forced it off the road. He abducted the driver, a 26-year-old white female, at gunpoint. She was found dead with multiple stab wounds to the chest. In January 1971, Lucas again killed, this time in Lubbock, Texas. The victim, a 54-year-old white female, was stabbed 24 times in the back and chest area, beaten with a flower vase, and burned on her breast area.

On September 29, 1971, Lucas unsuccessfully attempted to abduct a 15-year-old girl at gunpoint in Lenawee County, Michigan. He was arrested for attempted kidnapping and subsequently pleaded guilty to the charge, receiving a sentence of four to five years in Jackson Prison. Prior to his guilty plea he was committed to the Center for Forensic Psychiatry in Ypsilanti, Michigan, to determine his competency to stand trial. Lucas was found competent to stand trial. He was paroled in August 1975 from Michigan.

In December 1975, Lucas married a woman with two children in Elkton, Maryland. His wife was formerly married to Lucas's late cousin. He states he only married her to take care of the kids. Lucas left his wife in July 1977, never to return. He stated that he "couldn't have sex with her."

In 1976 Lucas became friends with Ottis Elwood Toole, a homosexual living in Jacksonville, Florida. They had first met in Avondale, Pennsylvania, in 1975 on what Lucas describes as a "date." Lucas lived with Ottis in Jacksonville and met Rebecca Powell, Ottis's seven-year-old niece. Lucas called her Becky, and she became his companion during his travels. Until 1983 Lucas traveled across this country with Becky, her younger brother Frank, and Ottis. At times Lucas traveled by himself, but much of the time he traveled with Ottis, Becky, and Frank.

On June 11, 1983, Lucas was arrested by the Montague county Sheriff's Office for carrying a weapon while on parole and incarcerated in the county jail in Stoneburg, Texas. Four days later Lucas began confessing to the killing of scores of people across the country. (For a summary of criminal convictions for homicide subsequent to this arrest, see Table 7.1)

In addition to the four homicides committed prior to his final stay in prison in Michigan, the task force has confirmed through official communication and correspondence with law enforcement agencies, homicide victims killed by Lucas and his accomplices in 27 states between August 23, 1975 and June 10, 1983, or approximately one victim every two weeks.

Lucas's home during the operation of the task force was a private cell in the Williamson County Jail in Georgetown, Texas, about 25 miles north of Austin. He had a color television, hot coffee always available, a tape recorder, and an oil painting set. A number of partially finished oil paintings were hung on the cell wall or stood in one corner. Scores of letters from reporters, preachers, writers, and relatives of missing persons were stuffed under his mattress.

A Catholic lay sister had become Lucas's trusted friend. She taught him how to paint, prayed with him, bought him religious books, and helped him answer his mail. She baptized him in January 1984.

Lucas seemed to enjoy his celebrity status. Sought out by the major networks for interviews, writers trying to get the rights to his story, and journalists from numerous states seeking his time; he could pick and choose whom he agreed to see. From about 9:00 a.m. to 5:00 p.m., five days a week and sometimes on weekends, he sat in a small interview room on the first floor of the jail talking to law enforcement officers from all over the country. As he sat drinking coffee

Table 7.1
Homicide Convictions of Henry Lee Lucas Following His Arrest, June 11, 1983

Date	Victim	Location	Sentence
8-9-70	Linda Phillips	Kaufman Co., Texas	Life
8-3-76	Clemmie E. Curtis*	Cabel Co., W. Virginia	Life
11-1-77	Lillie Pearle Darty	Harrison Co., Texas	60 years
10-31-79	Unidentified Caucasian Female	William Co., Texas	Death**
4-26-81	Dianne Lynn Bryant	Terry Co., Texas	75 years
8-24-82	Frieda L. Powell	Denton Co., Texas	Life
9-16-82	Kate P. Rich	Montague Co., Texas	75 years
12-19-82	Glenna B. Biggers	Hale Co., Texas	Life
3-17-83	Unidentified Caucasian Female	Montgomery Co., Texas	Life
4-18-83	Lura Jean Domez	Montgomery Co., Texas	Life

* on-duty police officer.
** All appeals to state appellate courts have confirmed conviction.

and chain-smoking filterless cigarettes, he recounted his killings in vivid, and frequently excruciating, minute detail.

He has been convicted of murder ten times, receiving long sentences and the death penalty in the state of Texas. He claims to have killed at least 360 people in 36 states as well as Canada and Mexico. Henry Lee Lucas may well become the most prolific killer in the country's history. The following case study analysis provides a more specific description of background and definitional dimensions of this serial murderer.

Social Environment

Lucas has been described as always having lived at a very low economic level. The house he lived in until age 14 is described as a two-room shack which had no electricity until 1951. The house had no flooring and was furnished with only the bare necessities. Lucas mentions the fact that he frequently stole the food that his family ate.

Lucas was in the first grade for the first three years of his schooling. His first grade teacher remembers him as "a very humble little boy who was a little slow and little dirty." He finished the fourth grade at age 14. He began but never finished the fifth grade at Beaumont Training School for Boys in 1953. This was his last known exposure to formal education other than some vocational training while in prison.

Much of his time, when not "doin' all the work for the family," was spent playing with knives and terrorizing animals. He learned how to have sex with animals from his mother's live-in boyfriend, Bernie. He experimented by killing cows, sheep, goats, dogs, and cats. He states he would frequently "shoot dogs and cats when they would come around the house—just to get rid of them."

His goal in life was to travel: "I wanted to travel and have adventure." Lucas made numerous attempts to run away from home and at age 14 was successful. He would travel thousands of miles and never return. He states, "I ain't got no roots."

His focal concern in life was survival. He has stated, "I don't leave witnesses." For Lucas, no living witnesses guaranteed his survival. In order to survive, he kept moving and he kept killing. He was always on the move when not incarcerated. There was no such thing as a steady job. He felt it was a "burden to be tied down." Remaining in one place "causes me to have thoughts of escape. It becomes more of a pressure—not bein' able to get up and go." He boasts of sometimes traveling 24 hours a day, keeping himself awake with "black beauties, marijuana, and PCP." For years he lived among the rootless, the searching, the homeless, and roaming of this country, living out of his car, stealing, murdering hitchhikers and stranded travelers. All but three of these victims were strangers to Lucas.

Lucas spent a great deal of his life behind bars. While he doesn't talk kindly of his keepers in prison, his discussions of life in prison never reach the intensity and hatred with which he describes his home life. For Lucas, prison was where he got his degree in criminality. He states, "It was a learnin' to do crime." He says he spent many years in the Michigan prison as a records clerk. During this time, Lucas says he studied crimes committed by the inmates and "learned to do 'em." He further states, "I just became part of the record." He seems to be saying that these records became his reference for his future crimes. He frequently did favors for incoming inmates, who in return described the crimes they had committed. For him, "It was like bein' in the big city." Compared with the poverty-stricken mountain country of western Virginia, this was indeed the big city.

Because Lucas spent most of his life in institutions of correction since age 14, he never really learned to live by the rules of society. If the rules benefited him, he went along. If they did not, he broke them.

The last year of his travels seemed to signal his demise, for he was apparently trying to settle down. For almost a year he continued to return to Stoneburg, Texas, from his murderous trips. He would return to his "home," a small trailer on a former chicken ranch owned by a lay minister who had befriended him. With Becky, now 15 years old, they lived in the trailer as man and wife until he killed her and dissected her body in a farmer's field. It was the day after his forty-sixth birthday in 1982.

Family Background

Lucas has been described by a psychiatrist as having a poorly developed moral sense due to undesirable ancestry. Lucas's family consisted of his father and mother, a brother, three half-brothers and four half-sisters. He was reportedly closest to one of his half-sisters who lived in Tecumseh, Michigan. The first 14 years of his life were spent growing up in a two-room cabin, living with his mother, a man he remembers as his father (records indicate the man was not his real father), his older brother, and his mother's boyfriend.

Lucas describes his parents: " [T]hey lived together, but my father didn't have no legs and he stayed drunk and my mother, she drank and was a prostitute. And that's the way I growed up, until it was time to get out on my own."

Lucas remembers that his father was either drinking or trying to sell pencils, his mother was either gone or having sex with different men and that his brother was gone most of the time. His mother was the head of the family who dominated everyone. " Nothin' was good enough for her," he says. According to Lucas, she forced him to do unpleasant tasks and severely mistreated him. "I grew up like 'at and watched prostitution with my mother till I was 14 years old. And then, since then, I started to steal and do everything else I could think of doin' to get away from home."

Lucas calls his mother, "Mom." He describes her as a Cherokee Indian of muscular build weighing 150 to 160 pounds. He states his mother "didn't work, she'd rather sell her body. [She] believed just in sex. Didn't try to provide for anyone." Lucas states the worst thing he remembers about his family was being forced to watch his mother having sexual intercourse with various men. He states, "She made me stand and watch 'em."

He states his father never argued with anybody: "We had a good relationship. He didn't misuse me. He asked [rather than told] me to do things." Lucas remembers his grief at his father's death in 1949: "Oh, it hurt! I just missed him. Bein' close to somebody and then losin' 'em." He states his mother's comment was, "Good riddance!"

His brother joined the Navy when Lucas was 14. Lucas remembers him: "He had a halfway decent life. He wasn't allowed to do too much around home. He was bigger 'en me and stronger." His brother is reported to have once suffered a nervous breakdown. He was killed in a construction accident in Tampa, Florida, in 1958.

Authorities describe Lucas's mother as a woman who drank heavily and was a bootlegger. Her daughters remember her as always cleaning homes and restaurants to support them. She was 51 years old when she gave birth to Lucas. Authorities at the Beaumont Training School for Boys report that Lucas desired to return to the home of his mother when released. A pre-sentence investigation (following Lucas's conviction of killing his mother) included an interview of the deceased woman's granddaughter. The granddaughter stated to the investigating probation officer that her grandmother was "a dirty old woman who chewed snuff and a kind of person you would not want to be around.''

The man Lucas calls his father, Anderson Lucas, had worked for the railroad and lost his legs when he reportedly fell under a train. Some of the residents of Blacksburg, Virginia, allege that he fell under the train on purpose in order to collect welfare. He was described by one caseworker as being illiterate and had a bad reputation as a bootlegger.

From as early as he can remember, Lucas was apparently confused as to his own gender. ''I grew up from four years old, best I can remember, till about seven years old as a girl. I lived as a girl. I was dressed as a girl. I had long hair as a girl. I wore girls' clothes.'' His half-sister in Maryland still keeps a childhood picture of Lucas with long curls in girls' clothing (Scott Simon, National Public Radio, ''Morning Edition,'' Feb. 25, 1985).

In the first grade at age seven, Lucas had his hair cut after his school teacher complained about its length. After the haircut, according to Lucas, there was ''a complete change of reality.'' Lucas claims his mother got ''meaner.'' He states he was forced to carry heavy objects, to steal, cut wood, carry water, and take care of the hog.

Lucas remembers no good times in his childhood, because if he had fun, he ''would get beat for it.'' He states that his mother wouldn't let him do anything with his brother. He would sneak into town occasionally and his brother would take him to the movies. If his mother learned of this, he was severely beaten. He has a scar on the back of his head which he claims resulted from his mother striking him with a two-by-four piece of wood. He reports that he was unconscious for 11 hours following this beating and that his skull was fractured.

Lucas refers to his childhood as one of constant abuse or neglect. When the author stated that many other people have had bad childhoods who turned out all right, he responded,

They ain't got, I don't think, a human being alive that can say he had the childhood I had. Bein' beaten every day. Bein' misused every day. Have'en to cook my own food, have'en to steal my own food. Eat 'en on the floor instead of the table. Bein' treated like what I call the hog of the family. It's a lot harder than what people can imagine. Growing up with hatred, without any kind of friendship, without any kind of companion to be around or anything.

To him, ''The best thing was leavin' home.''

Lucas apparently became very attached to Ottis Toole's mother when he lived with the Tooles in Jacksonville, Florida. When she died of cancer he describes her death as one of his most unpleasant memories.

His accomplices in crime could be described as his substitute, self-made family. He was very close to Ottis, a pyromaniac as a child, a homosexual, and an admittedly sexually sadistic killer. Lucas states that in their sexual relationship, he ''took the place of Ottis's wife.'' The two children, Becky and Frank, were treated like "my own children," he says. Ironically, he seems to have been doing to these two children what he alleges his mother did to him. Lucas states, "I would avoid actually killing anyone in front of them, and a lot of times they would sneak around to see what I was doin' and I would catch 'em and I would scold 'em for it."

Peer Group Associations and Personal Relationships

Lucas's half-sister in describing her brother states, "He always seemed like he wanted someone to love. He never seemed to be able to keep a friend for some reason." He was described as being reticent to initiate any conversation with other boys or girls while in school. In retrospect, those who knew Lucas as a boy characterize him as either socially inept or hostile.

His eye injury appears to have had a major impact on his interaction with children his own age. Following the damage to his eye and its reinjury a few months later, the eye socket would drain constantly. His appearance due to the empty eye socket and subsequent implant of an artificial eye apparently caused children to shun him or avoid direct contact with him. This restriction of peer relationships was intensified by his mother, whom Lucas claims would not allow him to play with other children, including his own brother.

The lack of any significant peer relationships combined with his treatment at home resulted in an overwhelming hatred, which Lucas refers to frequently.

I've hated since I can first remember, uh, back when I was a little kid I've hated my family and anything. Anytime I went out, uh, to go some play [with other children] or some show, or something, I never could get anybody to go with me.

Lucas became a pariah in childhood. "I never could make friends and I just hated people. Nobody would accept me 'cause of my left eye. [I] looked like garbage! No girls would go out with me. No boys would have anything to do with me. They just wanted to stay away from me." Upon leaving home, Lucas states, "[I] didn't believe in association with anybody." Ironically, Lucas also states, "Other 'en killing, I have been nice to everybody all my life."

Until his early twenties, Lucas relates he had "no, what I would call, a true relationship." He met a young woman in Tecumseh, Michigan, while living with his half-sister. He claims she was special and was planning to marry her until his mother intervened and was killed. In addition to this young woman, Lucas had few close relationships in his life. For Lucas, the true relationships in his life have been Becky Powell, Ottis Toole, a lay minister in Stoneburg, Texas, who provided him with housing, and the lay sister who visited him, taught him how to paint, and baptised him in the Williamson County Jail.

Lucas sought out membership with groups of inmates while in prison in order to "have companionship, just someone to associate with." In describing further attempts to establish relationships, he states, "I tried married life and it didn't work. I tried to go back with my family and that didn't work. I went to Florida, met Ottis and just started travelin'.''

In describing his relationship with Ottis Toole, Lucas states, "It was a male-to-female type relation. To me he was queer. That's the way I looked at it. I did it more or less for him, as a favor. As far as a sexual relationship, there wasn't nothin there. We were together all the time and he always had sex with me.'' Lucas met Toole the first time in 1975 in Avondale, Pennsylvania. "We went out as friends. We had our arguments, as far as arguments we worked 'em out. Me and Ottis never been in a fist fight. Friendship is further than anything else.''

He stated that Becky "more fit into my kind of life. She accepted everything I done. I could tell her things. She understood. This took off the pressure that was there. Before, I had the urge to destroy anything within my reach. Becky took some of the pressure away.'' In describing his relationship with her, he says, "Yeah, uh it's, uh weird. My love for her was like a daughter—you know, a father to daughter. I never thought of her as sexual.'' He stated that he only had sexual intercourse with her three times in order to satisfy her. "I loved her, but I don't think she felt love,'' he said.

Psychiatrists who have talked to Lucas characterize him as poorly socialized with an exaggerated need to feel powerful and important, who views others as objects to be manipulated. They describe his mindset as putting trust in no one except himself. Lucas's relationships are described by psychiatrists as solely for self-aggrandizement and exploitation, in which he will ultimately be in control.

Contact with Defining Agencies

Lucas's first documented contact with law enforcement officers was at age 14 or 15. His first contact with correctional personnel was in 1952 when incarcerated at Beaumont, Virginia. During this period he was assigned to a correctional caseworker.[1] His first documented contact with correctional psychologists occurred when he was in prison in Michigan. His first known psychiatric diagnosis occurred in July 1961 involving his transfer to Ionia State Hospital.

While Lucas appears to enjoy playing detective in "solving" his crimes, which he refers to as "my cases," he appears to have little regard for law enforcement in general. He states, "The police didn't know who done it. They never would have knowed who done it. They'd never know who done it unless I'd told 'em.'' He frequently reiterates, "Unless I tell 'em, they'd never clear these cases.'' He characterizes many of the hundreds of law enforcement officers who have interviewed him by stating, "I've seen better kids play cops than that!''

The procedures utilized by the task force in coordinating the investigations and interviews of officers from law enforcement agencies all over the country certainly tend to increase the reliability of Lucas's confessions. All officers who traveled to Georgetown to interview Lucas on homicides were thoroughly briefed by the task force on ways to handle Lucas and specific procedures to follow.

Lucas is shown a live picture of the victim or a number of pictures including the victims. He is told the state, jurisdiction, and the date of the incident. If Lucas remembers the victim, he describes the crime in great detail. He has a phenomenal memory for details.

Lucas describes his daily activities:

I have to give 'em every detail . . . how it happened, where it happened at, the description of the person, what was used, uh every type of, uh where the body was left, parts of bodies missing. I have to tell them what parts are missing, if they've been shot, I have to tell them that. If they were stabbed, cut, whatever. They don't give me no details. . . .

I've turned a lot of law enforcement, as far as people know it today, upside down. It took years of practice, years of understanding criminal law. In prison I knew what crime was. I knew how it was committed, where it was committed, what was left at the scenes, and where it was left. I could tell you practically every case that come in—between 5,000 cases that lived in the state penitentiary in Michigan. I read each record that come in there. And I knew what was goin' on.

From January 1, 1952, when he was incarcerated in juvenile detention in Richmond, Virginia, to June 11, 1983, when he was arrested in Stoneburg, Texas, Henry Lee Lucas spent over 21 years living behind bars under the control of various correctional authorities. In other words, 70 percent of his life during these thirty and one-half years was spent under someone else's control. Lucas contends that he was beaten and even shot by "law enforcement" while in prison. He threatened to kill himself while in prison in Michigan and is reported to have attempted suicide by cutting his left wrist. Prison authorities did not consider this a serious suicide attempt. He states that he was trying to change and get help in prison by talking to doctors and prison officials. During his first confession in Stoneburg, Texas, he exclaimed, "I begged them for help and couldn't get it!" He says, "They were just there for a job. Their purpose is just to keep an inmate calm. No attempt to change 'em. Don't treat inmates as a man."

Lucas consistently maintains he requested that he not be released from prison when paroled in 1975: "I kept insisting, you know, that they not release me until they could find out what was wrong with me and they talked until '75 and they said it was time for me to leave. They said, 'You're discharged.' And the day I got out on discharge I killed four people that day." Five murders committed by Lucas have been confirmed by the task force during the remainder of 1975. One of these murders was committed on the same day that he was married. Lucas further states that when he was released from the Boys Training School in 1953 he refused to be released to his mother. He states, "I told 'em that if they made me go back to my mother's that I would end up killin' her. So we agreed there in Virginia that I wasn't to go back there, that I was goin' to Michigan." No one would disagree with him now, when referring to both releases, that "they shouldn't have let me out." Between the times he was diligently reporting to his parole officer in Maryland following his first release from prison in Michigan, he was traveling across this country and leaving the remains of his victims in a number of states.

The results of psychological testing while Lucas was incarcerated reveal that he reads at the sixth-grade level, spells at the fifth-grade level and understands mathematics at the fourth-grade level. Institutional psychological examinations conducted in Michigan show Lucas to have a total average of 65 on the Standard Achievement Test and an IQ of 89 as determined by the Army General Classification Test. He placed in the sixtieth percentile on the revised Minnesota Paper Form Board. Lucas was further administered the Minnesota Multi-Phase Personality Inventory, the Figure Drawing Test, and the Rosenzweig P.H. Study. A summary of the interpretation of these tests written by psychologists on July 14, 1961, is as follows:

[W]hile contraindicating and underlying psychotic process as well as incapacitating neurotic qualities, tests results are suggestive of a basically insecure individual who has a relatively well crystalized inferiority complex and who is grossly lacking in self confidence, self reliance, will power and general stamina. There is also some evidence of a preoccupation with sexual impotence, the same which is believed to exist as only another reflection of his deflated impression of personal qualities in general. According to Rosenzweig P.H. Study he was found more value oriented than he is need oriented, but due to his lack of will power and self confidence he does not characteristically engage in behavior which is aimed at an implementation of his values. The anxiety and hostility caused by threats to the ego are usually directed intropunitively toward himself or inpunitively toward the frustrating situation. *He does not have the courage to* blame others for mistakes or misfortunes or to *engage in aggressive social behavior* aimed at alleviating some of his discomfort. (emphasis added)[2]

The clinical psychologist providing the above interpretative summary qualified his diagnostic impression due to the absence of pertinent and general background information on Lucas. In fact, prior to writing the above, he had never seen Lucas. He stated that his report should be a working hypothesis.

The following psychiatric diagnoses completed on Lucas while incarcerated were provided to law enforcement officials in 1984 in the form of narrative reports:

July 14, 1961: Psychiatric Clinic Ward, Jackson Prison (second admission)

DSM II–301.81 *Passive-aggressive personality* with a significant [sic] inferiority complex and general lack of self confidence, self reliance, will power and *perseverance* (emphasis added).[3]

DSM II–295.0 *Schizophrenia, simple type, chronic, severe.* Transfer to Ionia State Hospital recommended, prognosis fair.[4]

August 10, 1961: Ionia State Hospital

DSM II–295.90 *Schizophrenia, chronic undifferentiated type* sex deviate, sadist.[5]

January 28, 1965: Ionia Staff Conference on Lucas

> The patient's affect during the staff interview was definitely inappropriate. He is *potentially dangerous*.[6]

November 17, 1971: Center for Forensic Psychiatry

> DSM II-301.81 *Passive aggressive personality*. Found competent to stand criminal trial for kidnapping. "It is not felt that there is much outside an incarceration setting which would be effective in modifying the defendant's presently erratic social behavior." [7]

"I needed medical help, there's no doubt about it," was the layman's diagnosis offered by Lucas himself.

Offense Behavior

While his first deviant act, labeled as such, was theft, Lucas killed animals for sexual gratification in his very early teens and began using alcohol at age nine. He also became fascinated with knives in the first grade. They would ⅄ become one of the tools of his "trade." The knife was his favorite weapon since it was silent and quick, its target the throat and chest area of his victims.

Lucas has stolen numerous automobiles during his criminal career. Many of his killings were the result of burglary, theft, and armed robbery. His most frequent target for robbery was the 24-hour convenience store.

His criminal career was diffuse and intermittent, yet involving ever increasing forms of aggression. His first homicide was a 17-year-old girl in Virginia in 1951. His second was his mother, nine years later. For Lucas,

> It was just an impulse thing that if I wanted to kill somebody, I'd go and kill 'em. I wouldn't plan it, how I was gonna do that. Then I would sit and plan how to get rid of the body. Whether I would just dump it out on the road or whether I would leave it partially clothed or would leave anything around the body or whether I'd leave the body cut up, how I would leave the body, ya know.

Based on information provided to the Texas Rangers from law enforcement agencies in 27 states, some limited empirical data have been aggregated on the crimes committed by Lucas. The age range of victims was from 4 to 84 years, with a mean of approximately 31 years. Three-fourths of the victims were female. Over 90 percent of Lucas's victims were caucasian, the remainder either Afro-American, Hispanic or American Indian. Over 30 of his victims were hitchhiking immediately prior to their death. The most frequent location from which Lucas, sometimes with Ottis Toole, abducted these victims was a nearby business providing short-term service to people in transit. Over 40 different types of weapons were used by Lucas. The average victim was caucasian, female, 31 years of age, killed outdoors away from her residence, and sexually assaulted either before or after death. No significant sequential or non-sequential pattern or correlation of victim characteristics was found in this aggregated, albeit second-hand data. However, many of these victims fit within the definition developed by Egger (1985) (see Chapter 1).

In describing his killing, Lucas states,

We killed them every way there is except one. I haven't poisoned anyone. . . . [W]e cut 'em up. We hanged 'em. We ran 'em down in cars. We stabbed 'em. We beat 'em, we drowned 'em. There's crucifixion—there's people we filleted like fish. There's people we burnt. There's people we shot in cars. . . . We strangled them by hand. We strangled them by rope. We strangled them by telephone cord. We even stabbed them when we strangled them. We even tied them so they would strangle themselves.

All methods have been confirmed by the task force except hanging and crucifixion. Lucas talks about some of his victims being used for target practice. Synopsis of two confirmed homicides by the task force reveal one victim being shot while standing at a car wash and another shot while hanging up clothes in her backyard. They were shot as Lucas and Toole drove by in a car.

Lucas graphically describes one of his killings: "I stabbed her several times. . . . I took a knife and cut her throat. She was cut from ear to ear. After I got done I seen she was dead and I had sex with her." He admits to being a necrophiliac, although the term had to be explained to him: "In most of my cases, I think you'll find that I had sex with them after death, uh the other way I'm not satisfied."

"I've had people in houses, I've had people in stores, I've had people in banks," states Lucas. During the last year of his confinement in the Williamson County Jail in Texas he continued to stick to the number 360. "Well, I've got 360 people. I've got 36 states and three different countries [USA, Mexico, and Canada]." Law enforcement officers used to scoff at his claims. They don't anymore.

One reason he gives for his killings is, "I didn't leave no witnesses. I've never left witnesses." A witness for Lucas, in addition to his felony murders was, "whoever was on the street or in the area." He states, "After the first few, ya know, I felt the next one was covered. I'd just kill that one so they couldn't say I was there. If I came into contact with somebody, I couldn't afford to let 'em live."

Lucas claims to have been drinking prior to most of his killings. His argument with his mother in 1960, which led to her death, began in a tavern. He has reportedly used numerous amphetamines, PCP, LSD, and marijuana. He states, "I stayed on dope and I stayed on alcohol and those was what I lived on. I just wanted to stay high all the time." He remembers two instances of hallucinations or visions. While lying on a bed he felt himself rise off the bed and float in the air. While traveling on a highway, he states, "The center line came up and hit me in the face. . . . I drank beer with acid [LSD] and this took away hallucinations. This numbed all my feelings and I stayed that way." He states that the drugs he took kept him relaxed and kept him awake so he could travel a lot. "Drugs allowed me to stay on the road, to get out of the victim's neighborhood." For Lucas, being on drugs increased his degree of awareness.

Lucas and his accomplices used many vehicles in their travels. Several old cars were purchased in Jacksonville, Florida. When a car they were using broke down, they would abandon it and hitchhike or steal another car. Sometimes they would briefly use the cars of their murder victims.

Lucas was constantly and almost ceaselessly moving about the country. He took care not to be seen or to leave behind clues, and rarely repeated in the same area the ways in which he murdered. Lucas talks of a "force" that kept him moving and traveling with no specific destination in mind. For Lucas, it was as if he had heeded the advice of Harry King, the Boxman, who stated, "The only way you can beat the law is by moving all the time. The law is easy to beat as long as you keep moving. But you have to continuously move" (King and Chambliss, 1972, 91).

In many of his killings Lucas took the clothes of his victim. "It's just something I been doing for years. I just gather up their clothes and throw them away. I don't know why I do it. I don't think it'll cover the girl's identity or anything like that."

Many of his victims have been subjected to what the task force refers to as overkill. Lucas explains this by referring to the "force" that causes him to mutilate and frequently dissect the body of his victims. At other times he has stated, "A person doesn't think the person is dead." Further, he states, "If I cut up a body I'd use plastic bags and leave parts throughout the area." He and his accomplices claim to have carried the head of one victim through two states.

Very little physical evidence has been found to link Lucas to the crime scenes of his murders. A partial latent fingerprint was found in a robbery murder in a Louisiana motel. Victims' hair has been found in cars used by Lucas. Blood has been found at crime scenes that matches his blood type, found in less than two-tenths of 1 percent of the population. Also, a composite drawing made by a police artist from witnesses' descriptions of an abduction closely resembles Lucas.

Lucas contends that he constantly changed the way he killed in order to confuse law enforcement. By the time one of his murders was discovered he might be two or three counties away, killing in a different way. Sergeant Bob Prince, a Texas Ranger in charge of the task force, states, "Lucas has 16 homicides within a 50-mile radius of Georgetown [Texas]. If you laid these cases out on a table and asked investigators not familiar with Lucas to evaluate them, the officers would undoubtedly talk about numerous different killers instead of just one" (Bob Prince, personal communication, Feb. 20, 1985).

Self-Concept

Lucas frequently speaks of being driven by hatred. He attributes this hatred to the way he was brought up by his mother. "When I first grew up and can remember, I was dressed as a girl. And I stayed that way for two or three years and then after that I was treated as, uh, what I'd call the dog of the family.'' This, the beatings by his mother, and being forced to watch her in sexual intercourse caused, according to Lucas, "deep embedded hatred which I couldn't get rid of.''

He was killing and sexually experimenting with animals at age nine, and states he "never thought about killing anyone till I was 14 years old. Everything I had was destroyed.'' When asked if he ever really thought about himself, Lucas replied, "Once in 1970. I knew what I was gonna do.'' He says he thought someone would eventually shoot him before long. He says he didn't care.

Many detectives who have questioned him, report that Lucas is not reliable. He has admitted to crimes and then denied them. He has confused confessed places and dates. In some respects he brags about his murders: "Well, most of your other people leaves evidence. I don't. I've never left evidence in any of my cases.'' During a subsequent interview, Lucas claimed to have specifically left evidence on purpose.

Lucas states he was trying to "show people I can do anything I want to. Outsmart everybody else. It's your responsibility to catch me.'' Lucas's braggadocio is very evident when he states, "Anything I wanted to do, I could do. Outsmart a burglar alarm. Get around electric alarms. No kind of safety device I can't get out of.''

He is apparently impotent. In discussing sexual relations he always refers to not getting anything out of it. He attributes this to a stab wound requiring surgery to his groin while in prison. After that, he states, "I could only get a feeling but no liquid.'' He sees himself as sterile.

Lucas states that at one time he had a problem, "but I wasn't sick.'' In reference to his past killings, he states, "From 14 years old all I can say is I killed. I just lived a criminal life.'' As to his specific killings he says, "To me, it's as if I haven't killed anyone, yet I have. . . . It's like bein' two people. I could see myself commit 'em, the crime, but I couldn't feel myself committin' it.'' Lucas further states, "It's like living in two different worlds. You want to do what is right, and yet, ya can't do it.''

Lucas has described himself as

irritable, not willin' to associate with people. I guess my hatred showed more than it does now. I just wouldn't take nothin' from nobody. People that don't even know me, don't know anything about me and try to be a bully with me back then—I'd just as liable to shoot 'em right there on the spot. That's just the way it was.

Lucas, although frequently claiming to the contrary, seemed to enjoy his "celebrity" status. For a change, he had something others wanted—information. Lucas was now in the limelight, no longer going unnoticed. When he spoke, many people were listening!

Attitudes

Lucas now claims remorse for his victims. However, a big smile crosses his face when he is identified as having committed a homicide and he clears another of his "cases." The smile on his face is either because he had gotten away with a murder for so long or that he had, as he calls it, "solved his case."

One detective who interviewed Lucas stated, "When you first talk to him, you'd get the impression that he was a bum, a road child, that's grown old. He gives the impression that he's not a threat to anyone." Having cleared six homicides as a result of his long interviews with Lucas, the detective no longer doubts him.

To value human life seems beyond his capability. When asked why more of his victims weren't males, he replied, "That's somethin' I very seldom do, unless it's an emergency and have to do it." For him, the victim was an object: "Only one that ever bothered me was Becky." As for his mother, "No, 'cause I didn't kill her, she died of a heart attack after I hit her with the knife." He doesn't see any responsibility for his mother's death since she was beating him with a broom when she was killed. He views it as self-defense.

Lucas does not like to admit that some of his victims were young children. He blames most of those deaths on his accomplice, Toole. He claims to have believed a four-year-old victim was 15 years old.

He seems to have traveled from one victim to the next: "I'd go from one to the other and wouldn't think about the last one I'd killed. I never had no feeling for that person at all."

Most of his female victims were, for him, prostitutes. "Most of the girls I've met on the highway has turned out to be prostitutes. [They] has been either out sellin' theirselves to truckers or people on the highway and I, uh have always, since I was a little kid, hated prostitutes."

Recall of Events

His memory is described as including an excruciatingly intense wealth of detail. Law enforcement authorities have found Lucas to have a remarkable recall for road numbers, mileages, and landmarks. They have frequently taken Lucas into the countryside and let him direct them to the crime scene. In one instance in Texas, Lucas was driven past a commercial building when he said that he and an accomplice had killed a man and woman in an armed robbery of "that liquor store over there." The officer noted that the building was not a liquor store, but later learned that it had been when the proprietors were killed in a robbery. In another instance, a rural crime scene was so remote that the officer could not find his way back to it. Lucas led the officers directly to the crime scene. Following these and numerous similar instances, Lucas's credibility was decidedly enhanced.

When questioned about his memory, Lucas stated, "Yeah, I can't recall how I do it, really . . . there's so many of 'em. They just seem to come back clear as crystal. It's like something in a movie, like watching a movie over and over." Lucas is confessing to his murders because "the Lord told me to." As for his phenomenal memory, he states, "That was done by Jesus himself. That was from a light comin' into my cell and uh, go back to the bodies, and give complete descriptions of the bodies through Him. And that's the only way I can do it."

A more plausible explanation of his recall ability is referred to by psychologists as hypermnesia, an unusually exact or vivid memory. His ability to remember his victims can also be attributed to an eidetic memory, causing mental images that are unusually vivid and almost photographically exact.

Concluding Remarks by Henry Lee Lucas

Lucas, while under control of the task force, enjoyed painting landscapes in his private cell and doing his "religious work." He stated that in addition to this he was trying to teach law enforcement how to catch criminals like himself.

When asked by the author how to conclude his case study, he responded, "I've changed from what I used to be. I was a killer. Let's put it plain out. The type of life I lived. I mean that thing was nothin' but crime. I didn't do nothin' else. It got so killin' somebody meant nothin' to me."

When asked why he has changed, he responded:

Seein' what I've done. It's my own personal feelings. What I've seen, what I've done. Stuff like' at. That's caused me ta change. Since I've learned about the families. I've learned about the sufferin' they went through. How much sufferin' I've caused. It hurts! It would cause anybody to change. Seein' the misery 'cause of what I've done. I'd never dreamt of that before.

When asked about his death sentence and eventual execution by the state of Texas he stated, "I'm not afraid of death. I know where I'm goin'. Goin' ta Heaven."

The Controversy and Aftermath

On April 19, 1985, a federal district judge in Austin, Texas ordered Henry Lee Lucas transferred from the Williamson County Jail in Georgetown to San Antonio to appear before a federal grand jury in that city the following week. The Friday before Lucas was taken from Georgetown to Waco he had testified before a state grand jury just prior to the judge's order. Two days following Henry's trip to Waco, on Sunday, April 14, the *Dallas Times Herald's* front page headline asked the question, "Mass murderer or massive hoax?" The extensive reporting and investigative journalism in the pages that followed would certainly help the *Herald* in their battle with the local competition, the *Dallas Morning News*. In all, the *Herald* devoted five full pages to the story, which charged that Lucas had perpetrated a hoax to embarrass authorities and keep himself off death row. The article, written primarily by Hugh Aynesworth, who at one time talked Lucas into signing an exclusive contract giving Aynesworth rights to Lucas's life story, went into great detail regarding Henry's travels and his alleged victims. For the task force, it was the end of their work with Henry.

The Lucas Task Force, which came to an end, and more importantly, the Texas Rangers, were to become the targets of criticism by the news media and the attorney general of Texas, who under the Texas constitution was ironically charged with defending the Rangers in a civil or criminal court of law. The Lucas Task Force had been a unique organization during the 17 months it was operating. Never before in the history of law enforcement had the coordination of hundreds of homicide investigations been conducted in over 30 states on one suspect and his accomplices. One might think for such an endeavor there might be margin for some error, but the charge that all of it had been a hoax was hard for many to believe. A Texas newspaper was indeed making news by charging literally hundreds of police agencies in 27 states with falsifying information for the purpose of increasing their homicide clearance rates! What could possibly be the motive of the Texas Rangers, the Williamson County Sheriff's Office, and law enforcement agencies from all over the country in perpetrating such a hoax? Others would ask a different question. What could possibly be the motive of the attorney general of Texas in making such charges against the Texas Rangers, one of the oldest and most respected police agencies in the United States? Henry Lee Lucas is indeed a serial killer, being convicted of 11 homicides. Henry Lee Lucas probably did not kill the 360 people he claims. However, it is very difficult for the trained social scientist to question the clearances of all 162 homicides attributed to Lucas by police agencies in 27 states.

Briefly, the evidence used by the reports of the *Dallas Times Herald*, which the attorney general relied on almost exclusively, amounts to very little of a probative nature. Much of their evidence is based on recollections of Henry's half-brothers and half-sisters, searching their memories as far back as eight and nine years ago. Other evidence is based on weak assumptions that Henry could not have driven 11,000 miles in a month, or an average of approximately 367 miles per day. Documentary evidence of payroll records comes from the Jacksonville, Florida roofing company records when Lucas and Toole were working there. Further, the dates of Lucas's endorsements on his payroll checks were also crucial to the newspaper's charges since these dates coincided with the dates of some of his killings hundreds of miles away.

As a result of the Texas attorney general's staff investigation, a report was issued on the task force and the alleged homicides committed by Lucas. This report was never made public. After the Texas Rangers prepared a four-volume, extensively documented response to this report, the attorney general's report was substantially modified and revised. The Texas Rangers report was not made available to the public by order of the Texas attorney general. Such an order certainly appears to have been self-serving and placed Mr. Mattox, the Texas Attorney General in a definite conflict of interest position.

The Texas attorney general's *Lucas Report* issued in April 1986 was, in effect, an indictment of law enforcement investigators in 27 states and more directly an attack on the various judicial systems that found Lucas guilty of 10 of his 11 homicides.

It is also interesting to note that the report relied almost exclusively on the investigative reporting of the *Dallas Times Herald* for documentary evidence. Over 80 percent of the evidence described in the report comes directly from the *Dallas Times* article of April 14, 1985.

To provide the reader with the contextual flavor of this report, the following comments are excerpted from Jim Mattox's transmitted letter in the introduction to the report (Mattox, 1986):

Questions about Henry Lee Lucas will be debated for decades. This report is not offered as a *final answer* [emphasis added]. There may never be a final answer . . . .

[W]e find numerous discrepancies between Lucas' confessions and obtainable evidence regarding his whereabouts . . .

[Staff] conducted interviews with law enforcement officers around the country. [There is no evidentiary documentation to these interviews in the report and other reliable evidence strongly indicated that the majority of the law enforcement agencies that believe Lucas to have been the killer of the victims were never contacted by the attorney general's staff.] . . .

[T]here is a notable lack of physical evidence linking Lucas to the crimes to which he confessed. Lucas did not (sic) lead authorities to any bodies of victims. [This last statement is patently misleading according to numerous law enforcement agencies, since they have video and audio tape evidence of the fact the Lucas did lead them unassisted to the scene of his killings.]

We have found information that would lead us to believe that some officials ''cleared cases'' just to get them off the books. [Nowhere in this report is the term ''some'' quantified!] (pp. i-ii)

Henry Lee Lucas currently sits in death row at the Texas Department of Corrections, outside Huntsville, Texas. He continues to deny his confessions, but periodically and gleefully admits to having killed numerous people in his lifetime.

On May 5, 1989, grand juries in Holmes, Jackson, and Washington counties, Florida returned indictments charging Henry Lee Lucas and Ottis Elwood Toole in the deaths of four residents of this three-county area in 1980 and 1981. Apparently, authorities in Florida paid little attention to unsubstantiated allegations of the *Lucas Report* or the *Dallas Times Herald*. Extradition proceedings for Lucas to stand trial for these killings in Florida are currently pending.

NOTES

1. His first contact with correctional psychologists was undoubtedly in 1954 when he was incarcerated at the state prison in Richmond, Virginia. However, correctional records from this institution are not available to the author.

2. Henry Lee Lucas—Transfer Summary to Ionia State Hospital, July 14, 1961, p. 4.

3. Ibid.

4. Ibid, p. 5.

5. Henry Lee Lucas—Ionia State Hospital diagnosis, August 10, 1961, p. 4.

6. Henry Lee Lucas—Ionia State Hospital record, January 28, 1965, p. 13.

7. Henry Lee Lucas—Psychological Evaluation, Center for Forensic Psychiatry, Ypsilanti, Michigan, November 17, 1971, p. 4.

SOURCE MATERIAL

Henry Lee Lucas Homicide Task Force Investigative Reports: Index of Confirmed Homicides; Court Action Involving Henry Lee Lucas; Index to Supplements of Synopsis; Synopsis of Confirmed Homicides; Daily Log Activities of Lucas and Toole.

Interviews with Henry Lee Lucas: June 5, 1984; June 22, 1984; July 18, 1984; August 2, 1984; August 14, 1984; September 25, 1984; February 8, 1985; March 22, 1985.

Newspaper Articles

The Atlanta Constitution, April 10, 1985.

The Atlanta Journal, Dec. 21, 1984; April 22, 1985.

Austin American Statesman, June 29, July 3, Nov. 23, Dec. 8, 1983. March 9, 12, April 4, 18, 24, May 11, July 26, 1984. April 21, 1985.

Avalance Journal, (Lubbock, Texas), June 3, 4, 5, 6, 28, Sept. 2, October 31, 1984.

The Baltimore Sun, Feb. 20, 1984.

Beaumont Enterprise, July 1, 29, 1984.

Dallas Morning News, June 30, July 7, August 3, 11, 25, Dec. 8, 1983. June 8, August 1, 2, 9, October 28, 1984.

Dallas Times Herald, Aug. 11, 1982. June 24, 26, August 13, 25, 26, Nov. 26, 1983. April 5, 7, 11, 14, 23, 27, May 11, 17, Oct. 6, 27, Sept. 7, 1984. April 14, 15, 16, 17, 18, 19, 20, 23, 24, 1985.

El Paso Herald Post, Oct. 26, 27, 1984.

Fort Worth Star Telegram, Jan. 16, 29, 1984.

Herald Dispatch (Huntington, W. Virginia), Dec. 11, 12, 13, 14, 16, 1984.

Houston Chronicle, Oct. 11, 17, 28, 1983. April 7, 13, 23, May 12, June 2, 17, 23, Aug. 1, Sept. 7, Oct. 6, 1984. Jan 14, April 15, 16, 18, 19 20, 1985.

Law Enforcement News, Sept. 24, 1984.

New York Times, April 18, 24, 29, 1985.

Rocky Mountain News (Denver, Colorado), Sept. 13, 1984.

Tampa Tribune, June 9, 1985.

The Toledo Blade, Jan. 17, 19, 20, 1960.

Psychiatric Reports

Transfer to Ionia State Hospital (Michigan), July 14, 1961.
Ionia State Hospital Diagnosis, Aug. 10, 1961.
Ionia State Hospital Record, Jan. 28, 1963.
Psychological evaluation, Center for Forensic Psychiatry, Ypsilanti, Michigan, Nov. 17,
    1971.

REFERENCES

Call, M. (1985). *Hand of Death: The Henry Lee Lucas Story.* Lafayette, LA: Prescott
    Press, Inc.
Charmaz, K. (1983). The grounded theory method: An explication and interpretation. In
    Emerson, R. M. (ed.), *Contemporary field research: A collection of readings.*
    Boston, MA: Little, Brown and Co., pp. 109–26.
Cuba, N. (1985, July). "The Life & Deaths of Henry Lee Lucas." *Third Coast,* 4(12),
    44–59.
Denzin, N. K. (1978). *The research act.* New York: McGraw-Hill.
Egger, S. A. (1985, March). *Case Study of Serial Murderer Henry Lee Lucas* (copyright).
    Paper presented at the Academy of Criminal Justice Sciences 1985 annual meeting,
    Las Vegas, Nevada.
Gibbons, D. C. (1965). *Changing the lawbreaker.* Englewood Cliffs, NJ: Prentice-Hall.
Glaser, B. and Straus, A. L. (1967). *The discovery of grounded theory: Strategies for
    qualitative research.* Chicago: Aldine.
Hammersley, M. and Atkinson, P. (1983). *Ethnography: Principles in practice.* New
    York: Tavistock Publications.
King, H. and Chambliss, W. J. (1972). *Harry King: A professional thief's journey.* New
    York: John Wiley and Sons.
Klockars, C. B. (1974). *The professional fence.* New York: The Free Press.
Letkemann, P. (1973). *Crime as work.* Englewood Cliffs, NJ: Prentice-Hall, Inc.
Mattox, J. (1986). *Lucas report.* Austin, TX: Office of Attorney General.
McCall, G. J. (1975). *Observing the law: Applications of field methods to the study of
    the criminal justice system.* Rockville, MD: National Institute of Mental Health.
Polsky, N. (1967). *Hustlers, beats, and others.* Chicago: Aldine.
Regional Organized Crime Information Center. (1985). *Travel Movements of Henry Lee
    Lucas and Ottis Elwood Toole, 1952–1985.* Nashville, TN: ROCIC.
Webb, E. J., Campbell, D. T., Schwartz, R. D., and Sechrest, L. (1966). *Unobtrusive
    measures: Non-reactive research in the social sciences.* Chicago: Rand McNally.

III

Law Enforcement's Response to Serial Murder: Problems and Solutions

In this part of the work I develop a term I coined in 1984 called "linkage blindness" by further explaining this myopic view and its resultant problem of interagency communication, cooperation, and coordination in a serial murder investigation. Following an explanation of the problem of linkage blindness, I document this problem by highlighting its existence in a number of well-known serial murder cases. An analysis of the problem of linkage blindness concludes Chapter 8.

In Chapter 9, I provide a taxonomy of nine different investigative responses to the phenomenon of serial murder. I warn the reader not to construe this taxonomy as an indictment of law enforcement's response to serial murder. Notwithstanding the aggregate failures of this taxonomy, the developing responses should be viewed as the foundation of more effective investigative responses in the future. The chapter is concluded by noting that each of these responses in the taxonomy shares a common focus of reducing the extent to which linkage blindness occurs in a serial murder investigation.

8

Linkage Blindness:
A Systemic Myopia

STEVEN A. EGGER

DEFINING THE PROBLEM

The fact that linkage blindness exists across the various components and role sectors of the criminal justice system, and more specifically among the thousands of law enforcement agencies in the United States, is not really debatable. The existence of linkage blindness has been documented in retrospective interpretations in an analysis of serial murder cases by Egger (1985). The problem has become obvious to those journalists, researchers, and governmental officials who have examined numerous cases of serial murder. This is certainly true for the better-known nationally recognized cases such as Bundy, Lucas, Gacy, or Rameriz and also for those lesser known or less publicized cases of Eyler, Gary, or Hatcher.

Police officers, and particularly homicide investigators from Maine to Texas, are quick to agree that linkage blindness (when it is explained) exists. However, numerous police chiefs, sheriffs, and police commanders respond with a negative and, unfortunately, contrary opinion, arguing that agencies (more specifically, their agencies) communicate with one another on a daily basis, frequently across hundreds of miles of geography.

In discussing the mobility of serial killers and the difficulty of a multi-law enforcement agency investigation, Keyes (1986) describes Columbus, Ohio Homicide Sergeant Bill Steckman's thinking about what he was facing in the investigation of the ".22 caliber murders":

[M]ost serial murderers moved from city to city, stalking their victims across city, county or state lines, over weeks, months and even years. Because different law enforcement agencies were involved—county sheriff's deputies, city police and the FBI, each concerned primarily with their own cases—detectives often didn't notice the patterns. Conflicting investigative methods, interdepartmental jealousies, and prosecutors overreacting to the political pressures of a fearful and outraged public, often gave serial killers the advantage. Among the most difficult criminals to apprehend, most often, when they were arrested, it was by accident. (p. 77)

It is thus difficult for the author to provide an optimistic or positive prognosis to the control or amelioration of serial murder in this country. It is equally disheartening when one realizes that the phenomenon of serial murder, that is, law enforcement's response to this phenomenon, is only symptomatic of the greater and all-encompassing problem of serial criminality. The traveling criminal who repeats his criminal acts in different law enforcement jurisdictions is indeed exploiting this systemic weakness which frequently contributes to his or her continued immunity from detection or apprehension.

In a stranger-to-stranger murder lacking in physical evidence or witnesses, criminal investigators are left to deal with a very large set of suspects, with only a small probability of this set including the offender. A review of serial murders occurring over the last few years reveals that most serial murderers are caught by chance or coincidence and not by ratiocination or scientific investigation. Law enforcement agencies today are simply not adept at identifying or apprehending the murderer who kills strangers and moves from jurisdiction to jurisdiction and crosses state lines. Why, in this age of information and rapidly advancing computer technology, are multi-jurisdictional crimes of murder so difficult for law enforcement to solve?

Linkage blindness is the cause. Law enforcement investigators do not see, are prevented from seeing, or make little attempt to see beyond their own jurisdictional responsibilities. The law enforcement officer's responsibility stops at the boundary of his or her jurisdiction. The exception is generally only when hot pursuit is necessary. The very nature of local law enforcement in this country and a police department's accountability and responsiveness to its jurisdictional clients isolates the department from the outside world.

The National Crime Information Center provides officers access to other agencies indirectly in order to obtain information on wanted persons and stolen property. However, the sharing of information on unsolved crimes and investigative leads is not a function of this extensive nationwide information system. Reciprocal relationships between homicide investigators are at best informal and usually within relatively limited geographical areas.

Linkage blindness exemplifies the major weakness of our structural defenses against crime and our ability to control it. Simply stated, the exchange of investigative information among police departments in this country is, at best, very poor. Linkage blindness is the nearly total lack of sharing or coordinating investigative information and the lack of adequate networking by law enforcement agencies. This lack of sharing or networking is a prevalent condition of today's law enforcement officers and their agencies. Thus, linkages are rarely established among geographic areas of the country between similar crime patterns or modus operandi. Such a condition directly inhibits an early warning or detection system of the serial murderer preying on multiple victims. In those instances in which serial murders are discovered or suspected, they are frequently being committed within a relatively small geographic area and therefore subject to obvious inferences. A law enforcement agency operates on information, yet agencies fail to seek it out, use or process it from the "outside", or share it with colleagues or their counterparts in other agencies.

Empirical analysis, albeit retrospective in nature, reveals numerous instances of linkage blindness in the investigations of serial murder across the United States. It should also be noted that this failure in communication and networking is not a problem unique to this country, as evidenced by the Yorkshire Ripper investigation in England (see Doney, Chapter 5).

While it should be readily apparent to the informed reader that the concept of linkage blindness is applicable to all types of criminal mobility, examples will be limited to that of the serial murderer.

Joel Norris (1988) misuses the term "linkage blindness" by defining it as professionals in disparate disciplines failing to relate causalities of behavior to one another's area of understanding and study. Norris also failed to understand the concept when it was first explained to him by the author in 1983 (see Darrach and Norris, 1984). True, the term does generally apply to faulty communication linkages among like players in similar circumstances with similar responsibilities. But the term was coined and applied specifically to the law enforcement criminal investigation function. More importantly, the term was coined to denote a major investigative problem in the response to serial crime, not serial murder alone.

The editors of *Forensic Science International* (1985) appear to be much too optimistic in their appraisal of U.S. law enforcement's response to the problem of linkage blindness. These editors state:

The development of close communication and systems of accumulation of nationwide data has brought very important results especially the respect of law enforcement organizations at various levels and in various locations for each other. These organizations have thus realized that their problem is shared by others. (p. 135)

The relatively recent development of VICAP by the FBI and the development of task forces in response to the Williams case in Atlanta, the Stano case in Florida, the Lucas-Toole case in Monroe, Louisiana, and the Green River case in Seattle are the only evidence the authors present to substantiate their optimistic assessment of law enforcement's response to the problem of linkage blindness. While these cases are of course noteworthy and VICAP's effort indeed laudable, they represent the efforts of a relatively few agencies, while VICAP is in effect the effort of only one federal agency.

Levin and Fox (1985) state that unless the serial murderer leaves a distinct or unique signature at the crime scene, the police may not recognize the similarity of the killings. They also contend that if a pattern does exist, it may go undetected, due to the sheer volume of cases, particularly in large cities. For example, the Corll, Henley, and Brooks killings of 27 young boys from 1971 to 1973 in the Houston, Texas area was completely unknown to the police until they received a telephone call from Henley in August 1973. In this case the police failed to thoroughly investigate missing persons reports or to correlate similarities in these reports (Levin and Fox, 1985, pp. 177–81).

Levin and Fox (1985) state:

Seeing a common element in several reports of missing or murdered persons in one large city is difficult enough. Seeing it across city or state lines magnifies the problem. Some killers are able to kill on the move so that they are already hundreds of miles away before police discover the crime. (p. 182)

Goldstein (1977) refers to an acknowledgment by the New York City Police Department in September 1974 that it had failed to recognize the overall pattern in eight different murders and two assaults of women which occurred in the same hotel over a period of one and one-half years. This pattern was discovered when the killer confessed after being charged with another murder that occurred near the hotel (p. 67). This failure to identify patterns in different homicides may be the reason that the Houston, Texas Police Department has recently initiated a number of internal changes in its homicide division in response to a homicide clearance rate of only 64 percent. Two new shifts were created within the division which would overlap existing shifts to allow detectives more time to discuss cases and follow-ups with each other and possibly identify across-shift patterns.

Levin and Fox (1985) conclude that serial killers "may be hiding in the anonymity of large urban centers" (p. 186) or traveling across the country. In either case the police will probably not detect their pattern of killing. This failure to detect a pattern appears to be the result of a law enforcement communication failure.

Documenting the Problem

Many of Theodore Bundy's murder victims were reported missing by friends or relatives to the police. In most cases, the victims' disappearances were treated as routine missing person reports by the police. In one instance in Utah, the police failed to officially file a missing report when a victim's mother reported her daughter's disappearance.

It was not until the fourth victim was reported missing in May 1974 that the police established that there were some similarities among the disappearances of girls reported missing in Seattle, Olympia and Ellensburg, Washington and Corvallis, Oregon. It was not until early fall of that year that the missing girls' skeletal remains began to be discovered.

The task force in Seattle, Washington established in March 1975 was a delayed response to the problem of missing and murdered girls. No victims missing specifically from Seattle's jurisdiction had been discovered until March of that year. However, the girls disappearing from Lake Sammamish in July 1974 and the discovery of their bodies in September of that year should have been sufficient, coupled with all the other disappearances, to have warranted joint investigative action much sooner (see Larsen, 1980; Rule, 1980; and Winn and Merill, 1980). The task force had a limited automated capability to cross-reference their information. Even so, when Bundy was arrested in Salt Lake City, he was one of the task force's top 100 remaining suspects to be checked.

Parents of the murdered girl in Utah County, Utah asked the local sheriff's office to obtain assistance in their investigation from the Salt Lake City police. The sheriff's office refused, indicating that they didn't need any assistance.

Following the Chi Omega Sorority House murders in Tallahassee, Florida, officers from Washington and Colorado notified the Leon County sheriff's office to look for Ted Bundy as a suspect. This tip was apparently ignored by the sheriff's office. The sheriff's office also provided little cooperation to Colorado police interested in investigating Bundy's jail escape.

When John Wayne Gacy's crimes were discovered, he was in custody. Gacy had been separately connected to four of his victims who had been reported missing. However, the fact that Gacy was a common link to all of these missing boys was not identified by the Chicago police. The Des Plaines police had connected him to this thirty-third and last victim, who had been reported missing in Des Plaines, Illinois. Then, through their investigation, the Des Plaines police connected him to other missing boys, who turned out to be Gacy's victims. Nine of Gacy's victims were never identified by the police (see Linedecker, 1980 and Sullivan and Markew, 1983).

Four complaints had been lodged against Gacy in Chicago between 1971 and 1978 for homosexual assaultive behavior. One was still pending when he was arrested. However, since Gacy was never identified as a common link to the missing boys, this criminal information on Gacy was never linked to the boys' disappearances.

It was not until Kenneth Bianchi acted on his own and killed in Washington that he became a suspect in the "Hillside Strangler" murders. He was arrested for a double homicide in Bellingham, Washington. The Bellingham police notified the Los Angeles County sheriff's office since Bianchi had recently moved from there (see Schwartz, 1981 and Barnes, 1984).

The first three victims in Los Angeles County had been found within three separate law enforcement jurisdictions. The Los Angeles police department, the Los Angeles County sheriff's office, and the Glendale police department were each investigating a murder.

When homicide investigators from the sheriff's office viewed the body of the third victim where she had been found in Glendale, they immediately saw similarities with the second victim, found in their jurisdiction (F. Salerno, personal communication, August 1, 1985). From this point on, the investigators from the Los Angeles police department began exchanging information with the other two jurisdictions. However, it was not until November 22, 1977, and the discovery of five additional victims, that these law enforcement jurisdictions met formally to share information on the killings and decided to form a joint task force to investigate the murders.

Bianchi had been personally contacted in connection with the Hillside murders on at least three separate occasions, twice by the Los Angeles officers and once by a Glendale police officer. These contacts were in response to tips called in to the police. On a fourth and fifth occasion Bianchi's name was reported to the police, but no officer responded to this information. In all these cases, the information on Bianchi was either evaluated as unimportant, cleared with no additional follow-up, or lost among the thousands of tips given to police during late 1977 and 1978.

The task force formed in November 1977 grew to involve 130 officers assigned full-time from three police agencies at the height of their investigation in early 1978. The size of the task force is reported to have created internal communication and coordination problems among its members, who were working around the clock to solve the murders. Of possibly more importance is the fact that the three police agencies were physically separated, working in different facilities, working their own clue tips separately, and providing only summary information which was computerized without cross-referencing capability (F. Salerno, personal communication, August 30, 1985). Establishing linkages and common elements from all this data that was collected, transmitted, and stored in this manner became a difficult task.

No patterns to Henry Lee Lucas's homicides were known to have been identified prior to his arrest and subsequent confessions, except for those homicides occurring between 1978 and 1980 along Interstate 35 from Austin, Texas to the Texas-Oklahoma border north of Dallas, which Lucas is strongly suspected of having committed. A law enforcement conference was held to discuss these murders and share information among the various Texas jurisdictions involved.

The Lucas Task Force was formed after Lucas had been arrested and began confessing to the murders. Four major conferences in Texas, Louisiana, and California were held specifically to discuss Lucas and his killings. All of these efforts were, however, after the fact (see Egger, 1985).

In the Bundy and Gacy cases the police responded to a number of reports on missing persons, most of them in their teens. While responding to reports on missing young persons in a routine and perfunctory manner does not necessarily relate to linkage blindness, as defined, it does suggest the unwillingness of the police to make an effort to look for linkages among missing reports when they are considered routine, assumed to be reports of runaways, not really a law enforcement problem, and not potentially life-threatening. A similar problem is apparent in the Lucas case, although not well documented.

The Bundy and Lucas cases provide some examples of local and state agencies not sharing information or assisting one another. In the Bundy case there were numerous examples of sharing across local and state jurisdictions. However, there were at least two instances of a refusal to share information, seek assistance from another agency, or cooperate with an investigation. The Lucas case represents the lack of sharing or coordination at a macro level, across numerous states as well as local jurisdictions. The difference here is that no patterns were identified to require interagency or interstate cooperation. However, the lack of such cooperation or mechanism with which to communicate means that the patterns, identifiable in some cases on a large geographic scale, were not identified until after his arrest.

In the Gacy and Lucas cases all coordinated responses to their killings were after the fact. No patterns to Lucas's criminal behavior were identified until after his arrest. The police in the Gacy case did finally begin to discern a pattern in his behavior, but only after 33 deaths.

In the Hillside and Bundy cases, police responded with a multi-jurisdictional task force operation. Both were delayed responses to a problem, with Seattle being the more delayed. Neither task force had adequate automated cross-referencing capability. In the Hillside case, the task force was also so decentralized that the problem of coordinating and sharing their information was undoubtedly magnified rather than reduced.

The subjectivity of hindsight is not necessarily a fair or reliable measure of the effectiveness or efficiency of the numerous law enforcement agencies responding to these four serial murderers. Also, an after-the-fact assessment when all the facts are known, combined with recommendations beginning with phrases such as "They should have," or "If they had only," do not substantiate a cause and effect relationship and may facilitate very little change in the present intra- and inter-law enforcement communications. However, if the occurrences of linkage blindness found in the police response to these serial murderers are representative of the differing levels and degrees of this problem, workable solutions emerge and are the next logical step.

LINKAGE BLINDNESS: AN ANALYSIS

Interorganizational relations within the criminal justice system emerged as a major policy issue in the late 1960s and early 1970s. Recommendations of national commissions during this period attest to this concern.

In 1967, the President's Commission on Law Enforcement and the Administration of Justice recommended more cooperation between criminal justice agencies at the local level.

In 1969, the National Commission on the Cause and Prevention of Violence called for local jurisdictions to establish criminal justice coordinating councils.

In 1973, the National Advisory Commission on Criminal Justice Standards and Goals acclaimed those local areas which had adopted local criminal justice councils, then further recommended all major metropolitan areas consider adopting this criminal justice linkage model. (Johnson, 1977, pp. 5–6)

Gray and Williams (1980) define coordination as the planned and self-conscious interdependence of two or more organizations. They note that coordination of functional and jurisdictional elements is an agreed goal of the Omnibus Crime Control and Safe Streets Act of 1969 as amended (p. 138). However, neither the three commissions referred to above, nor the Safe Streets Act, refers specifically to coordination and communication between separate law enforcement agencies for the purpose of sharing information on unsolved crimes. The emphasis in these commission reports and legislation is on the communication and coordination among components of the criminal justice system (police, prosecution, courts, and corrections), and not on the interagency relations of law enforcement agencies.

Most references in the literature to the lack of communication, coordination, or networking among law enforcement agencies attribute this problem to the decentralized nature and local control of U.S. policing. Vollmer concluded in 1936 that American peace officers employed by various units of government operated under a highly decentralized plan of organization with virtually no coordination among these governmental units (Vollmer, 1936, p. 236). Bruce Smith (1960) makes a similar observation:

There is therefore no such thing in the United States as a police system, nor even a set of police systems within any reasonably accurate sense of the term. Our so-called systems are mere collections of police units having some similarity of authority, organization, or jurisdiction; but they lack any systematic relationship to each other. (pp. 20–21)

V. A. Leonard (1980) discussed governmental fragmentation and the police:

The American system of government is based on a political philosophy of decentralized power and local control. As a result, governmental structures, including police agencies, have proliferated and often overlap one another. Semi-autonomous governments (for example, towns, villages, cities, and the like) have established a wide variety of police agencies with differing formal structures and functions. (p. 11)

In discussing the organizational scale of U.S. law enforcement, Bayley (1977) stated:

The United States has the most decentralized police system in the world. Bruce Smith's famous figure is that there are 40,000 separate police forces in the United States. A more accurate figure may be 25,000. The United States does not really have a system, in the sense of development in accord with a considered plan; it has abutting and overlapping jurisdictions predicated on separate units of government. Like Topsy, the American police just grew. The strength of this tradition has been seen recently in the prevalence of the slogan "Support your local police." (p. 232)

Colton (1978) referred to the fragmented nature of law enforcement work:

Although there are federal police services (e.g., the Federal Bureau of Investigation, the Secret Service, etc.) the guiding principle in the United States is that police work is generally a local function and that recruiting, training, and levels of compensation are provided by local control. (p. 8)

In discussing why U.S. police operate differently from their counterparts in England and France, James Q. Wilson (1978) stated:

The essential problem is that whereas other nations have either a national police force (as does France) or at least a single police force for each city (as does England), police responsibilities in the United States are divided among local, state, and federal authorities, each with a constitutionally distinct basis for existence. Federalism, in short, creates a system of different and even rival police organizations sharing powers over common problems. (p. 58)

In advocating a regional approach to policing, McCauley (1973) stated:

The demand for local autonomy and "home rule" has created rigid jurisdictional limitations. Traditionally, today's law enforcement officer has authority only within the confines of his territorial jurisdiction. Likewise, the responsibility for maintaining public peace and order is esoterically funneled, thus effecting a condition whereby law enforcement and the "national crime problem" are viewed as local problems. The implication, then, is that crime must be prevented and controlled primarily at the local levels of government. (p. 1)

Thibault, Lynch and McBride (1985) state that there is an abundance of police forces in this country due to the federal system of government and the wish of local communities to have control over their police. As a result, they find certain organizational realities in U.S. policing today:

1. Active competition between police organizations for calls, resources, and, at times, personnel.

2. De facto spheres of influence arranged by formal and informal agreements between agencies. For instance, while the state police have statewide jurisdiction, many will normally not answer calls in a village that has a police department; the village police, in the same light, will not go outside municipal limits except in pursuit of an offender.

3. Informal relationships, usually based upon how well certain officers or agency heads get along, determine the distribution of intelligence information, assistance to other departments during emergencies, and the success or failure of interagency projects. (p. 319)

In addition to the decentralization, fragmentation, or balkanization of police agencies, references in the literature were also found that attributed the problem of linkage blindness to a jealousy or competitiveness among agencies, and in some cases, among individual officers. Alpert (1984) cited professional jealousy as a hindrance to interagency cooperation. He stated:

Although investigations are an integral part of police work, the organization of detectives and other personnel can interfere with good police work. For example, if both a police department and the district (or state) attorney's office have investigators, professional jealousy and the desire to receive credit for an arrest may hinder cooperation. If more than one jurisdiction is involved, whether it be a city, a county, or a state and a federal one, professional jealousy may be harmful to effective and efficient law enforcement. (p. 45)

In determining critical problems facing smaller police agencies, McCauley (1973) said that "interdepartmental conflicts and jealousies inhibit coordination and cooperation" (p. 4). He also noted, "Cooperation between state and local police is not always genuine" (p. 229). McCauley (1973) believed this spurious cooperation is a product of status manifestation due to the differential compensation, standards, equipment and working conditions between state and local police agencies.

Bruce Smith (1960) argued that the competition among law enforcement agencies results from personalities and leadership style. He stated:

The relationship between the varied types of police forces is difficult to explore in a system fashion. Partly it rests upon the personalities of the chief figures in the departments involved. As between forces in such specialized fields as narcotics suppression and liquor enforcement there is intense rivalry, based upon competition for informants and prestige. Numerous department heads imagine that interagency rivalry will develop a spirit among their own subordinates: rivalry thus becoming a device for leadership. (p. 23)

Strecher (1957) referred to both fragmentation and competitiveness among law enforcement agencies as contributing to coordination and communication problems. In his case study of the well-known Sam Shepard murder case of 1954 in the Cleveland, Ohio metropolitan area, Strecher (1957) found that the administrative deficiencies in the investigation of Marilyn Shepard's murder occurred due to the jurisdictional overlapping and interagency rivalry of the law enforcement agencies involved. Strecher stated:

The reaction of each of the assisting officials cognizant of the interagency rivalry and the distribution of legal power among rival officials, was to hasten into the investigative activity, assuming as large a role as possible without entirely supplanting any other organization. It is problematical, even if one competent official had assumed total responsibility for the inquiry, whether he could have elicited the cooperation of rival officials or their personnel. (p. 115)

Robert Daley (1983), a writer and former police commissioner of the New York City Police Department commented on the jealousy, competitiveness, and territoriality of police officers in a recent work of fiction, which for many, is fact disguised as fiction:

Like politicians they fought over jurisdiction, over protocol. Like actors they fought for credit for a headline. Given the chance to make a major arrest, to break an important case, they were willing, figuratively speaking, to destroy each other. (pp. 125–26)

Law enforcement personnel deal in secrets every day. Indeed their business relied on secrets almost exclusively. Which was not to say they were good at keeping them. Juicy tidbits were revealed to girl friends, to barmen and to the press almost as a matter of habit. Secrets were kept habitually—and with an almost religious fervor—only from each other. (p. 283)

Robert Keppel, who was involved with the Ted Bundy investigation in Seattle, Washington, and a consultant to the current Green River killings task force, found evidence of direct and intentional resistance to cooperation and coordination among police agencies. After trying to link serial killings in Seattle with murders in other locales, Keppel discovered some police agencies wanted no part of a serial murder investigation. Keppel stated, "I've had experience where police departments say, 'you've got your problems there in the big city. Stay away from us' " (*Newsweek*, Nov. 26, 1984, p. 106).

Forensic investigative services provided to many law enforcement jurisdictions, particularly in rural areas of this country, can create difficulties. The lack of access by small rural police agencies to qualified forensic investigative support services causes them to rely on state or large police agencies for these services, which must be allocated to many geographic areas. In addition, the medical examiner or coroner is frequently an elected official who is not a forensic pathologist. This problem of forensic support is further exacerbated by a lack of standardized procedures in many agencies for the collection and processing of physical evidence.

Structural dimensions of the typical law enforcement agency's organizational arrangement is another factor contributing to linkage blindness. The phenomenon of single-complaint policing rather than problem-based responses such as a problem-oriented approach (see Goldstein, 1979) results in police patrol units reacting to situations without identifying multiple situations of a similar nature as a problem or pattern to be resolved. The same is true for the organization and resource allocation of the criminal investigation function. Here, the "case" basis of investigative assignment also precludes a rapid identification of a developing crime pattern.

As indicated earlier, law enforcement's response, or lack thereof, to reports of missing persons fails to create the necessary information from which a readily identified pattern may emerge. While this has recently been changing in many agencies across the country, there are still many agencies unwilling to respond actively to reports of missing persons or treat them as serious and potentially violent criminal acts.

Linkage blindness also frequently occurs due to the inability of policing organizations to deal with large amounts of information. Brooks et al. (1988) found that historically,

the Achilles' heel of most prolonged serial murder investigations has not been that of the investigation function per se, but the viability of the law enforcement agencies involved to manage the massive amounts of information received and generated.

In most serial murder investigations, the vast amount of information and its rate of accumulation quickly exceeds human capabilities for effective management. While most governmental agencies in large metropolitan areas have installed computerized operations to increase the efficiency of their services, law enforcement agencies have, for the most part, been far behind the cutting edge of this development. Computer-assisted dispatching and automated records systems are commonplace today in many agencies; however, the development of computerized information systems to support investigations has lagged far behind. With the development of VICAP at the national level and HALT-like systems at the state level, the acceptance and utilization of these important tools, particularly for cross-jurisdictional information sharing, remains far from the normal operations of law enforcement agencies.

Further, law enforcement agencies are generally accustomed to operating as self-contained units specifically devoted to responding to service to the public within their respective jurisdictional boundaries. The organizational structure hierarchically designed for vertical (downward and upward) communication is poorly suited to communication and coordination with those agencies outside their jurisdiction.

Linkage blindness is the real and ever-present cause of law enforcement's inability to respond to serial murder in a timely and effective manner. As indicated earlier, linkage blindness has been defined as the lack of sharing or coordination of investigative information and the lack of adequate networking among law enforcement agencies and law enforcement officers in this country. Numerous references to the communication problem have been directly or indirectly referred to by others. Further, this problem has been documented above in the four well-known serial murder cases of Bundy, Gacy, the "Hillside Strangler," and Lucas.

In the day-to-day operations of law enforcement agencies in this country, little serious attention or resource allocation has been given to interagency communication, cooperation, or coordination of the criminal investigation function. Today the chances of linkage blindness occurring within the law enforcement community are very good due to the decentralized and fragmented nature of policing, resulting in thousands of law enforcement jurisdictions. The regionalization of policing services as well as the consolidation of police agencies have met with only limited success in this country.

Jealousy, a sense of interagency competitiveness, and "turf" battles only add to the problem of linkage blindness, facilitating a systemic myopia. Limited forensic services with coroners ill-prepared to support criminal investigations is another contributor.

Structural factors such as single-complaint policing and "case" based investigative assignments within hierarchically designed levels of control in most police agencies greatly inhibit interagency communication and increase the probability for linkage blindness to occur.

Law enforcement's response to reports of missing persons, although currently changing, has also clouded the lenses of many agencies in their view of these cases and evolving crime patterns. Fortunately, many such reports are beginning to be viewed with increased awareness of their potential criminality.

Untimely and ineffective information management has also contributed to increased instances of linkage blindness. The inability to support criminal investigation with effective information management will greatly inhibit multijurisdictional investigations of serial murder.

By the late 1990s, most police departments will have access to computer services (Bennett, 1989). Access is, however, only the first step. Standardized formats for the information and data processed by these services must be the next step. Failing this, the benefits of this automation will be wiped out due to the incompatibility of data formats, thus exacerbating the problem of linkage blindness.

REFERENCES

Alpert. G. P. (1984). *The American system of criminal justice*. Beverly Hills, CA: Sage.

Barnes, M. (producer and director). (1984). "The mind of a murderer." Videotape. Washington, DC: Public Broadcasting Service.

Bayley, D. H. (1977). "The limits of police reform." In David H. Bayley (ed.), *Police and society*. Beverly Hills, CA: Sage, pp. 219–36.

Bennett, G. (1989). *Crime-warps: The future of crime in America* (rev. edn.). New York: Anchor Books.

Biondi, R. and Hecox, W. (1988). *All his father's sins*. Rocklin, CA: Prima.

Brooks, P. R., Devine, M. J., Green, T. J., Hart, B. L., and Moore, M. D. (1988). *Multi-agency investigative team manual*. Washington, DC: U.S. Department of Justice.

Colton, K. W. (1978). *Police computer technology*. Lexington, MA: Lexington Books.

Daley, R. (1983). *The dangerous edge*. New York: Dell.

Darrach, B. and Norris, J. (1984). "An American Tragedy." *Life Magazine 7* (8), 58–74.

Egger, S. A. (1985). *Serial murder and the law enforcement response*. Unpublished

dissertation, College of Criminal Justice, Sam Houston State University, Huntsville, Texas.

Goldstein, H. (1977). "Improving policing: A problem-oriented approach." *Crime and Delinquency, 25*, April, 236–58.

Gray, V. and Williams G. (1980). *The organizational politics of criminal justice*. Lexington, MA: Lexington Books.

Johnson, K. W. (1977). *Police interagency relations: Some research findings*. Beverly Hills, CA: Sage.

Keppel, R. D. (1989). *Serial murder: Future implications for police investigations*. Cincinnati, OH: Anderson.

Keyes, D. (1986). *Unveiling Claudia: A true story of beauty, madness and murder*. New York: Bantam.

Larsen, R. W. (1980). *Bundy: The deliberate stranger*. Englewood Cliffs, NJ: Prentice-Hall.

Leonard, V. A. (1980). *Fundamentals of law enforcement*. St. Paul, MN: West Publishing Co.

Levin, J. and Fox, J. A. (1985). *Mass Murder*. New York: Plenum.

Linedecker, C. L. (1980). *The man who killed boys*. New York: St. Martin's Press.

McCauley, R. P. (1973). "A plan for the implementation of a statewide regional police system." Unpublished doctoral dissertation, Sam Houston State University, Huntsville, Texas.

Norris, J. (1988). *Serial killers: The growing menace*. New York: Doubleday.

O'Toole, L. and Montjoy, R. S. (1984). "Interorganizational policy implementation: A theoretical perspective." *Public Administration Review*, November/December, 491–503.

Rule, A. (1980). *The stranger beside me*. New York: W. W. Norton.

Schwartz, T. (1981). *The Hillside Strangler: A murderer's mind*. New York: Doubleday & Co.

"Serial murders: Another forensic challenge." (1985). *Forensic Science International, 27*, 135–44.

Smith, B. (1960). *Police systems in the United States* (rev. 2nd edn., Smith, B., Jr.). New York: Harper and Row.

Strecher, V. G. (1957). "An administrative analysis of a multiple-agency criminal investigation within the suburban district of a large metropolitan area." Unpublished master's thesis, Michigan State University, East Lansing, Michigan.

Sullivan, T. and Markew, P. T. (1983). *Killer clown: The John Wayne Gacy murders*. New York: Grosset & Dunlap.

Thibault, E. A., Lynch, L. M., and McBride, R. B. (1985). *Proactive police management*. Englewood Cliffs, NJ: Prentice-Hall, Inc.

Vollmer, A. (1936). *The police and modern society*. Berkeley, CA: Regents of University of California.

Wambaugh, J. (1989). *The blooding*. New York: William Morrow.

Wilson, J. Q. (1978). *The investigators: Managing FBI and narcotics agents*. New York: Basic Books, Inc.

Winn, S. and Merrill, D. (1980). *Ted Bundy: The killer next door*. New York: Bantam.

9

Taxonomy of Law Enforcement Responses to Serial Murder

STEVEN A. EGGER

Murder has traditionally been a crime in which police show a high clearance rate. However, part of the well-kept secret of this success is that a criminal homicide is a relatively easy crime to investigate and solve. Once the victim is identified, the investigator simply begins to reduce the number of associates, friends, and relatives of the victim who have a high probability of having committed the crime. In most cases, the killing will have been committed by persons in one of these categories. About 66 percent of murderers are in custody within 24 hours. If murders are not solved within 48 hours, the chance of solving the case and apprehending the killer drops markedly (Danto, 1982, p. 7). A study of Memphis murders from 1974 to 1978 found that all those involving persons related to one another were solved within 24 hours; 84 percent were solved in a day if the persons were known to each other but were not relatives; and only 69 percent were solved if they were strangers (Atkinson, 1984, p. A-14).

Review of *Uniform Crime Reports* for the last 20 years reveals that murder and non-negligent manslaughter have numerically increased by 300 percent, and the rate per 100,000 population has doubled during this period. The most dramatic change during this period is that police clearance rates for this crime have dropped

Expanded from ''The Investigative Challenge of Serial Murder'' by Steven A. Egger in *Criminal Investigation: Essays, Readings and Cases* edited by James N. Gilbert, © 1990 Merrill Publishing Company, Columbus, Ohio.

from 93 percent in 1962 to 70 percent in 1987. Currently, over one-quarter of all murders are not solved by law enforcement. This drop is generally attributed to the dramatic increase in stranger-to-stranger homicides. Wilbanks (1984) found an increase in stranger murders in Dade County, Florida between 1917 and 1988. In the last seven-year period, murders with unknown motives have increased by 270 percent on the national level. For this same period, murder has increased approximately 12 percent. It appears that police effectiveness in apprehending murderers has been substantially reduced in part because of the dramatic rise in seemingly motiveless murders and stranger-to-stranger murders. While police today may be solving a greater percentage of these types of murders, the clearance rate for serial murder comprises most of the unsolved category.

Luckenbill (1984) notes that the criminal justice system treats murder as a high priority offense more likely to be cleared by arrest than most other crimes. However, the relatively high clearance rate for homicide may be due to the nature of the crime itself, rather than, or in addition to, a system priority. Skogan and Antunes (1979) account for this high clearance rate by noting that most killings involved people who know one another. They state, "If a crime were committed by someone known to the victim, the circle of investigation would encompass only one person, and the job of the police would be reduced to finding the suspect" (p. 221). However, as Sanders (1977) states, "without some informative link in the more primary relationships, an investigation is opened to a larger and less manageable universe of inquiry, making the task of identifying the suspect that much more difficult" (p. 178).

Robert Keppel states that catching multiple murderers "is very, very difficult. Police departments aren't organized to catch serial killers. They're organized to catch burglars and robbers and to intervene in family fights" (Lindsey, 1984, p. 1). The crimes of serial murderers are more difficult to solve than the far more numerous murders in which a connection can be found between victim and killer, as noted above. Pierce Brooks, formerly a homicide detective and FBI consultant, states, "They [serial murderers] are very mobile, they don't leave a great body of physical evidence, and they kill strangers" (Garland, 1984, p. 1). Levin and Fox (1985) state, " [S]ome time may pass before law enforcement investigators realize that a series of seemingly unrelated homicides is actually the work of a single individual—by that time, he may be long gone" (p. 232). There is a greater suspicion today that many unexplained homicides are committed by serial murderers crossing city, county, and state lines. Terrence Green, former head of Oakland, California police department's homicide division, maintains that, "Every police department in the United States has dealt with a serial murder, perhaps without realizing it" (Garland, 1984, p. 1).

According to Wilmer (1970):

As the population continues to grow and as the modern criminal becomes more mobile, it is reasonable to expect that the probability of an average policeman missing a piece of information potentially of great value, by misinterpreting it, will continue to increase.

Of the different types of information obtained during a homicide investigation, each item can, in principle, alter the level of uncertainty regarding a pool of potential suspects. (p. 26)

Technically, the unsolved murder is never closed. Other murders occur and "old" cases receive reduced priorities. Resources are scarce and must be allocated on a cost-effective basis. Higher solvability factors as well as currency of the event lead to higher priorities and allocation of investigative manpower. When unsolved murders are identified as part of a serial sequence, either by confessions of an apprehended serial murderer or through the occurrence of a number of similar murders in a relatively small or contiguous geographical area, the police must respond. A documentation of the various ways in which law enforcement has responded to serial murder can be grouped into several categories: holding conferences with involved or potentially involved agencies; acting as a clearinghouse of information on the serial crimes; the formation of a task force for the coordination of multiple jurisdiction investigations; the uses of an outside investigative consultant team; or the use of psychological profiling. All of these responses are, of course, after the fact and reactive in nature. A less reactive response, although certainly not preventive in a pure sense, is the development of a centralized point of analysis from which to identify patterns of serial murders as they emerge and to communicate such patterns to the appropriate agencies for necessary and combined action. There are other responses to serial murder used less frequently than the aforementioned categories. These responses include utilizing specially developed computer software programs; geoforensic pattern analysis; and paying an identified serial killer for criminal evidence necessary to locate all his murder victims. Each of these categories of law enforcement response to serial murder is described in this chapter.

Prior to our description and analysis of various responses by law enforcement to serial murder we must, however, restate the major conclusion of Chapter 1 and, in effect, the premise of this book. Our systematic search of the current literature and research on serial murder reveals that very little of scholarly substance and empirical knowledge has been developed on the phenomenon of serial murder. Without such an empirically validated knowledge base, law enforcement's response to the serial murder is very frequently unsuccessful and, when successful, more a product of chance than of a sophisticated and carefully planned approach. The statement by Jenkins (1988) in his description of the status of research on serial murder—"the very rudimentary state of our knowledge of serial murder, even when our access to the facts of particular cases is extensive (p. 2)"—should be a warning to those who construe the following taxonomy as an indictment of law enforcement's investigative skills. In other words, those armed with the knowledge of this taxonomy and its apparent aggregate failures should temper the ease with which they are too quick to criticize.

The following list delineates each response of this taxonomy described in the remainder of this chapter:

1. conferences
2. information clearinghouses
3. task forces
4. investigative consultant teams
5. psychological profiling
6. centralized investigative network (international, national, and statewide efforts)
7. computerized analysis system (not included in 1–6)
8. geographical pattern analysis
9. paying a serial murderer for evidence

Conferences

Law enforcement conferences are almost a tradition in police work. They are normally convened on an annual basis by professional associations to socialize, share new techniques and technology, and generally be brought up to date on the particular world of policing germane to the specialization of the attendees or members. Recently, conferences have been convened to address specific problems facing multiple law enforcement jurisdictions and only very recently have such conferences attempted to deal with serial murder. Conferences dealing with serial murder have been of two types: those dealing with numerous unsolved murders, and those responding to the ramifications of the identification and confessions of a serial murderer.

One such conference dealing with numerous unsolved murders was convened at the Texas Department of Public Safety Training Center in Austin, Texas, on October 28–30, 1980. The discovery of an unidentified homicide victim found along Interstate 35 near Waco, Texas, and numerous other unsolved homicides occurring along this highway in a three-year period was the catalyst for the conference. The conference was requested by Jim Boutwell, sheriff of Williamson County, Texas, who stated, "We have a killer (or killers) still on the loose, traveling I-35. We know that the M.O. is not the same in all murders. Guns, knives, and strangulation have been utilized in killing these victims. Some may have been raped; some haven't" (J. Boutwell to F. Hacker, personal communication, August 29, 1980). Representatives from 32 cities, counties, and political jurisidictions in Texas attended this conference and 19 new leads to unsolved area crimes were developed as a result of the information shared among law enforcement officers (Personal communication, Texas Telesystems, 1980). Boutwell stated four years later, "If we'd only known about Henry [Henry Lee Lucas] back then!" (James Boutwell, personal communication, July 18, 1984).

Other such conferences have been held in response to the Green River killings in the Seattle, Washington area (1983); the "Michigan Murders" in the Ann Arbor-Ypsilanti, Michigan area (1968); and the "Hillside Strangler" case in the Los Angeles, California area (1979).

An example of conferences convened in response to an identified and confessed serial murderer, were the two conferences organized by the Monroe, Louisiana police department in October 1983 and January 1984. In a direct response to the arrest and subsequent confessions of serial murderer Henry Lee Lucas in Texas, more than 150 investigators from 24 states met during these two conferences and compared notes on unsolved murders in their area and were briefed by the Texas Rangers regarding Lucas's known travels and modus operandi. Similar conferences were held in 1984 in Wisconsin and Georgia focusing primarily on Henry Lee Lucas and unsolved murders in those states (Gest, 1984; Lindsey, 1984).

A more recent example was the conference on December 10, 1984, organized by Florida agencies following the arrest of Robert Joe Long, who was charged with eight counts of sexual battery, nine counts of kidnapping, one count of aggravated assault, seven counts of murder, and one count of first degree murder in the Tampa, Florida area. Hillsborough County, Florida sheriff's office, Tampa police department, the Florida Department of Law Enforcement officers, the Georgia Bureau of Investigation and the Regional Organized Crime Information Center in Nashville, Tennessee, attended. Information was shared on Robert Long and unsolved murders and rapes in Florida and Georgia that could possibly be attributed to Long (*ROCIC Bulletin*, 01–85, p. 13).

Information Clearinghouse

A response similar to the conference approach is that of the information clearinghouse. Again, such a response may occur due to the apprehension of a serial murderer or due to a number of unsolved murders involving multiple law enforcement jurisdictions. An example of the former, on a national scale, was the Lucas Homicide Task Force in the state of Texas. Formed by authorization of the governor of Texas in November 1983, the task force was comprised of Texas Rangers, the Texas Department of Public Safety and the Williamson County sheriff's office. This task force operated until April 1985. This organization, while entitled a task force, performed the function of an information clearinghouse by communicating with law enforcement agencies requesting information on Lucas, coordinating interviews of Lucas conducted by law enforcement investigators from numerous states, compiling and distributing information on Lucas to requesting agencies, conducting preliminary interviews of Lucas for agencies that sent investigative information by mail, and providing for the security of Lucas. In addition, the Texas Rangers directly investigated 16 homicides committed in Texas in which Lucas was a suspect and assisted in numerous other investigations within the state in accordance with their authorized state powers as peace officers. Between November 11, 1983 and April 12, 1985, approximately 600 different law enforcement agencies had interviewed Lucas. Total interviews of Lucas were conducted by 1,000 different people from 40 states and Canada. By the end of February 1985, a total of 210 homicide cases had been cleared by the task force, at that time 189 of which were directly attributed to Lucas (B. Prince, personal communication, May 21, 1985). A more detailed description of this task force is documented in the Lucas case study in Chapter 7.

A more current example of an information clearinghouse may be found in Tennessee. The Tennessee Bureau of Investigation began serving as an information clearinghouse on April 24, 1985, for law enforcement agencies from five different states (Pennsylvania, Kentucky, Tennessee, Mississippi, and Arkansas) and the FBI in response to eight unsolved homicides of unidentified females occurring since October 1983. The clearinghouse provided information to all jurisdictions and was the catalyst for a network among them (*Tennessean*, April 25, 1984, p. 1).

Task Force

Gilbert (1983) contends that, due to the increase of stranger criminal homicide, police administrators must seek nontraditional methods of case reduction such as aggressive patrol activity and interdepartmental task forces (pp. 162–63). However, the formation of a task force is one of the most traditional methods of responding to a multiple jurisdictional crime investigation.

In the early summer of 1969 a task force comprised of the Michigan state police, Ann Arbor police department, Ypsilanti police department, Eastern Michigan University police, and the Washtenaw County sheriff's office was established in Ann Arbor, Michigan, by the Washtenaw County prosecutor's office in response to six unsolved homicides of young females that had occurred in the county in the last two and one-half years. On July 28, 1969, a seventh young female homicide victim was found and on July 30, 1969, the governor of Michigan ordered the Michigan state police to take charge of the investigations, "to concentrate and coordinate the efforts of all state and local agencies" (*Detroit News*, July 30, 1969, p. 1). John Norman Collins was arrested on August 1, 1969, for the murder of the seventh homicide victim and subsequently convicted. Homicide Captain Daniel C. Myre, Michigan state police, who participated in this task force and later directed it after the governor's order, refers to a task force as a crime center in his book *Death Investigation* (1974). Myre states:

The investigation of a major crime sometimes requires various police departments to unite and form a single investigative unit with a central headquarters. Such major crime investigative centers are only as good as their organization and information retrieval systems. To eliminate duplication of effort and insure that evidence is handled properly by all investigators, a major crime center must have a definite command structure and well-defined rules of procedure. (p. 153)

Levin and Fox (1985) state that the usual law enforcement response in handling difficult investigations is to form a task force, which they argue "has never proven to be overly successful" (pp. 168, 169). The task force in the "Hillside

Strangler'' case was, for Levin and Fox (1985), too large and decentralized. They contend that had Bianchi not killed on his own in Washington, the killings would have never been solved. ''Until his arrest in Washington, however, the Los Angeles Task Force had been stumped for a year and had been labeled a total failure'' (Levin and Fox, 1985, p. 169).

In July 1980 Chief Lee Brown announced the formation of a task force to look into the problem of missing and murdered children in the Atlanta, Georgia area. The original task force consisted of five police officers (Dettlinger and Prough, 1983, p. 68). This task force effort, which was to grow a great deal larger, eventually resulted in the arrest and conviction of Wayne Williams for murdering two of 28 homicide victims and suspected as being responsible for the deaths of many of the other victims. Chet Dettlinger, formerly a police planner with the Kentucky Crime Commission and a former assistant to Atlanta's chief of police, is extremely critical of the Atlanta Task Force, particularly for its failure to place some homicide victims on a list of victims related to task force efforts and their analysis of the geographic distribution of the homicides (Dettlinger and Prough, 1983). Levin and Fox (1985) are also critical of the Atlanta Task Force for not being formed earlier and for its failure to consider the geographic evidence in a broader context.

Levin and Fox (1985) are also critical of the ''Boston Strangler'' task force, which for them was poorly focused, with techniques as diverse as traditional forensics and the use of psychics. They state: ''The capture of Albert DeSalvo actually resulted from his arrest by the Cambridge Police for a breaking and entering and an assault, rather than for one of the stranglings'' (Levin and Fox, 1985, p. 171).

Darrach and Norris (1984) contrast the Atlanta Task Force with the Green River Task Force, set up to investigate the killings of over 30 young women found in the general vicinity of the Green River in the Seattle, Washington area. They state:

Everything that went wrong in the Atlanta investigation has been going right in Seattle. The Green River Task Force, set up to investigate the killings, now includes 30 talented detectives and is clearly one of the best organized, least politicized and most effective units in the country. Protected by a strong sheriff, the group has shrewdly controlled the release of information to prevent hysteria and keep the killer guessing. (Darrach and Norris, 1984, p. 64)

However, as of November 1988, no arrests have been made by the Green River Task Force.

Past experience in multi-jurisdictional task forces reveals the crucial need for a well-managed and coordinated response. To meet this need, specific guidelines in the form of a manual—the *Multi-Agency Investigative Team Manual* (MAIT)— was developed as a result of a National Institute of Justice grant of funds to the Criminal Justice Center, Sam Houston State University in 1986. This manual resulted from the documentation and synthesis of a two-week conference of experienced serial murder investigators held in August 1986.

While the MAIT manual was seen as a disappointment for some because of its traditional approach to organization and management and its "cookbook" approach to the problem, there are indeed some particular points worth high-lighting.

The serial murderer often selects his victim from an urban area but disposes of the body in the privacy of a rural area, crossing jurisdictions in the process (p. 1). . . . Law en-forcement agencies are generally accustomed to operating as self-contained units and often do not have the organizational structure, personnel or inclination for coordinating with other agencies (p. 7). . . . Historically, the Achilles' heel of most prolonged serial murder investigations has not been that of the investigative function per se, but the viability of the law enforcement agencies involved to:

• Manage the massive amounts of information received and generated.

• Effectively communicate internally or externally with other involved agencies (p. 23). . . .

With most serial murder investigations, the amount of information and the rate of ac-cumulation far exceeds human capabilities for management (p. 27). . . . Case coordina-tion, review and analysis provides an opportunity to examine all investigative activities so that leads are not overlooked or links between them missed. (p. 49)

Investigative Consultants

In October 1980 the late chief of police of Stamford, Connecticut, Victor Cizanckas, contacted Commissioner Lee Brown, Department of Public Safety, Atlanta, Georgia, and offered his assistance regarding the missing and murdered children investigation in Atlanta. Specifically, Chief Cizanckas offered to loan Atlanta one of his skilled investigators with experience in a similar case. Further discussions ensued between Cizanckas, Brown, and the Police Executive Re-search Forum, to which both men belonged. As a result of these discussions, the Police Executive Research Forum agreed to underwrite a cooperative effort of providing a team of qualified investigators with experience to assist in dealing with the Atlanta child killings (Brooks, 1982). The Forum's ultimate goal in providing this investigative consultant team to Atlanta was "in the hope that it would serve as a model and prompt others to undertake similar efforts in the future" (Brooks, 1982, pp. v, vi).

A group of investigators was selected for the team by contacting homicide detectives in police departments from all regions of the country and asking them to name investigators in their area with expertise to deal with the Atlanta problem. Five investigators were selected from this nominated pool. Pierce Brooks, retired police chief of Eugene, Oregon, and formerly a homicide investigator with the Los Angeles, California police department, was selected as the team leader. Other members were Detective Alex Smith, Oakland, California; Detective Gil

Hill, Detroit, Michigan; Detective George Mayer, Stamford, Connecticut; and Detective Charles Nanton, New York City. On November 11, 1980, this team traveled to Atlanta and served in the capacity of investigative consultants for two weeks. The Police Executive Research Forum paid the $7,000 cost for this team to travel and live in Atlanta.

The responsibility of this investigative consultant team was

to come to Atlanta as consultants to the task force investigators and share with them any insights they might have by virtue of their experience in working complex cases in their respective jurisdictions. To that end, they were expected to review the case files and interact with the investigators responsible for the investigation involving the missing and murdered children. (Brooks, 1982, p. iii)

Commissioner Brown noted that the team's role "was akin to lawyers asking for consultation from other lawyers or doctors receiving consultation from other doctors—in short, asking for a second opinion" (Brooks, 1982, p. iii).

Brooks (1982) notes that the team could be considered the experimental product of established methods of interagency assistance: the formal mutual aid agreement and the informal one-on-one exchange of information between detectives. While the use of this team did not directly result in a successful resolution to the Atlanta homicides, Brooks states:

The November 1980 venture of the Investigative Consultant Team (ICT) in Atlanta is believed to be the first time police investigators, all from separate departments, were invited to participate as consultants in a major criminal investigation in a city other than their own. (p. 6)

While the utilization of psychiatrists, psychologists, forensic pathologists, and even psychics has been adopted by police as outside consultants to difficult criminal investigations, the participation of officers from other agencies not involved in the investigation was a bold and, for many, creative step by the Atlanta police.

Psychological Profiling

Another response to serial murder has been the use of psychological profiling in an attempt to provide investigators with more information on the serial murderer who is yet to be identified. Hazelwood and Douglas (1980) define a psychological profile as

an educated attempt to provide investigative agencies with specific information as to the type of individual who committed a certain crime. . . . A profile is based on characteristic patterns or factors of uniqueness that distinguishes certain individuals from the general population. (p. 5)

Reiser (1982) states:

> The arcane art of psychological profiling of suspects in bizarre and multiple murder cases is actually a variant of psycho-diagnostic assessment and psycho-biography. It involves an amalgam of case evidence, statistical probabilities based on similar cases, available suspect and victim psychodynamics, knowledge of unconscious processes, and interpretation of detectable symbolic communications. The factual materials and speculative possibilities are combined using an inferential-deductive process. (p. 53)

The actual origins of criminal profiling are obscure (Ault and Reese, 1980). However, it is known that during World War II, the Office of Strategic Services (OSS) employed a psychiatrist, William Langer, to profile Adolf Hitler (Ault and Reese, 1980, p. 23). The material assembled by Langer included a psychological description of Hitler's personality, a diagnosis of his condition, and a predictive statement suggesting how Hitler would react to defeat (Pinnizzotto, 1984, p. 32). Furthermore, such cases as the "Boston Strangler" and the "Mad Bomber" of New York City in the 1960s were profiled in a similar manner by Dr. James A. Brussels (Geberth, 1983, p. 399).

The FBI became involved in psychological profiling in 1970, when Agent Howard Teten began developing profiles. Teten was teaching an applied criminology course at the FBI Academy at that time and students from various police departments would bring their criminal cases to him (Porter, 1983). The FBI began formally developing psychological profiles shortly thereafter, for as Ressler et al. (1984) states: "The FBI Agents at the Behavioral Science Unit have been profiling murderers for approximately twelve years" (p. 12). Roger L. Depue, director of the FBI's Behavioral Science Unit, states: "We believe that in most crime scenes, the killer leaves his signature there. If you're sensitized to what these things are, you can construct a profile of the killer" (Kessler, 1984, p. A-16).

Ressler, Burgess, Douglas and Depue (1985) describe psychological profiling as "the process of identifying the gross psychological characteristics of an individual based upon an analysis of the crimes he or she committed and providing a general description of the person, utilizing those traits" (p. 3). Ressler et al. (1982) state that the process normally involves five steps:

1. a comprehensive study of the nature of the criminal act and the types of persons who have committed this offense

2. a thorough inspection of the specific crime scene involved in the case

3. an in-depth examination of the background and activities of the victim(s) and any known suspects

4. a formulation of the probable motivating factors of all parties involved

5. the development of a description of the perpetrator based upon the overt characteristics associated with his/her probable psychological makeup (p. 3).

Swanson, Chamelin and Territo (1984) concisely state the purpose of the psychological profile:

The purpose of the psychological assessment of a crime scene is to produce a profile; that is, to identify and interpret certain items of evidence at the crime scene which would be indicative of the personality type of the individual or individuals committing the crime. The goal of the profiler is to provide enough information to investigators to enable them to limit or better direct their investigations. (pp. 700, 701)

FBI Agent Robert K. Ressler, a member of the profiling team in the Behavioral Science Unit, states:

All people have personality traits that can be more or less identified. But an abnormal person becomes ritualized even more so and there's a pattern in his behavior. Often times, the behavior and the personality are reflected in the crime scene of that individual. ... [B]y studying the crime scene from the psychological standpoint, rather than from the technical, evidence-gathering standpoint, you could recreate the personality of the individual who committed the crime. If the crime scene is abnormal, it would indicate their personality is abnormal. (*Law Enforcement News*, December 22, 1980, p. 7)

Geberth (1983) discusses the utility of psychological profiling:

Psychological profiling is usually productive in crimes where an unknown subject has demonstrated some form of psychopathology in his crime. For example,

• sadistic torture in sexual assaults
• evisceration
• postmortem slashing and cutting
• motiveless fire setting
• lust and mutilation murders
• ritualistic crimes
• rapes

Practically speaking, in any crime where available evidence indicates a mental, emotional, or personality aberration by an unknown perpetrator, the psychological profile can be instrumental in providing the investigator with information which narrows down the leads. It is the behavior of the perpetrator as evidenced in the crime scene and not the offense per se that determines the degree of suitability of the case profiling. (pp. 400, 401)

Roy Hazelwood, a member of the FBI's profiling team states: "We don't get hung up on why the killer does the things he does. What we're interested in is that he does it, and that he does it in a way that leads us to him" (Porter, 1983, p. 6).

In 1982 the FBI Behavioral Science Unit received a grant from the National Institute of Justice, U.S. Department of Justice to expand their profiling capabilities by building a file of taped interviews with convicted murderers (Porter, 1983; Ressler et al., 1984). As of September 18, 1984, 36 convicted sexual murderers representing solo, serial, and mass murderers had been interviewed (Ressler et al., 1984, p. 5).

The results or evaluations of psychological profiling found in the literature have not been conclusive. Godwin (1978) is very critical of profiling. He characterizes it as dull, tedious, and of little use to the police. He states:

They play a blindman's bluff, groping in all directions in the hope of touching a sleeve. Occasionally they do, but not firmly enough to seize it, for the behaviorists producing them must necessarily deal in generalities and types. But policemen can't arrest a type. They require hard data: names, faces, fingerprints, locations, times, dates. None of which the psychiatrists can offer. (p. 276)

Dr. John Liebert, a Bellevue, Washington psychiatrist and consultant to Seattle's Green River Task Force, is distrustful of psychological profiles put together by police agencies and the FBI. He states, "I think the state of the art [profiling] leaves a lot to be desired" (McCarthy, 1984, p. 1).

Liebert further urges that law enforcement officers involved in a serial murder investigation utilize the services of a psychiatric consultant. He warns against phenomenological generalizations about the murderer and states that "Superficial behavioral scientific profiling that rigidly reduces serial murder to a few observable parameters can lead an investigation astray" (Liebert, 1985, p. 199).

Levin and Fox (1985) characterize psychological profiles as vague and general and thus basically useless in identifying a killer. They state:

As with most things, however, the value and validity of a psychological profile depends mostly on the skills and experience of the profiler. Unlike a psychologist who might consult with police investigators on an occasional, ad hoc basis, a full-time team of FBI agents trained in behavioral sciences as well as law enforcement techniques prepares approximately three hundred criminal profiles a year. Because FBI profilers have extensive experience, they construct the most useful profiles. Unfortunately, this tool, no matter how expertly implemented, is inherently limited in its ability to help solve crimes (p. 174).
... The FBI's own recent evaluation of its profiling efforts, in our minds, underscores the limitations of this approach. A survey of 192 users of these profiles indicated, first, that less than half the crimes for which the profiles had been solicited were eventually solved. Further, in only 17% of these 88 solved cases did the profile help directly to identify the subject. While a "success" rate of 17% of those 88 cases may appear low (and even lower if one includes the unsolved cases), the profiles are not expected, at least in most instances, to solve a case, but simply to provide an additional set of clues in cases found by local police to be unsolvable. Indeed in over three-fourths of the solved cases, the profile did at least help focus the investigation. (p. 175)

Holmes and DeBurger (1988) warn against a trend in law enforcement of contacting federal agencies to assist them in the development profiles. They argue that since federal agencies have little experience in murder cases, rather than the local agencies using a "specialist," it would be far better to train their homicide investigators in the recognition of psychological motives and other characteristics of the unknown killer that can be inferred from the crime scene.

Levin and Fox (1985) also indicate that the profile is intended to be a tool in order to focus in on a range of suspects, rather than pointing precisely to a particular suspect. Campbell (1976) sees intensive investigative work to locate a suspect and find corroborating evidence following the development of a psychological profile, due to its general and non-specific descriptors. Reiser (1982), however, notes that the profile may provide a starting point or focus from which an investigation can proceed.

The FBI itself urges caution in perceiving profiling as an automatic solution to a difficult case. Hazelwood, Ressler, Depue, and Douglas (1987) state:

Profiles have led directly to the solution of a case, but this is the exception rather than the rule, and to expect this will lead to failure in most cases. Rather, a profile will provide assistance to the investigator by focusing the investigation towards suspects possessing the characteristics described. (p. 147)

Psychological profiling is a relatively new tool in criminal investigation and has had some success in assisting in a serial murder investigation. Pinnizzotto (1984) states: "Currently, the Behavioral Science Unit of the Federal Bureau of Investigation is developing a variety of research methods to statistically test for reliability and validity [of profiling]" (p. 37).

West (1987), in his discussion of psychological profiling states: "It can be seen that profiling owes more to experience and imagination than to scientific deduction. All the same, matches between the actual and predicted characteristics of an offender are sometimes very striking" (p. 183).

Geberth (1983) notes that the psychological profile "can be a valuable tool in identifying and pinpointing suspects; however, it must be noted that the profile has its limitations. It should be utilized in conjunction with the sound investigative techniques ordinarily employed at the scene of a homicide" (p. 399).

Most homicide investigators appear to be convinced of the potential value of the psychological profile. Geberth, an experienced homicide investigator of the New York police department, argues that the serial murderer is a type of personality that can be profiled. Geberth (1986) states, "A description of the salient psychological and behavioral characteristics which identify personality and behavioral traits or patterns can be used to classify and distinguish such an individual from the general population" (p. 495).

The Behavioral Science Unit of the FBI is currently developing an artificial intelligence software program to enhance the investigative tool's effectiveness. It should also be noted that recently private vendors have developed software programs for personal computers with an application for psychological profiling referred to as computer-oriented profiling.

Psychological profiling by FBI agents of the Bureau's Behavioral Science Unit has indeed received a great deal of criticism, as noted above. These profiles are not, however, without substantial support. Park Elliott Dietz, a noted forensic psychiatrist and a professor of law, behavioral science, and psychiatry at the University of Virginia, argues that the FBI profiles have no peers. Dietz has stated, "I think I know as much about criminal behavior as any mental-health professional and I don't know as much as the bureau's profiles do" (Michaud, 1986, p. 42).

Centralized Investigative Network

Control is currently law enforcement's only viable strategy in responding to the phenomenon of serial murder. In this sense, control means to identify, locate, and apprehend; identifying means verifying that similar patterns or modi operandi are present, suggesting a serial murder. This usually requires information from different jurisdictional sources. Once this information is collated and the strong suggestion or probability of the serial events is identified, the collator at a central point can then distribute the information, from which a pattern has been determined, to the original sources. These sources, a group of discrete investigative agencies, can then share this information in order to coordinate investigative action. The collator is necessary in order to ensure that a valuable piece of information is not missed (Wilmer, 1970, p. 32). A central point of analysis prevents this from happening. An investigative network is then in a position through state-of-the-art investigative techniques to attempt to locate and apprehend the serial murderer.

Such a centralized investigative network or system is currently operational at the national and state level in the United States, and on a national level in Britain and, to some extent, in Canada. The U.S. network is referred to as the Violent Criminal Apprehension Program (VICAP, spelled VI-CAP until 1984) and is located at the FBI National Academy in Quantico, Virginia, as a component of the National Center for the Analysis of Violent Crime (Conceptual Model, July 1983). The Behavioral Science Unit at the Academy is the central site for this system and the unit performs the aforementioned functions of collator. This unit of agents also currently provides a psychological profile of the perpetrator of an unsolved violent crime when requested by a local agency.

VICAP is reported to have been the brainchild of Pierce Brooks, retired police chief of Eugene, Oregon, and a former homicide investigator with the Los Angeles, California police department, and other police officials in the Pacific Northwest. The VICAP concept was first operationalized during a multi-jurisdictional investigation of the killing of young children in Oakland County, Michigan, in 1976 and 1977 (Levin and Fox, 1985; see also McIntyre, 1988). This systematic approach coordinated the collection and distribution of case information to the team of investigators from different law enforcement jurisdictions in the county. The Oakland County Task Force, the result of a Law Enforcement Assistance Administration (LEAA) grant, was to have served as a model in criminal investigation to other agencies facing a serial murder investigation. However, the task force's efforts have never been made available in document form to the law enforcement community.

Further developments concerning VICAP came in the form of a technical assistance task plan submitted to Integrated Criminal Apprehension Program (ICAP) program manager Robert O. Heck of the Law Enforcement Assistance Administration in September 1981. This plan, written by Pierce Brooks, stated:

VI-CAP, a product of ICAP, is a process designed to integrate and analyze, on a nationwide basis, all aspects of the investigation of a series of similar pattern deaths by violence, regardless of the location or number of police agencies involved. The overall goal of the VI-CAP is the expeditious identification and apprehension of the criminal offender, or offenders, involved in multiple murders (also referred to as serial murders, sequential murders, or random and motiveless murders). (Brooks, 1981, p. 1)

Brooks (1981) also provided a statement of the problem, which the proposed VI-CAP system would address:

The lack of a centralized automated computer information center and crime analysis system to collect, collate, analyze and disseminate information from and to all police agencies involved in the investigation of similar pattern multiple murders, regardless of date and location of occurrence, is the crux of the problem. Research of almost every multiple murder investigation indicates an absolute need for a centralized information center and crime analysis function as a nationwide all-agency resource. . . . [T]here is no question that on a number of occasions multiple killers could have been apprehended much sooner if the several agencies involved in the investigation could have pooled and correlated their information. Each agency alone had "bits and pieces" of suspect identity—together their information would have provided the murderer's complete identity and early on apprehension. (p. 2)

Between November 1981 and May 1982, four VI-CAP planning sessions were held in Colorado, Texas, and Virginia. These sessions were funded from ICAP monies and participants were investigators and crime analysts from law enforcement agencies involved in ICAP projects. As indicated in the notes of the first planning session, the definition, purpose, and goal of VI-CAP were as follows:

VI-CAP Defined: VI-CAP is a centralized computer information center and crime analysis system designed to collect, collate and analyze all aspects of the investigation of similar pattern multiple murders, on a nationwide basis regardless of location or number of police agencies involved;

VI-CAP Purpose: Through analysis and evaluation of data received, to identify the existence of similar characteristics (M.O., suspect description, physical evidence, etc.) that may exist in a series of deaths by criminal violence; and

VI-CAP Goal: The overall goal of VI-CAP is to provide police agencies reporting similar pattern homicides with the information necessary to initiate a coordinated multi-agency investigation to expedite the identification of the criminal offender, or offenders, responsible for the murders. (Brooks, 1981, p. 1)

Due to the demise of the Law Enforcement Assistance Administration, funds were suspended for any further VI-CAP planning efforts following the last planning session in May 1982. VI-CAP procedures, budget, and forms had been developed as a result of these planning sessions. A third revised VI-CAP crime report form with instructions and summary sheets was the product of the final session (Briggs, 1982).

On July 1, 1983, Sam Houston State University received a planning grant award from the Office of Juvenile Justice and Delinquency Prevention (OJJDP) and the National Institute of Justice, U.S. Department of Justice, entitled the "National Missing/Abducted Children and Serial Murder Tracking and Prevention Program" (NMACSMTP) (OJJDP Grant Award, 1983). Activities of this planning grant included task force and workshop activities to plan, develop, and implement a National Center for the Analysis of Violent Crime, to include the VI-CAP system. A program workshop meeting in July 1983 included the following activities:

Preliminary development of a conceptual model of a National Center for the Analysis of Violent Crime (NCAVC) consisting of four major program components:

    (1) training
    (2) research and development
    (3) profiling
    (4) the Violent Criminal Apprehension Program (VI-CAP)

The Behavioral Science Unit of the FBI Academy in Quantico, Virginia, was recommended as the site for the NCAVC. Preliminary development of the procedures and reporting mechanisms for collecting information on serial murders and incidents of missing/abducted children. Included here was the first draft of an offense report for the collection of VI-CAP murder-incident information. (OJJDP Memo, July 28, 1983)

An NMACSMTP workshop meeting in August 1983 included the following activities:

- A preliminary VI-CAP standardized form was developed for collecting murder-incident information. Selected members of the planning group were designated to perform content analysis on this form and field-test the document.
- The conceptual model of the National Center for the Analysis of Violent Crime to be located at the FBI Academy was further discussed and refined. Network linkages and collection, analysis and dissemination processes of NCAVC were discussed (OJJDP memo, Sept. 15, 1983).

The third workshop of the program, held in November 1983, included the revision of VI-CAP reporting forms (OJJDP memo, Nov. 20, 1983). As a result of program efforts and activities referred to above, specific planning was initiated within the U.S. Department of Justice to fund the National Center for the Analysis of Violent Crime. On March 31, 1984, the FBI received approximately $3.3 million to support the organizational development of NCAVC for 24 months. Funding for this development was provided by the Office of Juvenile Justice and Delinquency Prevention, the National Institute of Justice, and the Office of Justice Assistance and Research Statistics. Under this funding arrangement, the project stipulated that it would:

• Create, develop, and test a criminal justice operations center for a national multi-jurisdictional investigative research information and assistance program addressing selective violent crimes. The center will be under the direction and control of the FBI training center at Quantico, Virginia.

• Include four major organizational components that will include a research, training, and investigative support and information assistance program.

• Provide a research and analysis center for the nation's law enforcement and criminal justice system that can coordinate, assist, and provide comparative investigative assistance between multi-jurisdictional criminal justice agencies having similar murder patterns showing violent sexual trauma; mysterious disappearances of adults and children who may have been abducted, sexually exploited, molested or raped (OJJDP Interagency Agreement, December 19, 1983).

VICAP (the hyphen was deleted in 1984), a major component of the National Center for the Analysis of Violent Crime, currently operational, is a centralized data information center and crime analysis system that collects, collates, and analyzes all aspects of the investigation of similar-pattern, multiple murders, on a nationwide basis, regardless of the location or number of police agencies involved. VICAP is described by Brooks (1981) as a "nationwide clearinghouse . . . to provide all law enforcement agencies reporting similar pattern violent crimes with the information necessary to initiate a coordinated multi-agency investigation" (p. 41). VICAP attempts to identify any similar characteristics that may exist in a series of unsolved murders, and provide all police agencies reporting similar patterns with information necessary to initiate a coordinated multi-agency investigation.

Cases that currently meet the criteria for VICAP are:

1. solved or unsolved homicides or attempts, especially those that involve an abduction; are apparently random, motiveless, or sexually oriented; or are known or suspected to be part of a series

2. missing persons, where the circumstances indicate a strong possibility of foul play and the victim is still missing

3. unidentified dead bodies where the manner of death is known or suspected to be homicide (Howlett, Hanfland, and Ressler, 1986, pp. 15–16).

Levin and Fox (1985) argue that the value of VICAP is predicated in part on the assumption that serial murderers roam the country. They state: "Traveling serial killers like Bundy, Lucas and Wilder are in the minority to those like Williams, Gacy, Corll, Buono, and Berkowitz who 'stay at home' and at their jobs, killing on a part-time basis" (p. 183). However, this statement is based upon a data set of 42 offenders involved in 33 acts of multiple murder, and only ten of these were committed serially (see Fox and Levin, 1983, p. 4).

The success of VICAP will not be known for some time. It is dependent on a number of factors, not the least of which is local law enforcement cooperation in completing a very lengthy 16-page form and the transmittal of this form on unsolved cases to the FBI. The concept, however, appears to be moving in the right direction since no database from which to identify serial murders currently exists in this country. Depue notes that his VICAP system will be expanded to include the crimes of rape, child sexual abuse, and arson (Ressler 1985). Darrach and Norris (1984) state that for over 20 years the United States has had a national system for reporting and tracing stolen cars, but that no national computerized clearinghouse for reporting unsolved homicides currently exists. When VICAP develops the appropriate database, the hope is that the identification of patterns will stimulate the necessary interagency communication and sharing of information which is currently, with a few laudable exceptions, almost nonexistent.

By the mid 1980s a number of states initiated efforts to develop statewide analysis capabilities similar to the system evolving with VICAP. In 1986 there were 14 states involved in such an effort. The author was the project director of one such system for the state of New York, the first statewide system to become fully operational in 1987. The Homicide Assessment and Lead Tracking System (HALT) was developed with state funds by the New York Division of Criminal Justice Services and turned over to the New York state police in 1987 to be fully implemented. To date, HALT is far from realizing its full potential due to the short-sightedness of the executive-level personnel of this agency who have provided only one full-time investigator for the system. Nonetheless, HALT has become a model for other states to follow in terms of its design, computer software, functions, and established cooperative relationship with VICAP.

The development of HALT was a cooperative effort between the New York state police and the Criminal Justice Institute, Division of Criminal Justice Services. From the onset of program development, plans were made for the operational control of the program by the New York state police. This was a major planning assumption in program development.

The HALT program was initiated in January 1986, and was designed to provide a systematic and timely criminal investigative tool for law enforcement agencies across the state. Through computer analysis of case-incident information supplied by police agencies, HALT is able to determine when similar crime patterns exist in two or more jurisdictions. When patterns are identified, the appropriate local agencies are notified.

HALT is being developed in cooperation with the FBI's national effort addressing serial homicide so as to be compatible with its program (Violent Criminal Apprehension Program, or VICAP). However, HALT was not simply a conduit from New York to VICAP. The system is "value added" in order to provide communication linkages within the state, investigative support services, and a source center to refer law enforcement agencies to specific services or to provide the appropriate applied research information.

HALT became fully operational by the New York state police in 1987 and is considered to be a valuable resource in addressing the problem of serial violent crime in New York.

The program goals of HALT were developed:

1. To provide an informational and investigative resource for law enforcement agencies in the state by facilitating effective responses by local police agencies to serial homicides.
2. To promote and facilitate communication, coordination, and cooperation among law enforcement agencies in the state on unsolved serial homicides.
3. To be designed in a manner that will permit its extension to other serial crimes (Egger, 1986, pp. 1–2).

Those who watch "Mystery" on PBS television or consider themselves devotees of the British mystery novel will be familiar with the police sergeant who accompanies the inspector from Scotland Yard. This sergeant always has a box in which he maintains the records of the investigation. When the United Kingdom began to experience serial murder, the records of such an investigation necessarily outgrew this box. Today the box has been replaced in all police jurisdictions in the United Kingdom with a small portable computer running a software program appropriately labeled with the acronym HOLMES (Home Office Large Major Inquiry System). This software is based on standardized criminal investigation procedures developed for major criminal incidents. The location of such an investigation is referred to as the major criminal investigation incident room (see Doney, Chapter 5 for a more complete description).

The Major Crimes Files presently in operation in the Canadian Police Information Centre (CPIC) system is a national system that operates in a manner somewhat similar to VICAP and HOLMES. In contrast to VICAP, in which the analysis is conducted at a central site, the Major Crimes File allows the investigator to use the program for his own remotely located terminal (C. P. Clatney, personal communication, March 31, 1988). The utility of the system by a single investigator at a remote site is then similar to the function of HOLMES.

The objective of the Major Crimes File as stated by the Royal Canadian Mounted Police is:

to bridge the gaps among record systems maintained by member forces of the Canadian police community and encourage investigators to communicate, to share information and to link major crimes, initially those believed to involve homicide, thereby leading to the rapid apprehension of serial offenders. A crime-portrait computer file, where similarities and patterns are identified, can effectively compare a major crime in Vancouver with one in Montreal and may lead to a specific suspect. (C. P. Clatney, personal communication, March 31, 1988)

While little information is currently available on the extent to which serial murder is an international phenomenon (except for the research of Hickey, 1985 and Jenkins, 1988), one special international network should not be excluded from this discussion. Interpol, the International Criminal Police Organization, is an international network and communication system in place to respond to the transnational character of serial crime. It is the organization best suited to provide a centralized investigative network for the world.

Interpol is primarily a criminal information exchange service that provides its members with studies and reports on individuals and groups involved in crime conducted on an international scale. "The purpose of INTERPOL is to facilitate, coordinate, and encourage international police cooperation as a means for embattling crime" (Interpol General Secretariat, 1978, p. 94).

Interpol is becoming an increasingly important tool for criminal investigation in the United States to satisfy investigative leads that go beyond the borders of this country. To address the need for an international channel of communication for state and local law enforcement officials, each of the 50 states is setting up a point of contact within their own police systems to serve as a focal point for all requests involving international matters. This effort was initiated and is being coordinated by the National Central Bureau of the U.S. Justice Department. Illinois was the first state to implement the program of state liaison, establishing this function within the Division of Criminal Investigation of the Illinois state police.

While Interpol was not specifically designed to respond to serial murder, the in-place system of this organization is uniquely qualified to provide assistance to investigators of a serial murder with potentially transnational characteristics. As each of the 50 states develops its liaison program, Interpol will become better known to the law enforcement community as a tool for international information and assistance.

The extent to which conflict continues to exist between law enforcement agencies will contribute to a continuing communication problem. Notwithstanding this conflict, a centralized investigative network can substantially contribute to the reduction of such conflict. Where conflict remains between two organizations there may be less of it when an outsider (VICAP or HALT) holds an acknowledged monopoly of relevant information. Thus, the ability of these agencies to access and retrieve information from a centralized investigative network may further reduce the conflict between involved agencies.

Other Developing Responses to Serial Murder

In addition to the computer software applications referred to earlier, there are other software programs being developed to assist law enforcement agencies in responding to serial murder. One such program, which operates on a personal computer and was recently implemented by the Peel Regional Police Force in Brampton, Ontario, is the Dr. Watson Case Management System. This system, in some ways very similar to the HOLMES or the HALT systems, was implemented in early 1988. Since that time the agency has utilized the system on several lengthy homicide investigations and has been given very positive evaluations (M. S. Trussler, personnel communication; Jan. 27, 1989; also see "Police track serial killer with commercial DBMS," Dec. 5., 1986, *Government Computer News*, p. 78).

A number of agencies investigating a serial murder have attempted to conduct geographical analyses for pattern identification. However, only one forensic geographer has specifically researched this area and developed an analytical geoforensic capability. The late Milton B. Newton of Geoforensics, Inc. and formerly of Louisiana State University was in the process of developing a geoforensic analysis of localized serial murder when he was killed in an automobile accident in Mexico in 1988.

Dr. Newton presented a preliminary analysis of his research, entitled "Geoforensic Identification of Localized Serial Crime," to the Southwest Division, Association of American Geographers in Denton, Texas in October 1985. Newton's latest and final (unpublished) research was entitled, "Geoforensic Analysis of Localized Serial Murder: The Hillside Stranglers Located," coauthored with Elizabeth Swoope, which the author received from Newton in January 1987. In this work, Newton developed a method through a post hoc analysis using a geographic method with points of fatal encounter and body dumps resulting in a near geographic "hit" on Angelo Buono's home, where many of the murders had actually taken place.

Notwithstanding the loss of Milton Newton as a personal friend and colleague, the criminal investigation profession in the country, unknowingly, lost a very good friend. While it is true that Newton's analysis was conducted on a post hoc basis, his techniques could very easily be used as an integral part of an ongoing serial murder investigation. Had he lived, his further research would have undoubtedly provided this capability to an ongoing serial murder investigation. It is the hope of the author that Newton's research will be recognized by the small but evolving geoforensic community and that his research will be continued.

On January 14, 1982, Clifford Robert Olson pleaded guilty in a Vancouver, British Columbia courtroom to the rape and murder of 11 young boys and girls. Olson's plea was entered in exchange for a promise by Canadian authorities to establish a $90,000 trust fund for Olson's wife and son. The story of this controversial plea received a great deal of coverage in the Canadian press and was also reported extensively by the media in this country (*Criminal Justice Ethics*, Summer/Fall 1983, pp. 47–55). While the intense negative reaction from the public regarding this negotiated plea may preclude the probability of such an unusual event recurring, it is certainly worthy of note. One can only imagine the frustration of the criminal justice officials in Canada that caused such a negotiation to take place. It is not unrealistic to contemplate such a negotiation in this country in such well-known cases as Ted Bundy and Henry Lee Lucas to have resulted, in the very least, in a resolution of cases and an end to the painful uncertainty of the relatives of their victims.

All of the law enforcement investigative responses encompassed within this taxonomy share a common focus: to reduce the extent to which linkage blindness occurs in a serial murder investigation. Linkage blindness is a term coined by the author (see Egger, 1984) and was addressed in the previous chapter. In the future, criteria for the success of a serial murder investigation will necessarily include the extent to which this short-sightedness or cross-jurisdictional myopia is reduced or excluded (see Chapter 10).

REFERENCES

Atkinson, R. (1984, Feb. 20). "Killing puzzle." *Washington Post*, pp. 1, 14–15.

Ault, R. L. and Reese, J. T. (1980, March). "A psychological assessment of crime: Profiling." *FBI Law Enforcement Bulletin*, pp. 1–4.

Barrington, R. C. and Peace, D. M. S. (1985). "HOLMES: The development of a computerized major crime investigation system." *The Police Journal, 63* (3), pp. 207–23.

Briggs, T. (1982). *VI-CAP memo*. Colorado Springs police department, March 4, pp. 1–10.

Brooks, P. R. (1981). *VI-CAP*. Unpublished report.

———. (1982). *The investigative consultant team: A new approach for law enforcement cooperation*. Washington, DC: Police Executive Research Forum.

Brooks, P. R., Devine, M. J., Green, T. J., Hart, B. L., and Moore, M. D. (1987, February). "Serial murder: A criminal justice response." *The Police Chief*, pp. 37, 41–42, 44–45.

———. (1988). *Multi-agency investigative team manual*. Washington, DC: U.S. Department of Justice.

Campbell, C. (1976, May). "Portrait of a man killer." *Psychology Today*, pp. 110–19.

Danto, B. L. and Kutcher, A. H. (eds.) (1982). *The human side of homicide*. New York: Columbia University Press.

Darrach, B. and Norris, J. (1984, July). "An American tragedy." *Life Magazine*, pp. 58–74.

Dettlinger, C. and Prough, J. (1983). *The list*. Atlanta. GA: Philmay Enterprises.

Egger, S. A. (1985). *Serial murder and the law enforcement response*. Unpublished dissertation, College of Criminal Justice, Sam Houston State University, Huntsville, Texas.

———. (1986). *HALT briefing document*. Albany, NY: Division of Criminal Justice Services.

"FBI develops profile to change face of sex probes." (1980, Dec. 22). *Law Enforcement News*, p. 7.

Fox, J. A. and Levin, J. (1983), *Killing in numbers: An exploratory study of multiple-victim murder*. Unpublished manuscript.

Federal Bureau of Investigation. (1983). *Violent Criminal Apprehension Program: Conceptual model*. Unpublished working paper, July, pp. 1–4.

Garland, S. B. (1984, August 12). "Serial killings demand new ways to analyze unsolved homicides." *Houston Post*, p. 1., and Newhouse News Service.

Geberth, V. J. (1981, Sept.) "Psychological profiling." *Law and Order*, pp. 46–49.

———. (1983). *Practical homicide investigation*. New York: Elsevier.

———. (1986), "Mass, serial and sensational homicides: The investigative perspective." *Bulletin of New York Academy of Medicine*, 62(5), 492–96.

Gest, T. (1984, April 30). "On the trail of America's 'serial killers.' " *U.S. News and World Report*, p. 53.

Gilbert, J. (1983). "A study of the increased rate of unsolved criminal homicide in San Diego, California and its relationship to police investigation effectiveness." *American Journal of Police, 2*, 149–66.

Godwin, J. (1978). *Murder USA: The ways we kill each other*. New York: Ballantine Books.

Hazelwood, R. and Douglas, J. (1980, April). "The lust murderer." *FBI Law Enforcement Bulletin*, pp. 1–5.

Hazelwood, R. R., Ressler, R. K., Depue, R. L., and Douglas, J. E. (1987). "Criminal personality profiling: An overview." In R. R. Hazelwood and A. W. Burgess (eds.), *Practical aspects of rape investigation: A multidisciplinary approach*. New York: Elsevier, pp. 137–49.

Hickey, E. W. (1985). "Serial murderers: Profiles in psychopathology." Paper presented at annual meeting of Academy of Criminal Justice Sciences, Las Vegas, Nevada.

Holmes, R. M. and DeBurger, J. (1988). *Serial murder*. Newbury Park, CA: Sage.

Howlett, J. B., Hanfland, K. A., and Ressler, R. K. (1986). "The violent criminal apprehension program VICAP: A progress report." *FBI Law Enforcement Bulletin, 55* (12), 15–16.

Interpol General Secretariat. (1978). "The I.C.P.O.—Interpol." *International Review of Criminal Policy, 34*, 93–96.

Jenkins, P. (1988). "Myth and murder: The sexual murder panic of 1983–85." *Criminal Justice Research Bulletin, 3*(11).

Kessler, R. (1984, Feb. 20). "Crime profiles: FBI behavioral science unit paints psychological portraits of killers." *Washington Post*, pp. 1, 16, 18.

Levin, J. and Fox, J. A. (1985). *Mass murder*. New York: Plenum.

Liebert, J. A. (1985). "Contributions of psychiatric consultation in the investigation of serial murder." *International Journal of Offender Therapy and Comparative Criminology., 29* (Dec.), 187–99.

Lindsey, R. (1984, Jan. 21). "Officials cite a rise in killers who roam U.S. for victims." *New York Times*, pp. 1, 7.

Luckenbill, D. F. (1984). "Murder and assault." In R. W. Meier (ed.), *Major forms of crime*. Beverly Hills, CA: Sage, pp. 18–45.

McCarthy, K. (1984, July 7). "Serial killers: Their deadly bent may be set in cradle." *Los Angeles Times*, p. 1.

McIntyre, T., (1988). *Wolf in sheep's clothing: The search for a child killer*. Detroit: Wayne State University Press.

Michaud, S. C. (1986, Oct. 26). "The F.B.I.'s new psyche squad." *New York Times Magazine*, pp. 40, 42, 50, 74, 76–77.

Myre, D. C. (1974). *Death investigation*. Washington, DC: International Association of Chiefs of Police.

National Center for the Analysis of Violent Crime (Conceptual Model, July 1983). Unpublished report.

Newton, M. B. and Newton, D.C. (1985, Oct. 18). *"Geoforensic identification of localized serial crime."* Paper presented at the Southwest Division, Association of American Geographers meeting, Denton, Texas.

Newton, M. B. and Swoope, E. A. (1987). *Geoforensic analysis of localized serial murder: The Hillside Stranglers located*. Unpublished manuscript.

Palmiotto, M. J. (1988). *Critical issues in criminal investigation* (2nd edn.). Cincinnati: Anderson.

"Paying a murderer for evidence." (1983). *Criminal Justice Ethics*, Summer/Fall, pp. 47–55.

Pinnizzotto, A. J. (1984). "Forensic psychology: Criminal personality profiling." *Journal of Police Science and Administration, 12* (1), 32–36.

"Police track serial killer with commercial DBMS." (1986, Dec. 5). *Government Computer News*, p. 78.

Porter, B. (1983, April). "Mind hunters: Tracking down killers with the FBI's psychological profiling team." *Psychology Today*, pp. 55–60.

"Red-haired victims found along highways." (1984, April 25). *Tennessean*, p. 1.

Regional Organized Crime Information Center. (1985). *ROCIC Bulletin* (01–85), pp. 1–47.

Reiser, M. (1982, March). "Crime-specific psychological consultation." *The Police Chief*, pp. 53–56.

Ressler, R. K. et al. (1985). Violent crime. (Special issue reporting on research of the National Center for the Analysis of Violent Crime). *FBI Law Enforcement Bulletin, 54*(8), 1–31.

———. (1987). *Criminal profiling research on homicide*. Unpublished research report.

———. (1984). *Serial murder: A new phenomenon of homicide*. Paper presented at the annual meeting of the International Association of Forensic Sciences. Oxford, England.

Sam Houston State University Criminal Justice Center. (1983). *National Missing/Abducted Children and Serial Murder: Tracking and Prevention Program*. Grant application to Office of Juvenile Justice and Delinquency Prevention, U.S. Department of Justice, Huntsville, Texas.

Sanders, B. (1977). *Detective work*. New York: The Free Press.

Skogan, W. G. and Antunes, C. E. (1979). "Information, apprehension, and deterrence: Exploring the limits of police productivity." *Journal of Criminal Justice, 7*, 217–41.

"State police to take charge of co-ed murder investigation." (1969, July 30). *Detroit News*, p. 1.

Swanson, C. R., Chamelin, N. E., and Territo, L. (1984). *Criminal investigation*. New York: Random House.

West, D. J. (1987). *Sexual crimes and confrontations: A study of victims and offenders*. Brookfield, VT: Gower.

Wilbanks, W. (1984). *Murder in Miami*. Lanham, MD: University Press of America.

Wilmer, M. A. P. (1970). *Crime and information theory*. Edinburg: University Press.

IV

The Future: Investigation and Research

This final part of this work looks to the future and raises a number of important and critical challenges for law enforcement and the criminologist. Each of these two chapters briefly argues for a specific focus of emphasis in further investigation and research of serial murder.

Chapter 10 argues for the necessary changes, both structural and procedural, that law enforcement agencies must make as they move into the 1990s. Here I argue for a number of subtle and radical changes that must occur to more effectively respond to the problem of serial murder. Six primary curricular training areas are advocated for both patrol officers and criminal investigators. Following this recommended focus on training development, I argue for a new method of thinking about criminal investigation which includes a shared ecology of crime, more serious attention to reports of missing persons, more effective exploitation of evolving technologies such as "genetic fingerprinting," greater emphasis on problem-finding, corrected sight creating permeable jurisdictional boundaries, and increased networking resulting in greater interagency collaboration. In all of this new thinking the target is to reduce the extent of linkage blindness.

The final chapter of this work presents a research agenda for serial murder. For all the contributors of this work, the phenomenon of serial murder remains yet an elusive one. While some components or factors of serial murder have been unveiled and explicated, numerous others remain to be determined and explained. Throughout this agenda the future researcher can choose those questions that provide a focus and starting point for his or her research interests. It is hoped that many of the questions posed in this agenda will be addressed so that future criminologists can move into the twenty-first century with a solid framework with which to address the seriality of other violent crimes whose incidence is more common in all parts of this country.

10

The Future of Serial Murder Investigation

STEVEN A. EGGER

It will be no surprise to the reader that many of the recommendations in the chapter are designed to reduce the linkage blindness of law enforcement agencies and their officers. These recommended resolutions fall into one of four major categories: new and/or revised training programs for patrol officers as well as criminal investigators; the promotion and engenderment of a relatively new and different kind of thinking for managers and supervisors of the criminal investigation function; the more effective exploitation of developing technology by law enforcement agencies; and greater reliance on forensic investigative services and the encouragement of the further development of forensic support services.

The serial murderer does not fall solely within the province of the detective. As noted earlier, numerous serial murderers owe their captivity and identification to the efficient response of patrol officers subscribing to routine procedures. This makes it necessary for agencies to target patrol officers as well as detectives for training programs designed to reduce linkage blindness. There are six primary curricular training areas deserving attention in order to increase awareness and understanding of the phenomenon of serial murder:

1. definitions of serial murder

2. crime scene search and identification of physical evidence

3. linkage blindness

4. case law of serial murder cases on appeal

5. serial murder solvability factors

6. psychological profiling

The serial murder definitions provided in Chapter 1, particularly those of Egger (1988), Levin and Fox (1985), and Brooks, et al. (1988), should form the basis of an introductory curricular unit on the phenomenon. The component parts of each of these definitions could be provided to training participants in such a way as to develop them as flags for the patrol officer or investigator responding to a homicide. These flags would then alert the responding officers to the possibility or probability that such characteristics as severe mutilation of the body, economic status of the victim, appearance of the crime scene, apparent torture of the victim, and so on may mean that the victim is only one of a number of serial murder victims. Procedures for notification and cross-jurisdictional communication could then be specified within this curriculum component.

The utility of an extensively documented explication of a phenomenon that is not well defined or understood is nevertheless both directly operational and analytical. First, the various components of such a definition can be easily translated into data elements or flags for the person given responsibility for responding to a variety of situations in which the phenomenon may be present. These elements or flags then become operational tools for such an individual to determine the probability of the phenomenon. Thus, simply aggregating data elements and comparing them with the extent to which data elements are lacking or whose presence cannot be determined will provide an initial basis for determining the probability that a given situation is in fact the phenomenon in question.

The problem of such an operational tool is, however, the extent to which the finite components of an explication can be aggregated without concern for the weight of criticality given to each component. Components translated into data elements used to reconstruct a situation which may inductively point to the phenomenon may be misleading without a weighting or level of importance being placed on various elements. In addition, when the phenomenon in question lacks an empirical basis from which a statistically representative sample can be drawn, the weighting given to portions of a rational explication as well as the explanation alone can certainly be challenges to validity.

Since the value of crime scene evidence and its potential for identifying the murderer has been greatly enhanced due to technological advances in criminalistics in the last two decades, the search of the crime scene (or crime scenes if a point of fatal encounter and a body drop have been determined) and the identification of physical evidence of a probative nature are critical areas for necessary training. Not only should this training focus on criminalistics support to an investigation, but certain procedures for placing boundaries on the crime scene should also be addressed. Frequently, the crime scene of a homicide is defined within very narrow limitations of the struggle or actions of the murderer and his or her victim during the attack. A three-part premise must be inculcated into the thinking of responding officers: that is, the killer brought something to the point of fatal encounter, left something at the scene of the encounter, and took something away with him or her. This not only attunes an officer's thinking to searching for specific types of physical evidence based on the situation but forces one to think in broader spatial terms when reviewing the crime scene and the ingress and egress to the attack. Boundaries are quickly extended with this kind of thinking.

While stated earlier in Chapter 8 that most officers and detectives will agree to the ever-present existence of linkage blindness, this is frequently not the experience of the author until the term is defined. Thus, one focal point of training on serial murder investigation critical to any long-term effects of this training is to define linkage blindness and provide numerous examples of its existence in serial murder investigations. Once the term is defined with examples, the underlying causes of this problem must be explained and delineated, followed by group discussions focusing on its resolution. Defining, explaining, and resolving this problem would therefore be the charge given to the appropriate instructors.

Robert Keppel, criminal investigator for the State of Washington's attorney general's office, is the first author to retrospectively analyze mistakes made by law enforcement in the investigation of serial murders by reviewing appellate court cases. Keppel's book (1989) *Serial murder: Future implication for police organizations* highlights problems and errors of five well-known serial murder cases by conducting the analysis of appellate decisions of these cases. This book, specifically targeted for the law enforcement investigator, would provide excellent reading material for a training program on serial murder investigation. Other serial murder case appellate court decisions could be used in a similar fashion.

The utilization of solvability factors in a homicide investigation or, more specifically, in a serial homicide investigation may become practical in the near future pending the results of current ongoing research. The analysis of over 1,200 homicide cases in the state of Washington being conducted by Keppel and Weis (1986) should facilitate training in the use of these factors. One of the objectives of this research is "to determine the critical solvability factors present in homicide investigations in order to provide the ability of the police to apprehend murders" (p. 3).

Psychological profiling is a relatively new tool in a homicide investigator's arsenal. The tool is poorly understood by much of the law enforcement community. While it is not suggested that all appropriate officers targeted for training on serial murder be trained in the techniques of profiling, a better understanding of how this profiling is accomplished and how it may aid a serial murder investigation is recommended. Paramount in such a training approach is to explain the product of psychological profiling, and its utility to the investigator. How in some cases a profile may reduce the universe of suspects to a much more manageable number then becomes the focus of the training.

In order to become more effective in the investigation of serial murder in the future, homicide investigators will have to develop a different kind or method of thinking about the investigation. McGahan (1984) discusses a subjective ecology of crime which results from the police imagery of the urban environment. The ecological typifications that evolve with an officer's experience must become the grist of the data from which shared ecologies are distributed throughout a network of agencies and officers, formal as well as informal. In other words, the extent of the investigator's awareness of linkage blindness is exemplified by a familiarity of shared ecologies of crime in urban, suburban, or rural environments. It follows that accessibility to such a network then allows the investigator to refine thoughts of shared ecologies to comparative analysis and cooperative communication efforts.

The homicide investigator and the patrol officer will have to also modify his or her way of thinking about the report of missing persons. As in the example noted earlier in the John Wayne Gacy case, missing persons became serial murder victims. A timely response and more serious treatment of these reports will undoubtedly improve community relations, but more importantly, possibly save a life or lead to a serial murderer.

The rapidly developing technological advances of this decade, particularly with respect to computers and the processing of information, must be more effectively exploited by law enforcement agencies. As noted in the "Hillside Stranglers" investigation in Chapter 8, Kenneth Bianchi's name had been entered in the computer on three separate occasions; however, this information was not made available through information retrieval due to the limited cross-referencing capability of the computer software. At this time in the late 1970s the average student had access to library computer terminals that could provide the necessary searching and cross-referencing capability to provide numerous references to a specific individual or topic for a college term paper. Today, many law enforcement agencies using computers remain without this basic capability to cross-reference and retrieve aggregate data in a timely fashion.

The links that investigators make between pieces of information can be accomplished more quickly and efficiently for an exponentially larger body of facts with a computer. With the development and implementation of statewide automated information and retrieval systems in the late 1960s, patrol officers were able to rapidly determine whether an automobile was stolen prior to stopping the driver, whether the driver was wanted in other states, and the status of the driver's operator's license. These statewide systems, with communication interfaces to the National Crime Information Center in Washington, DC, greatly increased the effectiveness of patrol officers across the nation. However, it is only recently that such computing technology has been utilized for the support of criminal investigation. Most of the law enforcement resources following the development of statewide systems were allocated to provide management information for such functions as personnel resource allocation, records processing to generate crime statistics, or computer-aided dispatching. The utility of the information age and its geometric advancements was all but lost to the operational and day-to-day functioning of criminal investigation. The recent development

of automated crime analysis in agencies and the rapid implementation of automated fingerprint information systems (AFIS) on the state level has begun to
address the investigation function at the operational level.

Trade publications as well as mainstream periodicals have placed a great
emphasis on AFIS and its ability to make matches for identification from latent
fingerprints found at the scene of crimes. AFIS will indeed provide criminal
investigators with this function; however, the cost of such systems requires
government spending of millions of taxpayer dollars. Many analysts have begun
to question the cost-effectiveness of such expensive computer systems. Such
systems have undoubtedly greatly increased the ability of an investigator to link
criminal suspects to the scene of a crime, but at what costs?

A much more extensive method of tracing an individual to a crime scene
which is not limited to the use of latent fingerprints is the technique of genetic
identification or "bloodprint." Geneticist Alec Jeffreys developed a method of
examining genetic differences between people by identifying deoxyribonucleic
acid (DNA)—their genetic material—in England in 1984. This method, called
"genetic fingerprinting," is rapidly becoming important in forensic analysis. By
mid–1988, United States law officers had become very interested in genetic
fingerprinting, and variations called DNA typing or DNA fingerprinting. There
were criminal cases involving genetic fingerprinting prosecuted in Florida, Okla-
homa, New York, Pennsylvania, Virginia, and Washington—all with positive
results—and large companies in Maryland, California, and New York were doing
genetic fingerprinting analysis (Wambaugh, 1989, p. 284).

As genetic fingerprinting analysis continues to increase in its forensic application to criminal investigation, AFIS, by comparison, may become a very
expensive frill that many law enforcement agencies will not be able to defend
as a sufficiently necessary expenditure of scarce resources. As with the large
mainframe computers or large calculators, the demand for such forensic analysis
may rapidly reach the economies of scale and provide such service on a cost-
effective basis to U.S. law enforcement agencies.

Keppel and Weis (1986) correctly conclude that "to date, advances in the
quality of detective work have been motivated and accomplished only by the
ingenuity and drive of individual detectives" (p. 13). As noted in Chapter 1,
there is a significant and growing body of literature on serial murder. Law
enforcement organizations must exploit the results of this research to the benefit
of their criminal investigators so that their horizon will be expanded, both across
jurisdictions and over larger time frames.

The conceptualization of the working environment of the homicide investigator
within the city or county limits is totally inappropriate when considering the
spatial distribution of serial murder. Such a working environment must be re-
defined to reflect the mobility of the serial murderer. In other words, the investigator should think of his or her agency and its jurisdiction merely as a stable
geographic location or point of reference from which to seek out and network
with other jurisdictions. In effect, then, the homicide investigator, to be suc-

cessful in a serial murder investigation, becomes a problem-finder before he or she can hope to become a problem-solver.

The redefinition of the working environment requires a reshaping of the cognitive mental mapping of an investigator and the mental images such thinking represents. Such reshaping will not only cause the investigator to expand his or her vision of crime scene boundaries, but also to think through and beyond the agency's jurisdiction. These boundaries must then be viewed as totally permeable for purposes of the investigation.

Practically all criminal investigators have worked as patrol officers. As a patrol officer, he or she gradually developed cognitive representatives of the various areas of the law enforcement jurisdiction until an imagery was crystallized, causing a thinking or perceptual shorthand to occur which unconsciously ignored the space beyond agency responsibility. For McGahan (1984), this becomes the environment from which officers develop a subjective ecology of crime. When transferred or promoted to the position of detective, the concept of shared ecologies is foreign to the officer's mind. The crystallized imagery of a finite geographical area from which to operate is carried to this new role of investigation and places severe limitations on the ability of the investigator to respond to one of a series of homicides that happen to occur within his or her jurisdictional field of vision.

The criminal investigator of the future should be prepared to network with a variety of shared ecologies of crime; to exploit not only the most current research but also to became a problem-finder; and, foremost, to seek such problems in a collaborative manner by linking with the most important resource for such an undertaking—colleagues across whose turf the serial murderer has traveled and killed.

Law enforcement agencies must put professional competition, jealousies, turf-protecting, case-based investigative assignments, and jurisdictional myopia behind them in the interest of the common and greater good. These agencies must utilize those centralized investigative networks available to them and reward their employees with the necessary incentives that will facilitate networking across jurisdictional boundaries and the sharing of information on unsolved homicide with other agencies. Administrators and managers of law enforcement agencies in this country must look critically at the investigation of homicide and make the necessary and significant changes to reduce their agencies' linkage blindness. This will improve their capability and readiness to effectively respond to a serial murder by identifying and apprehending the serial murderer.

REFERENCES

Keppel, R. D. (1989). *Serial murder: Future implications for police organizations.* Cincinnati: Anderson.

Keppel, R. D. and Weis, J. G. (1986). *Improving the investigation of homicides and the apprehension rate of murderers.* Proposal to National Institute of Justice, U.S.

Department of Justice, Tacoma, Washington: Office of the Attorney General and University of Washington.

McGahan, P. (1984). *Police images of a city*. New York: Peter Lang.

Wambaugh, J. (1989). *The blooding*. New York: William Morrow.

11

An Agenda for Research of Serial Murder

STEVEN A. EGGER

If the reader has methodically read each of the chapters in this book in their order of presentation, he or she may be wondering, what is left? While the writer of each chapter has attempted to do justice to the chapter title, as the more conscientious readers will attest, each chapter has left more questions unanswered than the provision of definitive and complete descriptions of various perspectives on the phenomenon of serial murder.

The contributors to this book were specially selected because of their lack of answers and wealth of critical questions. Each was selected for his or her willingness to readily admit what was not known or determined, rather than for his or her all-knowing expertise. All, including the editor, consider themselves researchers or students of the phenomenon of serial murder and eschew the label of experts.

Thus, rather than summarize what has already been written, the intent herein is to provide the structure and implicit methodology of a research agenda for further study and research of the phenomenon of serial murder. A research agenda of a very tentative and preliminary nature was developed earlier by the editor (see Egger, 1986). Some of that agenda has hopefully been accomplished in this work. Additions and modifications to this agenda have resulted from those numerous unanswered questions posed by the contributors to this work.

While all answers to the questions posed in this agenda may never be answered, it is hoped that sufficient academic and practitioner research will result in answers or partial answers to many of them. If sufficient resources are allocated to this end, a paradigm shift should occur early in the next century so that the problem of linkage blindness can be applied to the much larger and complicated phenomena of serial criminality.

What follows is an agenda for the research of serial murder. This agenda should serve doctoral students seeking a dissertation topic, funding agencies developing priorities, and the rather intense and continuous curiosity of faculty members in criminology and criminal justice academic programs. It is hoped that no one who chooses to address a research question in this agenda will develop emotional calluses and that their research focus will continue to offend their sense of morality and value of life.

How can the incidence and prevalence of serial murder be more accurately determined?

Is the incidence of serial murder increasing in this country? If so, why?

What case study techniques or idiographic methodologies will better develop our understanding of the etiology of serial murder?

What clarifications or explanations of the phenomenon of serial murder are necessary in order to develop intervention, prevention or deterrent strategies and policies?

Is the working definition of serial murder by Egger or others noted herein (see Chapter 1) useful in facilitating a systematic framework from which to study the phenomenon?

How can the significance or importance of serial murder in this country be emphasized in order to warrant the necessary allocation of resources for its study?

What are the pre-adolescent and adolescent characteristics of serial murderers that would distinguish them from their birth cohort? And how can the identification of such characteristics be exploited to develop the necessary intervention techniques and strategies to prevent the maturity of these individuals into serial murderers?

Is the correlate of gender of most known serial murderers a significant characteristic of the phenomenon?

Are prestigeless or powerless groups of people the most common victims of the serial murderer or is their vulnerability a precipitating factor, creating ''soft'' targets for the serial murderer?

Does the problem of linkage blindness accurately depict law enforcement's major problem in responding to serial murder?

Do the characteristics of powerlessness or lack of prestige of most serial murder victims contribute to the initial priority that law enforcement gives to singular acts of homicide prior to any identification of a serial pattern?

How does the serial murderer select a victim and how have selected victims escaped death?

Why is a surprisingly large proportion of serial murders committed by multiple offenders? And do subcultural theories apply to this group participation in multiple homicide (see Jenkins, 1989)?

Is there a correlation between demographic or geographic patterns in this country and the incidence of serial murder? For instance, there would appear to be a disproportionate number of serial murderers who have killed in the Pacific Northwest (R. Keppel, personal communication, July 1985).

Is a national centralized investigative network such as VICAP the most effective system for assisting local law enforcement agencies with unsolved and potentially serial homicides or should other alternatives such as regional or state distributive networks be considered? A corollary is, obviously, how effective is VICAP in assisting local law enforcement in responding to serial murder?

What is the best method for developing a national database on serial murders, solved and unsolved?

Can at-risk populations reduce the probability of their victimization from a serial murderer?

What investigative strategies and techniques are the most successful for law enforcement's response to an unsolved and potentially serial murder?

Can the technique of developing solvability factors be utilized in assessing the investigation of a serial murder?

What is the most effective methodology for estimating the number of serial murderers currently operating in this country?

Is the collator concept, that is, collecting information on unsolved murders at a central location, the most effective method of reducing the linkage blindness of law enforcement?

Will the development of a typology of multiple homicide facilitate a clearer distinction between mass and serial murder and thus increase meaningful research and study of the latter?

What are the necessary curricular components in a training program for criminal investigators to increase their effectiveness and efficiency in the investigation of serial murder? (Implicit in this research question is a challenge to the age-old assumption that an effective patrol officer makes an effective criminal investigator.)

It is the fervent hope of the author that this research agenda will stimulate the necessary research and study beyond that which has been provided in this work to provide a basis for the development of tactics and strategies that can be readily shared with the law enforcement community to reduce the prevalence and increase control of the incidence of serial murder. For the phenomenon of serial murder must indeed become less elusive.

REFERENCES

Egger, S. A. (1986). "A challenge to academia: Preliminary research agenda for serial murder." *Quarterly Journal of Ideology, 10*(1), 75–77.

Jenkins, P. (1989). "Sharing murder: Understanding group serial murder." Paper presented at annual meeting of American Society of Criminology, Reno, Nevada, November 11, 1989.

Bibliography

Abrahamsen, D. (1973). *The murdering mind*. New York: Harper and Row.

Alpert, G. P. (1984). *The American system of criminal justice*. Beverly Hills, CA: Sage.

Altheide, D. L. and Fritz, N. J. (1987). "The mass media and the social construction of the missing children problem." *The Sociological Quarterly, 28*(4), 473–92.

American Psychiatric Association. (1987). *Diagnostic and statistical manual of mental disorders* (3rd edn. revised). Washington, DC: American Psychiatric Association.

———. (1968). *Diagnostic and statistical manual of mental disorders*. (2nd edn.). Washington, DC: American Psychiatric Association.

Andersen, K. (1983, Jan. 24). "An eye for an eye." *Time*, 28–39.

Atkinson, R. (1984, Feb. 20). "Killing puzzle." *Washington Post*, 1, 14–15.

Ault, R. L. and Reese, J. T. (1980, March). "A psychological assessment of crime profiling." *FBI Law Enforcement Bulletin*, 1–4.

Banay, R. S. (1956). "Psychology of a mass murderer." *Journal of Forensic Science 1*, 1.

Barnes, M. (producer and director). (1984). "The mind of a murderer" (videotape). Washington, DC: Public Broadcasting Service.

Bartol, C. R. (1980). *Criminal behavior*. Englewood Cliffs, NJ: Prentice-Hall, Inc.

Bauer, S. (1988, Sept. 12). "All new coroners to be tested." *News-Gazette*.(Champaign, IL) 3.

Bayley, D. H. (1977). "The limits of police reform." In D. H. Bayley (ed.), *Police and society*. Beverly Hills, CA: Sage, pp. 219–36.

Bennett, G. (1989). *Crime-warps: The future of crime in America* (rev. edn.). New York: Anchor Books.

Berger, J. (1984, Sept. 8). "Mass killers baffle authorities." *New York Times*, 1.

Berman, E. (1975, May). "Tested and documented split personality: Veronica and Nelly." *Psychology Today*, 78–81.

Bernstein, E. M. and Putnam, F. W. (1986). *Development, reliability, and validity of a dissociation scale*. National Institute of Mental Health, unpublished manuscript.

Best, J. (1987a). "Calculating the numbers of children abducted by strangers: Dark figures and child victims." Paper presented at the Pacific Sociological Association Meeting in Seattle, WA.

———. (1987b). "Dark figures and missing children: Defining stranger abduction." Paper presented at the American Society of Criminology Meeting, Montreal.

Bettelheim, B. (1979). "The individual and mass behavior in extreme situations." In B. Bettelheim, *Surviving and other essays*. New York: Harcourt.

Biondi, R. and Hecox, W. (1988). *All his father's sins*. Rocklin, CA: Prima.

Bjerre, A. (1981). *The psychology of murder: a study in criminal psychology* (reprint of 1927 edn.). New York: De Capo Press.

Black, D. J. (1970). "The production of crime rates." *The American Sociological Review*, *44*, 84–92.

Blackman, P. and Gardiner, R. (1986). "Flaws in the current and proposed uniform crime reporting program regarding homicide and weapons use in violent crime." Paper presented at the annual meeting of the American Society of Criminology.

Blank, A. S. (1985). "The unconscious flashback to the war in Vietnam veterans: Clinical mystery, legal defense, and community problem." In S. M. Sonnenberg, A. S. Blank, and J. A. Talbott (eds.), *The trauma of war: Stress and recovery in Vietnam veterans*. Washington, DC: American Psychiatric Press.

Blau, J. R. and Blau, P. M. (1982). "The cost of inequality: Metropolitan structure and violent crime." *American Sociological Review, 47*,. Feb. 114–29.

Bliss, E. L. (1983). "Multiple personalities, related disorders, and hypnosis." *American Journal of Clinical Hypnosis, 26*, 114–23.

Bliss, E. L. and Larson, E. M. (1984). "Sexual criminality and hypnotizability." *Journal of Nervous and Mental Disease, 173*, 522–26.

Boar, R. and Blundell, N. (1984). *The world's most infamous murders*. New York: Exeter Books.

Bogdan, R. and Taylor, S. J. (1975). *Introduction to qualitative research methods*. New York: John Wiley and Sons.

Bowers, W. J. and Pierce, G. L. (1975). "The illusion of deterrence in Issac Ehrlich's research on capital punishment." *Yale Law Journal, 85*, 187–208.

Brauer, R., Harrow, M. and Tucker, G. J. (1970). "Depersonalization phenomena in psychiatric patients." *British Journal of Psychiatry, 117*, 509–15.

Brearley, H. C. (1969). *Homicide in the United States*. Montclair, NJ: Patterson Smith (1932 reprint).

Briggs, T. (1982, March 4). *Memo Vi-CAP*. Colorado Springs Police Department, pp. 1–10.

Brittain, R. P. (1970). "The sadistic murderer." *Medical Science and the Law, 10*, 198–207.

Brooks, P. R. (1982). *"The investigative consultant team: A new approach for law enforcement cooperation*. Washington, DC: Police Executive Research Forum.

———. (1981). *VI-CAP*. Unpublished report.

Brooks, P. R., Devine, M. J., Green, T. J., Hart, B. L., and Moore, M. D. (1988).

Multi-agency investigative team manual. Washington, DC: U.S. Department of Justice.

———. (1987). "Serial murder: A criminal justice response." *The Police Chief, 54*, 37–45.

Brophy, J. (1966). *The meaning of murder*. New York: Thomas Y. Crowell Co.

Burgess, A. W., Hartman, C. R., Resseler, R. K., Douglas, J. E. and McCormack, A. (1986). "Sexual homicide: A motivational model." *Journal of Interpersonal Violence, 1*(3), 251–72.

Burnham, D. (1985, April 26). "U.S. to list suspects in white-collar crimes." *The New York Times*, 1.

Cahill, T. (1986). *Buried dreams*. New York: Bantam Books.

Campbell, C. (1976, May). "Portrait of a mass killer." *Psychology Today*, 110–19.

Cantor, D. and Cohen, L. E. (1980). "Comparing measures of homicide trends: Methodological and substantive differences in the Vital Statistics and Uniform Crime Report Time Series 1933–1975." *Social Science Research, 9*, 121–45.

Cattell, J. P. (1972). "Depersonalization phenomena." In S. Arieti (ed.), *American handbook of psychiatry*. New York: Basic Books.

Charmaz, K. (1983). "The grounded theory method: An explication and interpretation." In Robert M. Emerson (ed.), *Contemporary field research: A collection of readings*. Boston, MA: Little, Brown and Co., pp. 109–26.

Cleckley, H. (1964). *The mask of sanity* (4th edn.) St. Louis: C. V. Mosby Co.

Cocores, J., Santa, W. and Patel, M. (1984). "The Ganser syndrome: Evidence suggesting its classification as a dissociative disorder." *International Journal of Psychiatric Medicine, 14*, 47–56.

Cohen, B. (1980). *Deviant street networks*. Lexington, MA: Lexington Books.

Coleman, J. C., Butcher, J. N. and Carson, R. C. (1984). *Abnormal psychology and modern life*. Glenview, IL: Scott Foreman.

Colton, K. W. (1978). *Police computer technology*. Lexington, MA: Lexington Books.

Comiskey, R. J. (1983). "Paying a murderer for evidence, commentaries on the issue." *Criminal Justice Ethics*, Summer/Fall, 47–56.

Confer, W. N. and Ables, B. S. (1983). *Multiple personality: Etiology, diagnosis and treatment*. New York: Human Sciences Press.

Cormier, B. M. Angliker, C. C. J., Boyer, R., Mersereau, G. (1972). The psychodynamics of homicide committed in a semispecific relationship. *Canadian Journal of Criminology and Corrections, 14*, 335–44.

Curtis, L. A. (1974). *Criminal violence*. Lexington, MA: Lexington Books.

Daley, R. (1983), *The dangerous edge*. New York: Dell.

Daly, M. and Wilson, M. (1988). *Homicide*. New York: Aldine Degruyter.

Danto, B. L., Bruhns, J., and Kutcher, A. H. (eds.) (1982). *The human side of homicide*. New York: Columbia University Press.

Darrach, B. and Norris, J. (1984). "An American tragedy." *Life Magazine, 7*(8), 58–74.

de River, J. P. (1958). *Crime and the sexual psychopath*. Springfield, IL: Charles C. Thomas.

Denzin, N. K. (1978). *The research act: a theoretical introduction to sociological methods*. New York: McGraw-Hill.

Denzin, N. K. (ed.) (1970). *Sociological methods: A sourcebook*. Chicago: Aldine Publishing Co.

Department of Health and Human Services, Office of Inspector General. (1983). *Runaway and homeless youth, national program inspection.* Hyattsville, MD: Public Health Service.

Detlinger, C. and Prugh, J. (1983). *The list.* Atlanta, GA: Philmay Enterprises, Inc.

Dietz, M. L. (1983). *Killing for profit.* Chicago: Nelson-Hall.

Dixon, J. C. (1963), "Depersonalization phenomena in a sample population of college students." *British Journal of Psychiatry, 109,* 371–75.

Doerner, W. G. (1975). "A regional analysis of homicide rates in the United States." *Criminology, 13,* May, 90–101.

Dor-Shav, K. N. (1978). "On the long-range effects of concentration camp internment on Nazi victims: 35 years later." *Journal of Consulting Clinical Psychology, 46,* 1–11.

Douglas, J. E. and Burgess, A. E. (1986). "Criminal profiling: A viable investigative tool against violent crime." *FBI Law Enforcement Bulletin,* 55, 9–13.

Drapkin, I. and Viano, E. (1975). *Victimology: A new focus.* Lexington, MA: D.C. Heath and Company.

Dworkin, A. (1976). *Our blood: Prophecies and discussions on sexual politics.* New York: Harper and Row.

Egger, S. A.(1989). "Serial murder." In W. C. Bailey (ed.), *The Encyclopedia of police science.* New York: Garland Publishing, 578–81.

———. (1988). Definition of serial murder revised. (work in progress).

———. (1986a). "Utility of the case study approach to serial murder research." Paper presented at the American Society of Criminology Annual Meeting in Atlanta, Georgia, November 1986.

———. (1986b). "A challenge to academia: Preliminary research agenda for serial murder." *Quarterly Journal of Ideology, 10*(1), 75–77.

———. (1986c). *Homicide assessment and lead tracking system: HALT briefing document.* Albany, NY: New York Division of Criminal Justice Services.

———. (1985). *Serial murder and the law enforcement response.* Unpublished dissertation, College of Criminal Justice, Sam Houston State University, Huntsville, Texas.

———. (1984a). "A working definition of serial murder and the reduction of linkage blindness." *Journal of Police Science and Administration, 12* (3), 348–57.

———. (1984b). "Research in progress: Preliminary analysis of the victims of serial murderer Henry Lee Lucas." Paper presented at annual meeting, American Society of Criminology, Cincinnati, Ohio.

Eitzen, D. S. and Timmer, D.A. (1985). *Criminology.* New York: John Wiley & Sons.

Ellenberger, H. F. (1970). *The discovery of the unconscious: The history and evolution of dynamic psychiatry.* New York: Basic Books.

Ellis, A. and Gullo, J. (1971). *Murder and assassination.* New York: Lyle Stuart Inc.

Farmer, D. J. and Hooker, J. E. (1987). *Homicide policy and program analysis: Understanding and coping in local government.* (Commonwealth Paper). Richmond, VA: Virginia Commonwealth University, Center for Public Affairs.

Federal Bureau of Criminal Investigation, U.S. Department of Justice. (1987). *Uniform reports, 1978–1984: Supplementary homicide report.* Washington, DC: U.S. Government Printing Office.

Federal Bureau of Investigation, United States Department of Justice. (1986). *Crime in* the United States. *Uniform crime reports 1985*. Washington, DC: U.S. Government Printing Office.

———. (1985). *Crime in the United States: Uniform crime reports 1984*. Washington, DC: U.S. Government Printing Office.

———. (1985). *Missing person file data collection entry guide*. Washington, DC: U.S. Government Printing Office.

———. (1984). *Crime in the United States. Uniform Crime Reports 1983*. Washington, DC: U.S. Government Printing Office.

———. (1984). *The missing children*. Washington, DC.: U.S. Government Printing Office.

———. (1980). *Crime in the United States. Uniform Crime Reports 1979*. Washington, DC: U.S. Government Printing Office.

———. (1961). *Crime in the United States. Uniform Crime Reports 1960*. Washington, DC: U.S. Government Printing Office.

Fisher, C. (1945). "Amnesiac states in war neuroses: The psychogenesis of fugues." *Psychoanalysis Quarterly, 14*, 437–68.

Fliess, J. L., Gurland, B. J., and Goldberg, K. (1975). "Independence of depersonalization-derealization." *Journal of Consulting Clinical Psychology, 43*, 110–11.

Fox, J. A. and Levin, J. (1983). *Killing in numbers: An exploratory study of multiple-victim murder*. Unpublished manuscript.

Frankel, F. H. and Orne, M. T. (1976). "Hypnotizability and phobic behavior." *Archives of General Psychology, 33*, 1259–61.

Franklin, C. (1965). *The world's worst murderers*. New York: Taplinger Publishing Co.

Fullerton, D. T. et al. (1981). "Psychiatric disorders in patients with spinal cord injuries." *Archives of general psychiatry, 38*, 1369–71.

Garcia, C. (1987, July 27). "Casting a net at Green River: A serial murder manhunt remains a study in frustration." *Time*, 61.

Garland, S. B. (1984, August 12). "Serial killings demand new ways to analyze unsolved homicides." Newhouse News Service.

Garmire, B. L. (ed.) (1982). *Local government police management* (2nd edn.). Washington, DC: International City Management Association.

Gastil, R. D. (1971). "Homicide and a regional culture of violence." *American Sociological Review, 36*, June, 412–27.

Geberth, V. J. (1983). *Practical homicide investigation*. New York: Elsevier.

———. (1981, September). "Psychological profiling." *Law and Order*, 46–52.

Gest, T. (1984, April 30). "On the trail of America's 'serial killers.' " *U.S. News & World Report*, 53.

Gibbons, D. C. (1965). *Changing the lawbreaker*. Englewood Cliffs, NJ: Prentice-Hall.

Gilbert, J. N. (1983). "A study of the increased rate of unsolved criminal homicide in San Diego, California and its relationship to police investigative effectiveness." *American Journal of Police, 2*, 149–66.

Glaser, B. and Straus, A. L. (1967). *The discovery of grounded theory: Strategies for qualitative research*. Chicago: Aldine.

Godwin, J. (1978). *Murder USA: The ways we kill each other*. New York: Ballantine Books.

Goldstein, H. (1979). "Improving policing: A problem-oriented approach." *Crime and Delinquency, 25*, April, 236–58.

———. (1977). *Policing a free society*. Cambridge, MA: Ballinger.

Goldstein, J. H. (1975). *Aggression and crimes of violence.* New York: Oxford University Press.

Gove, W. R., Hughes, J., and Geerken, M. (1985). "Are uniform crime reports a valid indicator of index crimes? An affirmative answer with minor qualifications." *Criminology, 23*, 451–501.

"Governor orders state police to take over co-ed murder investigation." (1969, July 30). *Detroit News*, 1.

Gray, V. and Williams, G. (1980). *The organizational politics of criminal justice.* Lexington, MA: Lexington Books.

Graysmith, R. (1976). *Zodiac.* New York: Berkley Books, St. Martin's Press.

Greaves, G. B. (1980). "Multiple personality: 165 years after Mary Reynolds." *Journal of Mental Disorders, 168*, 577–96.

Grinker, R. R. and Spiegel, J. P. (1943). *War neuroses in North Africa.* New York: Josiah Macy, Jr. Foundation.

Groth, A. H. (1979). *Men who rape: The psychology of the offender.* New York: Plenum Press.

Guttmacher, M. (1960). *The mind of the murderer.* New York: Grove Press, Inc.

Hale, N. G. (ed.) (1975). *Morton Prince. Psychotherapy and multiple personality: Selected essays.* Cambridge: Harvard University Press.

Hammersley, M. and Atkinson, P. (1983). *Ethnography: Principles in practice.* New York: Tavistock Publications.

Harper, M. (1969). "Deja vu and depersonalization in normal subjects." *Aust NZ Journal of Psychiatry, 3*, 67–74.

Hazelwood, R. R. and Douglas, J. E. (1980, April). "The lust murderer." *FBI Law Enforcement Bulletin*, 1–5.

Hetzel, R. L. (1985). "The organization of a major incident room." *The Detective: The Journal of Army Criminal Investigation, 12*(1), 15–17.

Hewitt, J. D. (1988). "The victim-offender relationship in convicted homicide cases: 1960–1984." *Journal of Criminal Justice, 16*, 1, 25–34.

Hickey, E. W. (1987). *The etiology of victimization in serial murder: An historical and demographic analysis.* Submitted for publication.

———. (1986). "The female serial murderer." *Journal of Police and Criminal Psychology, 2*(2), 17–28.

———. (1985). "Serial murderers: Profiles in psychopathology." Paper presented at annual meeting of Academy of Criminal Justice Sciences, Las Vegas, Nevada.

Hilgard, E. R. (1977). *Divided consciousness: Multiple controls in human thought and action.* New York: Wiley & Sons.

Hindelang, M. J. (1974). "The uniform crime reports revisited." *Journal of Criminal Justice, 2*, 1–17.

Hollingshead, A. B. (1957). *Two-factor index of social position.* Unpublished manuscript.

Holmes, R. M. and DeBurger, J. (1988). *Serial murder.* Newbury Park, CA: Sage.

———. (1985). "Profiles in terror: The serial murderer." *Federal Probation, 49*, 29–34.

Howe, E. G. (1984). "Psychiatric evaluation of offenders who commit crimes while experiencing dissociative states." *Law and Human Behavior, 8*, 253–82.

Howlett, J. B., Haufland, K. A., and Ressler, R. K. (1986). "The violent criminal apprehension program—VICAP: A progress report." *FBI Law Enforcement Bulletin, 55*, 14–22.

Hudzik, J. K. and Cordner, G. W. (1983). *Planning in criminal justice organizations and systems*. New York: Macmillan Publishing Company.

Humphreys. L. (1985). *Tearoom trade*. New York: Aldine.

Jacobson, E. (1977). "Depersonalization." *Journal of American Psychoanalytic Association, 7*, 581–609.

Jenkins, P. (in press). "Serial murder in the United States 1900–1940: A historical perspective." *Journal of Criminal Justice*.

———. (1989). "Sharing murder: Understanding group serial murder." Paper presented at annual meeting of American Society of Criminology, Reno, Nevada, November 11, 1989.

———. (1988). "Myth and murder: The serial killer panic of 1983–5." *Criminal Justice Research Bulletin, 3*(11).

———. (1988). "Serial murder in England 1940–1985." *Journal of Criminal Justice, 16*, 1–15.

Jesse, F. T. (1924). *Murder and its motive*. New York: Alfred A. Knopf.

Johnson, K. W. (1977). *Police interagency relations. Some research findings*. Beverly Hills, CA: Sage.

Karlen, N. (1985, October 7). "How many kids missing?" *Newsweek*, 30–31.

Karmen, A. (1984). *Crime victims*. Monterey, CA: Brooks/Cole Publishing Company.

———. (1983). "Deviants as victims." In D. E. MacNamara and A. Karmen (eds.), *Deviants: Victims or victimizers?* Beverly Hills, CA: Sage, pp. 237–54.

Karpman, B. (1954). *The sexual offender and his offenses*. N.Y: Julian Press.

Katz, J. (1982). "A theory of qualitative methodology: The social system of analytic fieldwork." In Robert M. Emerson (ed.), *Contemporary field research*. Boston: Little, Brown and Co, pp. 127–48.

Kendall, E. (1981). The phantom prince: My life with Ted Bundy. Seattle: Madrona Publishers.

Keppel, R. D. (1989). *Serial murder: Future implications for police investigations*. Cincinnati: Anderson Publishing.

Keppel, R. D. and Weis, J. R. (1986). *Improving the investigation of homicides and the apprehension rate of murders*. Proposal to National Institute of Justice, U.S. Department of Justice, Tacoma, Washington: Office of the Attorney General and University of Washington.

Kessler, R. (1984, Feb. 20). "Crime profiles." *Washington Post*, 1, 16.

Keyes, D. (1986). *Unveiling Claudia: A true story of beauty, madness and murder*. New York: Bantam.

King, H. and Chamblis, W. J. (1972). *Harry King: A professional thief's journey*. New York: John Wiley & Sons.

Klockars, C. B. (1974). *The professional fence*. New York: The Free Press.

Kolb, L. C. (1985). "The place of narcosynthesis in the treatment of chronic and delayed stress reactions of war." In S. M. Sonnenberg, A. S. Blank, and J. A. Talbott (eds.), *The trauma of war: Stress and recovery in Vietnam veterans*. Washington, DC: American Psychiatric Press.

Kozenczcak, J. R. and Henrikson, K. M. (1987, August). "In pursuit of a serial murderer." *Law and Order*, 81–83.

Krystal, H. (1969). *Massive psychic trauma*. New York: International Universities Press.

Larsen, R. W. (1980). *Bundy: The deliberate stranger*. Englewood Cliffs, NJ: Prentice-Hall.

Leonard, V. A. (1980). *Fundamentals of law enforcement*. St. Paul MN: West Publishing Co.

Lester, D. and Lester, G. (1975). *Crime of passion: Murder and murderer*. Chicago: Nelson-Hall.

Letkemann, P. (1973). *Crime as work*. Englewood Cliffs, NJ: Prentice-Hall, Inc.

Levin, J,. and Fox, J. A. (1985). *Mass murder*. New York: Plenum.

Leyton, E. (1986). *Compulsive killers: the story of modern multiple murders*. New York: New York University Press. (Canadian title: *Hunting Humans: The use of the modern multiple murderer*.)

Lindsey, R. (1984, Jan. 21). "Officials cite a rise in killers who roam U.S. for victims." *New York Times*, 1, 7.

Linedecker, C. L. (1980). *The man who killed boys*. New York: St. Martin's Press.

Lipton, S. (1943). "Dissociated personality: A case report." *Psychiatric Quarterly, 17*, 35–36.

Luckenbill, D. F. (1984). "Murder and assault." In R. W. Meier (eds.), *Major forms of crime*. Beverly Hills, CA: Sage, pp. 19–45.

Ludwig, A. M. (1983). "The psychobiological functions of dissociation." *America Journal of Clinical Hypnosis, 26*, 93–99.

Lunde, D. T. (1976). *Murder and madness*. Stanford, CA: Stanford Alumni Association.

Lundsgaarde, H. P. (1977). *Murder in space city*. New York: Oxford University Press.

Macdonald, J. M. (1986). *The murderer and his victim* (2nd edn.). Springfield, IL: Charles C. Thomas.

Mattox, J. (1986). *Lucas report*. Austin, TX: Office of Texas Attorney General.

McCall, G. J. (1975). *Observing the law: Applications of field methods to the study of the criminal justice system*. Rockville, MD: National Institute of Mental Health.

McCarthy, K. (1984, July 21). "Serial killers: Their deadly bent may be set in cradle." *Los Angeles Times*, 1.

McCauley, R. P. (1973). *A plan for the implementation of a statewide regional police system*. Unpublished doctoral dissertation, Sam Houston State University, Huntsville, Texas.

McDonald, W. (1970). *The victim: A social psychological study of criminal victimization*. Unpublished doctoral dissertation, Ann Arbor, Michigan: University Microfilms.

McGahan, P. (1984). *Police images of a city*. New York: Peter Lang.

McIntyre, T. (1988). *Wolf in sheep's clothing: The search for a child killer*. Detroit: Wayne State University Press.

McKay, S. (1985, July 8). "Coming to grips with random killers." *Maclean's*, 44–45.

McKellar, P. (1977). "Autonomy, imagery and dissociation." *Journal of Mental Imagery, 1*, 93–108.

Meares, R. and Grose, D. (1978). "On depersonalization in adolescence." *British Journal of Medical Psychology, 51*, 335–42.

Megargee, E. I. (1982). "Psychological determinants and correlates of criminal violence." In M. E. Wolfgang and N. A. Weiner (eds.), *Criminal violence*. Beverly Hills, CA: Sage.

Meredith, N. (1984, Dec.). "The murder epidemic." *Science, 84*, 43–48.

Messner, S. F. (1983). "Regional differences in the economic correlates of the urban homicide rate: some evidence on the importance of cultural context." *Criminology, 21*, 477–88.

Milgram, S. (1967). "The small world problem." *Psychology Today, 1*, 61–67.

Morris, T. and Bloom-Cooper, L. (1964). *A calendar of murder*. London, England: Michael Joseph.

Mowday, B. E. (1984, July). "Computer tracking violent criminals." *Police Product News*, 26–29.

Murphy, G. (1947). *Personality: A biosocial approach to origins and structure*. New York: Harper & Row.

Myers, D. and Grant, G. (1970). "A study of depersonalization in students." *British Journal of Psychiatry, 121*, 59–65.

Myre, D. C. (1974). *Death investigation*. Washington, DC: International Association of Chiefs of Police.

Naisbitt, J. (1982). *Megatrends*. New York: Warner Books, Inc.

Nash, J. R. (1980). *Murder America: Homicide in the United States from the revolution to the present*. New York: Simon and Schuster.

National Center for Health Statistics. (1987). *Medical examiner's and coroner's handbook on death registration and fetal death reporting*. DHHS Pub. No. PHS87–1110, Public Health Service. Hyattsville, MD.

———. (1986). *Annual summary of births, marriages, divorces and deaths, United States. Monthly Vital Statistics Report*. Report no. 13DHHS, Public Health Service. Hyattsville, MD.

National Center for Missing and Exploited Children. (1988). *Memorandum*.

National Center for the Analysis of Violent Crime. (1985). *VI-CAP Crime Report*. Quantico, VA: Federal Bureau of Investigation.

———. (Conceptual model, July, 1983). Unpublished report.

National Crime Information Center. (1988). *Unidentified persons report, missing persons report*. Washington, DC: U.S. Government Printing Office.

———. (1985). *Missing person file, data collection entry guide*. Washington, DC: U.S. Government Printing Office.

Nelson, T. (1984, July). "Serial killings on increase, study shows." *Houston Post*, 1, 11.

Nemiah, J. C. (1981). "Dissociative disorders." In A. M. Freedman and H. I. Kaplan (eds.), *Comprehensive textbook of psychiatry* (3rd edn.). Baltimore: Williams & Wilkins.

Nettler, G. (1982). *Killing one another*. Cincinnati, Ohio: Anderson.

Newton, M. (1988). *Mass murder: An annotated bibliography*. New York: Garland.

Norris, J. (1988). *Serial killers: The growing menace*. New York: Doubleday.

Noyes, R. and Kletti, R. (1977). "Depersonalization in response to life-threatening danger." *Psychiatry, 18*, 375–84.

Noyes, R., Hoenk, P. R., and Kupperman, B. A. (1977). "Depersonalization in accident victims and psychiatric patients." *Journal of Nervous Mental Disorders, 164*, 401–7.

O'Brien, D. (1985). *Two of a kind: The hillside stranglers*. New York: Signet.

O'Brian, R. (1985). *Crime and victimization data*. Beverly Hills, CA: Sage Publications.

O'Hara, C. E. (1980). *Fundamentals of criminal investigation* (5th edn.). Springfield, IL: Charles C. Thomas.

O'Toole, L. and Montjoy, R. S. (1984). "Interorganizational policy implementation: A theoretical perspective." *Public Administration Review*, November/December, 491–503.

Oborne, D. J. and Clarke, M. J. (1975). "Questionnaire surveys of passenger comfort." *Applied Ergonomics, 6*(2), 97–103.

Office of Juvenile Justice and Delinquency Prevention. (1988). *OJJDP update on research.* Washington, DC: U.S Government Printing Office.

———. U.S. Department of Justice. (1986). *America's missing and exploited children: Their safety and their future.* Washington, DC: Government Printing Office.

———. (1983), *National missing/abducted children and serial murder tracking and prevention Program.* Washington, DC: U.S. Department of Justice.

———. (1983). *Memo,* November 20.

Office of Technology Assessment, (1982). *Assessment of NCIC.* Washington, DC: U.S. Government Printing Office.

Oppenheim, A. N. (1966). *Questionnaire design and attitude measurement.* New York: Basic Books.

Orne, M. T., Dinges, D. F., and Orne, E. C. (1984). "On the differential diagnosis of multiple personality in the forensic context." *International Journal of Clinical Hypnosis, 32,* 118–69.

Parikh, D., Sheth, A., and Apte, J. (1981). "Depersonalization." *Journal of Postgraduate Medicine, 27,* 226–30.

Parkinson, G. (1977). *Figuring it out: An evaluation of the police and community services project.* Province of British Columbia: Justice Development Fund.

Pettinati, H. M., Horne, R. L., and Staats, J. M. (1985). "Hypnotizability in patients with anorexia nervosa and bulimia." *Archives of General Psychiatry, 42,* 1014–16.

Pinnizzotto, A. J. (1984). "Forensic psychology: Criminal personality profiling." *Journal of Police Science and Administration, 12*(1), 32–37.

Pokorny, A. D. (1965). "A comparison of homicides in two cities." *Journal of Criminal Law, Criminology and Police Science, 56,* Dec., 479–87.

Polsky, N. (1967). *Hustlers, beats, and others.* Chicago: Aldine.

Porter, B. (1983, April). "Mind hunters." *Psychology Today,* 1–8.

Prince, M. (1909). "Psychological principles and field of psychotherapy." In N. G. Hale (ed.), *Morton Prince. Psychotherapy and multiple personality: Selected essays.* Cambridge: Harvard University Press.

Putnam, F. W. (1985). "Dissociation as a response to extreme trauma." In R. P. Kluft (ed.), *The childhood antecedents of multiple personality.* Washington: American Psychiatric Press.

Putnam, F. W. et al. (1986). "The clinical phenomenology of multiple personality disorder: 100 recent cases." *Journal of Clinical Psychiatry* (in press).

Regional Information Sharing Systems. (1984). *The RISS projects: A federal partnership with state and local law enforcement.* Washington, DC: Bureau of Justice Assistance.

Regional Organized Crime Information Center. (1985). *ROCIC Bulletin,* Jan., 13.

Reidel, M. (1987). "Stranger violence: Perspectives, issues and problems." *The Journal of Criminal Law and Criminology, 78*(2), 223–58.

Reinhardt, J. M. (1962). *The psychology of strange killers.* Springfield IL.: Charles C. Thomas.

Reiser, M. (1982, March). Crime-specific psychological consultation. *The Police Chief,* 53–56.

Reiss, A. Jr. (1980). "Victim proneness in repeat victimization by type of crime." In

S. Fineberg and A. Reiss, Jr. (eds.), *Indicators of crime and criminal justice: Quantitative studies*. Washington, DC: U.S. Department of Justice, 41–54.

———. (1961). "The social integration of queers and peers." *Social Problems, 9*, 102–20.

Remington, M. et al. (1979). "Comparative reliability of categorical and analogue rating scales in the assessment of psychiatric symptomology." *Psychological Medicine, 9*, 765–70.

Rendon, M. (1973). "The dissociation of dissociation." *International Journal of Social Psychiatry, 19*, 240–43.

Ressler, R. K., Burgess, A. W., Douglas, J. E., and McCormack, A. (1986). "Murderers who rape and mutilate." *Journal of Interpersonal Violence, 1*(3), 273–87.

Ressler, R. K., Burgess, A. W., Douglas, J. E., and Depue, R. L. (1985). "Criminal profiling research in homicide." In A. W. Burgess (ed.), *Rape and sexual assault: A research handbook*. New York: Garland, pp. 343–49.

Ressler, R. K. and Burgess, A. W. (1985a). "The split reality of murder." *FBI Law Enforcement Bulletin, 54*, 7–11.

———. (1985b). "Crime scene and profile characteristics of organized and disorganized murders." *FBI Law Enforcement Bulletin, 54*, 18–25.

Ressler, R. K. et al. (1985). "Violent crime." Special issue reporting on research of the National Center for the Analysis of Violent Crime, *FBI Law Enforcement Bulletin, 54*(8), 1–13.

———. (1984). "Serial murder: A new phenomenon of homicide." Paper presented at the annual meeting of the International Association of Forensic Sciences, Oxford, England.

———. (1982). *Criminal profiling research on homicide*. Unpublished research report.

Revitch, E. and Schlesinger, L. B. (1981). *Psychopathology of homicide*. Springfield, IL: Charles C. Thomas.

———. (1978). "Murder: evaluation, classification, and prediction." In I. L. Kutash et al. (eds.), *Violence: perspectives on murder and aggression*. San Francisco, CA: Jossey-Bass, pp. 138–64.

Rieber, R. W. and Green, M. R. (1988). *The psychopathy of everyday life*. Unpublished manuscript, New York.

Roberts, W. (1960). "Normal and abnormal depersonalization." *Journal of Mental Science, 106*, 478–93.

Rose, H. M. (1979). *Lethal aspects of urban violence*. Lexington, MA: Heath and Co.

Ross, H L. (1959). "The 'hustler' in Chicago." *Journal of Student Research, 1*, 13–19.

Rule, A. (1980). *The stranger beside me*. New York: W. W. Norton.

Sagarin, E. and Maghan, J. (1983). "Homosexuals as victimizers and victims." In D. E. MacNamara and A. Karmen (eds.), *Deviants: Victims or victimizers*. Beverly Hills, CA: Sage, pp. 147–62.

Sanders, W. B. (1977). *Detective work*. New York: The Free Press.

Sargent, W. and Salter, E. (1941). "Amnesic syndromes in war." *Proceedings of the Royal Society of Medicine, 34*, 757–64.

Schafer, S. (1977). *Victimology: The victim and his criminal*. Reston, VA: Reston.

Schwartz, H. and Jacobs, J. (1979). *Qualitative sociology*. New York: The Free Press.

Schwartz, T. (1981). *The Hillside Strangler: A murderer's mind*. New York: Doubleday & Co.

Sedman, G. (1966). "Depersonalization in a group of normal subjects." *British Journal of Psychiatry, 112*, 907–12.

Sedman, G. and Reed, G. F. (1963). "Depersonalization phenomena in obsessional personalities in depression." *British Journal of Psychiatry, 109*, 376–79.

"Serial murders: Another forensic challenge." (1985). *Forensic Science International, 27*, 135–44.

Shaw, C. (1930). *The jack-roller*. Chicago: University of Chicago Press.

Simon, R. I. (1977). "Type A, AB, B murderers: Their relationship to the victims and to the criminal justice system." *Bulletin of the American Academy of Psychiatry and Law, 5*, 344–62.

Skogan, W. G. (1975). "Measurement problems in official and survey crime rates." *Journal of Criminal Justice, 2*, 1–17.

Skogan, W. G. and Antunes, G. E. (1979). "Information, apprehension, and deterrence: Exploring the limits of police productivity." *Journal of Criminal Justice, 7*, 217–41.

Smith, B. (1960). *Police systems in the United States* (rev. 2nd edn.: Smith, B., Jr.). New York: Harper & Row.

Smith, D.A. and Visher, C. A. (1982). "Street-level justice: Situational determinants of police arrest decisions." *Social Problems, 29*, 167–77.

Snider, D. and Clausen, T. (1987). *A typology of serial murder*. Unpublished manuscript.

"Something in my head . . . clicks." October 27, 1986, *Tampa Tribune*, 3A.

Sonnenschein, A. (1985, Feb.). "Serial killers." *Penthouse, 32*, 34–35, 44, 128, 132–34.

Spector, M. and Kituse, J. (1987). *Constructing social problems*. New York: Aldine de Gruyter.

Spelman, W. (1988). *Beyond bean counting*. Washington, DC: Police Executive Research Forum.

Spiegel, D. (1984). "Multiple personality as a post-traumatic stress disorder." *Psychiatric Clinic of North America, 7*, 101–10.

Spiegel, H. (1963). "The dissociation-association continuum." *Journal of Nervous Mental Disorders, 136*, 374–78.

Staff. (1988, January 3). "Experts say mass murders are rare but on the rise." *New York Times*, 10, 15.

———. (1985, September 9). "Are serial killers on the rise?" *U.S. News and World Report*, 14.

———. (1982). *Homicide—United States. Morbidity and mortality weekly report. 31*(44), 594, 599–602.

———. (1982, December 5). "Child abductions a rising concern." *The New York Times*, 77.

———. (1980, Dec. 22). "FBI develops profiles to change face of sex probes." *Law Enforcement News*, 7.

Starr, M. et al. (1984, November 26). "The random killers." *Newsweek*, 100–6.

Storr, A. (1972). *Human destructiveness*. New York: Basic Books, Inc.

Strecher, V. G. (1957). *An administrative analysis of a multiple-agency criminal investigation within the suburban district of a large metropolitan area*. Unpublished master's thesis, Michigan State University, East Lansing, Michigan.

Sudnow, D. (1965). "Normal crimes: Sociological features of the penal code in a Public Defender office." *Social Problems, 33*, 255.

Sullivan, T. and Markew, P. T. (1983). *Killer clown: The John Wayne Gacy murders.* New York: Grosset and Dunlap.

Sutherland, E. (1937). *The professional thief.* Chicago: University of Chicago Press.

Swanson, C. R., Chamelin, N C., and Territo, L. (1984). *Criminal investigation.* New York: Random House.

Tavis, L. F., III. (1983). *"The case study in criminal justice research: Applications to policy analysis." Criminal Justice Review,* 8(2), 46–51.

Taylor, E. (1982). *William James on exceptional mental stress: The 1986 Lowell Lectures.* New York: Scribners.

Taylor, W. S. and Martin, M. F. (1944). "Multiple personality." *Journal of Abnormal Social Psychology, 39,* 281–300.

"The random killers." (1984, Nov. 26). *Newsweek,* 100–6.

Thibault, E. A., Lynch, L. M., and McBride, R. B. (1985). *Proactive police management.* Englewood Cliffs, NJ: Prentice-Hall, Inc.

Thornton, J. (1983, October 24). "The tragedy of America's missing children." *U.S. News and World Report,* 63–64.

Torrie, A. (1944). "Psychosomatic casualties in the Middle East." *Lancet, 29,* 139–43.

Tucker, G. J., Harrow, M., and Zuinlan, D. (1973). "Depersonalization, dysphoria and thought disturbances." *American Journal of Psychiatry, 130,* 702–6.

United States Department of Justice. Federal Bureau of Investigation. (1988). *Uniform crime reporting handbook.* Washington, DC: U.S. Government Printing Office.

U.S. House of Representatives. Committee on Government Operations. (1986a). *The federal role in investigation of serial violent crime.* 99th Congress, 2nd Session, House Report 99–888. Washington DC: U.S Government Printing Office.

————. (1986b). *Hearings before a subcommittee—The federal role in investigation of serial violent crime (April 9 and May 21, 1986).* Washington, DC: U.S. Government Printing Office.

U.S. House of Representatives. (1985). *Oversight hearing on the missing children's assistance act.* Hearings held by the Subcommittee on Human Resources, Committee in Education and Labor, May 21.

————. (1981). *The missing children act.* Hearings held by the Subcommittee on Civil and Constitutional Rights. Committee on the Judiciary. November 18, 30.

Visher, C. A. (1983). "Gender, police arrest decisions, and notions of chivalry." *Criminology, 21,* 5–28.

Vollmer, A. (1936). *The police and modern society.* Berkeley, CA: Regents of University of California.

von Hentig, H. (1979). *The criminal and his victim.* New York: Schocken.

Wambaugh, J. (1989). *The blooding.* New York: William Morrow.

Watkins, J. G. (1984). "The Bianchi (L. A. Hillside Strangler) case: Sociopath or multiple personality?" *International Journal of Clinical Experimental Hypnosis, 32,* 67–101.

Webb, E. J., Campbell, D. T., and Sechrett, L. (1966). *Unobtrusive measures: Non-reaction research in the social sciences.* Chicago: Rand McNally.

West, L. J. (1967). "Dissociative reaction." In A. M. Freedman, and H. I. Kaplan (eds.), *Comprehensive textbook of psychiatry* (2nd edn.). Baltimore: Williams & Wilkins.

White, R. W., and Shevach, B. J. (1942) "Hypnosis and the concept of dissociation." *Journal of Abnormal Social Psychology, 37,* 309–28.

Williams, K. R. and Flewelling, R. L. (1987). "Family, acquaintance, and stranger homicide: Alternative procedures for rate calculations." *Criminology, 25*(3), 543–60.

Willie, W. S. (1975). *Citizens who commit murder: A psychiatric study*. St. Louis: Warren H. Green.

Wilmer, M. A. P. (1970). *Crime and information theory*. Edinburgh: University Press.

Wilson, J. Q. (1978). *Varieties of police behavior: The management of law and order in eight communities*. Cambridge, MA: University Press.

———. (1978). *The investigators: Managing FBI and narcotics agents*. New York: Basic Books, Inc.

Wilson, P. R., (1987). " 'Stranger' child-murder: Issues relating to causes and controls." *International Journal of Offender Therapy & Comparative Criminology, 31*, 49–59.

Winn, S. and Merrill, D. (1980). *Ted Bundy: The killer next door*. New York: Bantam.

Wolfgang, M. E. (1958). *Patterns in criminal homicide*. Philadelphia: University of Pennsylvania Press.

Wolfgang, M. E. and Ferracuti, F. (1967). *The subculture of violence*. London, England: Tavistock.

Wulach, J. S. (1983). "Diagnosing the DSM-III antisocial personality disorder." *Professional Psychology: Research and Practice, 14*, 330–40.

Yin, R. K. (1984). *Case study research: Design and methods*. Beverly Hills CA: Sage.

Zahn, M. A. (1981). "Homicide in America: a research review." In I. L Barak-Glantz and R. Huff (eds.), *The mad, the bad and the different: Essays in honor of Simon Dinitz*. Lexington MA: Lexington Books.

———. (1980). "Homicide in the twentieth century." In J. A Inciardi and C. Faupel (eds.), *History and crime: Implications for criminal justice policy*. Beverly Hills, CA: Sage.

Zahn, M. and Sagi, P. C. (1987). "Stranger homicide in nine American cities." *The Journal of Criminal Law and Criminology, 78*(2), 377–97.

Author Index

Subject Index

Asterisked (*) cross-references can be found in the Author Index.

About the Author and Contributors

RICHARD H. DONEY is Principal Scientific Officer for the Home Office, Scientific Research and Development Branch, London, England. He is leader of a group of research scientists researching the application of technology to major crime investigation. He was previously a scientist with the General Electric Company, Hirst Research Centre. He is a chartered member of the Institute of Electrical Engineers. Mr. Doney received a B.S. degree in electronics from Southampton University.

STEVEN A. EGGER is Associate Professor, Social Justice Professions Program at Sangamon State University in Springfield, Illinois. He was formerly Project Director of the Homicide Assessment and Lead Tracking System for the state of New York where he directed the development of a computerized system to track and identify serial murderers. He has been conducting research into the phenomenon of serial murder since 1983. His other research interests include the epistemology of criminal investigation, decisionmaking models of criminality, and the future predator. Dr. Egger has worked as a police officer, homicide investigator, police consultant, and law enforcement academy director. His Ph.D. in Criminal Justice is from Sam Houston State University, where he completed the first dissertation in this country on serial murder.

DAVID A. FORD is a postdoctoral fellow at the Family Research Laboratory of the University of New Hampshire. He is an Associate Professor of Sociology at Indiana University at Indianapolis. Dr. Ford is a consultant to the Indianapolis Police Department for training and criminal investigation and was a member of the Central Indiana Multiagency Investigative Team. He is the principal investigator for the National Institute of Justice-funded field experiment evaluating the specific preventive impact of prosecution of wife-batterers.

ERIC W. HICKEY is currently Assistant Professor of Criminal Justice and Criminology at Ball State University, Muncie, Indiana. He has worked on the psychiatric staff of the Utah State Hospital and was a correctional officer in New Brunswick, Canada. His current research is in the etiology of serial murder victimization and he is finishing a book on serial murder. Dr. Hickey holds a Ph.D. in Sociology from Brigham Young University.

KENNA KIGER is a doctoral student in sociology at the University of Illinois. She is also Research Assistant on a National Institute of Justice grant, Criminal Careers and Crime Control. Her research interests are criminal career offending patterns and homicide.

HAROLD VETTER is a trained psychologist and the author of numerous journal articles and monographs. He was formerly chairman of the Criminology Department at the University of South Florida in Tampa. Much of his recent research has focused on the psychopathology of criminality. Dr. Vetter is presently Adjunct Professor at Portland State University in Oregon. He is currently collaborating on a work of fiction.